Looking Back

Harriet Devine was Literary Manager of the Royal Court Theatre from 1968 to 1969 and is daughter of George Devine, Founder and Artistic Director of the Royal Court from 1956 to 1965. She is Reader in English Literature at Edge Hill College in Lancashire, and has written and edited many books and articles on eighteenth- and nineteenth-century writers and poets.

Looking Back

Playwrights at the Royal Court, 1956–2006

interviews by
HARRIET DEVINE

faber and faber

First published in 2006
by Faber and Faber Limited
3 Queen Square London WC1N 3AU

Typeset by Country Setting, Kingsdown, Kent CT14 8ES
Printed in England by Mackays of Chatham plc, Chatham, Kent

A CIP record for this book
is available from the British Library

ISBN 978-0-571-23193-5
ISBN 0-571-23013-X

2 4 6 8 10 9 7 5 3 1

Contents

LOOKING BACK

Introduction

On 2 April 1956, the English Stage Company opened the first production of its first season at the Royal Court Theatre, Angus Wilson's *The Mulberry Bush*. My father, George Devine, had been appointed artistic director of the new company, with Tony Richardson as his associate. That it has kept its doors open for fifty years, and that its policies remain those of its first artistic directors, is truly remarkable, especially since it has survived numerous financial disasters and vicissitudes. In 1956 it was the first and only theatre to provide a permanent venue for new writing, while today almost every theatre in Britain, from the National Theatre to many tiny fringe venues, offers openings to new playwrights. Yet despite this competition and the fact that the theatre regularly comes under fire for failing to do whatever its various critics think it should be doing, the Royal Court survives and seems to have a special place in the hearts and minds of its writers and its audiences.

I was still a child when my father and Tony Richardson finally brought into being their plans for a 'vital modern theatre of experiment' that would produce 'hard-hitting, uncompromising writers [whose] works are stimulating, provocative and exciting'.[1] They wanted to reach out to a new audience, an audience of young people who would not, traditionally, be theatregoers, and above all this was to be done by a new emphasis on the dramatist: 'Ours is not to be a producers' theatre or an actors' theatre; it is a writers' theatre,' my father said in an interview just before the theatre opened in the spring of 1956. In order to support and encourage 'a contemporary style in dramatic work', writers were to be encouraged to 'look upon the Court as a workshop, and . . . come to any rehearsals, not only of their own plays but of other people's'.[2]

For me the story of the Royal Court in its early days and the story of my own growing up are intertwined. I spent a great deal of time at the theatre, as my mother and my aunt, Sophie, and Margaret (Percy) Harris, the theatre designers known as Motley, designed many of the early productions.

I saw every play that was done there, even running away from boarding school to go to the first night of Ionesco's *The Chairs*. I sat through rehearsals and helped to make props. I stayed up late for dinner parties, a silent listener to conversations between my parents and Beckett, the Ionescos, the Ardens. I visited the Weskers in their flat in Clapton, and John Osborne and Mary Ure in their house in Woodfall Street. As a shy and inhibited teenager, I'd been allowed to go to Bill Gaskill's Writers' Group classes, and hesitantly joined in improvisations with Ann Jellicoe, Arnold Wesker, Edward Bond, John Arden and Keith Johnstone.

My father died in 1966, and Bill Gaskill took over the running of the theatre. I knew Bill well – he'd been a frequent visitor to my mother's house in Lower Mall, Hammersmith, for several years. He asked me if I'd like to start reading plays, at ten shillings a script, which I did and found I enjoyed it. I seemed to have, as Timberlake Wertenbaker puts it, a nose. So it was that I became, after a while, the Royal Court's first literary manager. This sounds a rather glorious title but it was not a glorious job. I didn't have an office of my own, just a table in a corner of an office that belonged to two assistant directors, Robert Kidd and Barry Hanson. There were some shelves over the top of the table but too many scripts to fit on them, so they were piled on the floor under and around the table. A large part of my job consisted of trying to keep track of them, something I did with variable efficiency.

When scripts arrived I would farm them out to the readers, who were mostly writers themselves. They would come back with their written reports – some detailed, some just saying things like 'crap' – and I'd make my own judgement, read any that looked halfway promising, and pass anything interesting to the associate directors or to Bill. New writers were usually launched with a Sunday-night 'production without décor' and then graduated to a full-scale production. I was confident in those days and, like David Storey, believed I could tell after a page or two whether a play was worth reading further. My confidence may have been unfounded, though it is hard to say now. People sometimes ask me if I discovered any writers, and for a long time I used to say no. But when I started working on this book I remembered that I had made one good find – a writer called Adrienne Kennedy, whose two rather bizarre and powerful one-act plays, *A Lesson in a Dead Language* and *Funnyhouse of a Negro*, I pushed successfully to a Sunday-night performance. Adrienne Kennedy has become one of America's leading black women playwrights, and has written with affection about her experiences at the Royal Court.[3]

4

Nicholas Wright, a friend from drama school, started at the Court at the same time as I did, as the casting director. After a year or so Bill asked us both if we would like to have a go at directing a play for a Sunday night. Nicky said yes – in fact he directed his own play, *Changing Lines* – and I said no, no way. I was getting less interested in reading plays, and was spending more time at my cottage in Somerset. Eventually, and amicably, Bill and I agreed I should give up the job. Christopher Hampton took over, and a year or so afterwards David Hare came in too. This made me laugh, and I used to say that when I left they had to take on two people to replace me, though the truth was that Christopher had been trying to be the literary manager and the resident dramatist simultaneously.

Ten years went by, during which I did many things, all unconnected with theatre. I saw plays occasionally, sometimes met old friends like Bill, and Peter Gill, and Donald Howarth – Donald, together with George Goetschius, had bought Lower Mall in 1971. At the end of the 1970s I came back to London to do a degree in English Literature. A friend suggested I might like to read plays for the National Theatre, and for a short time I did. But I had completely lost my confidence. I could certainly still see what was dreadful and probably what was wonderful too, but I was totally defeated by the large middle ground and got into a panic about it. I suppose studying English made me too analytical, and I felt I'd been out of touch for too long. In any case the degree became increasingly absorbing and I concentrated on that.

I became an academic, specialising not in twentieth-century drama (to which I gave a wide berth) but in eighteenth- and nineteenth-century poets and women writers. Living and working in Lancashire, I visited London quite often, and managed the occasional trip to the Royal Court, to see a play or witness the presentation of the George Devine Award. Then, in early 2004, I was invited to join the selection committee of this award, given each year to a promising new playwright. Excited, if rather apprehensive, I agreed.

The committee met every week for six weeks in February and March. It was quite an experience for me, not least because we met in my old house at Lower Mall. We read through a record number of scripts before agreeing unanimously on that year's winner, Lucy Prebble, for her play *The Sugar Syndrome*. My fears that I might not be up to it diminished considerably as it became clear that instinct and subjectivity played a large part in the selection process. But I still had a suspicion there might be some criterion of Royal Court-ness that perhaps I was not aware of, and so I decided to set myself the task of finding out what, if anything, that might be.

A great deal of catching up was involved. I went to see everything that opened at the Court over the succeeding months, and started reading my way through many past productions I had missed. I tried to get my head around the characteristics of the different artistic directors' eras, and read all the books and articles I could find on the history of the Royal Court from my father's day up to the present. It struck me then that though books have been written about both the Court itself and about individual writers, no one had given a voice to the writers as a group. This seemed a strange omission, as the writers have always been the cornerstone of the theatre's existence. So I thought I'd better do it myself. As the fiftieth anniversary was approaching, the time for a reassessment seemed particularly auspicious.

Somewhere in the region of three hundred and fifty writers have had their plays performed at the Royal Court since April 1956. How many could I talk to, and how was I going to choose them? Many lists were made. I knew I wanted to cover, as far as possible, the whole fifty-year period. I was learning on my feet, and people got added as I saw, or read, and enjoyed their plays, or realised they were in some way important. But still the final list ended up being rather arbitrary, and it should in no way suggest that those who are not on it are being judged as less worthy. I realised very soon that I would have to limit myself in some way, and the writers I have talked to have all been British or Irish. So, no Americans – much as I would like to have met Arthur Miller, Sam Shepard, Wallace Shawn, Rebecca Gilman and others – and none of the exciting new writers who have emerged from the Royal Court's international programme. There were also quite a few playwrights I would like to have interviewed who chose not to be included: some refused politely and others simply didn't answer my letters.

Even so, I have tried to make the interviews represent writing from every era of the Court's history. Of those I have talked to, John Arden was the first writer whose play, *Waters of Babylon*, was performed during my father's era, closely followed by Ann Jellicoe, Arnold Wesker and Donald Howarth. Peter Gill's first play, *The Sleepers' Den*, had its Sunday-night performance in early 1965. David Cregan's *Miniatures* was one of the last productions in that period, and one of the last plays my father appeared in before he was taken ill. Bill Gaskill was artistic director when Christopher Hampton's *When Did You Last See My Mother?* was produced, and Bill was responsible for the first appearance at the Court of David Storey and Nicholas Wright. The so-called triumvirate – Bill Gaskill, Lindsay Anderson and Anthony Page – was running the theatre during the early 1970s, and David Hare, David Edgar and Snoo Wilson all emerged at this time. From 1972 to 1975 the theatre was under the direction of Oscar Lewenstein, whose interest in multiculturalism is represented here by one of his most important discoveries, Mustapha Matura. Hanif Kureishi's earliest contact with the Court was in 1976, when Nicholas Wright and Robert Kidd were joint artistic directors. Max Stafford-Clark, the longest running of the artistic directors (1979–1992) is justly celebrated for his championing of women writers, represented here by Louise Page, Timberlake Wertenbaker and April De Angelis. Other playwrights who emerged during his era were Terry Johnson and Martin Crimp. Stephen Daldry took over in 1992, and while he was artistic director the Court put on the first productions of plays by Kevin Elyot, Joe Penhall, Sebastian Barry and Ayub Khan Din. During this period there was a foray into verbatim theatre: *Body Talk* (1996), described here by one of the participants, Glyn Pritchard. Since 1998 Ian Rickson has been the artistic director, and his tenure is represented here by Conor McPherson, Simon Stephens, Roy Williams, Richard Bean, Leo Butler, Lucy Prebble and Simon Farquhar.

Once I started to make contact with the writers, I had to decide what questions to ask. It is apparent from the interviews that I have tended to go for the broad rather than specific – that is, I have focused less on each writer's individual plays and more on their experiences of writing and of theatre in general. For one thing, the process of writing has always fascinated me. When I talked to David Hare, who also had been a young literary manager working for Bill Gaskill, he asked me if I'd ever tried to write a play. My reaction was, 'Good Lord, no! I wouldn't have dared.' Perhaps this was partly a result of having been exposed to so many people being so harshly critical of much theatre work all through my formative years. Whatever the reason, any creative ability that I may have does not seem to manifest as drama: dialogue, which many of the writers I talked to have said is their preferred form of expression, is evidently not my forte, and I am happiest writing consecutive prose. So I wanted to know what the experience of writing a play was like, from the first conception to the final produced presentation.

Clearly, even from this small survey, it is not the same for everyone. At one extreme there is David Storey, who told me he 'started with a first line, and, "Let's see what happens",' and who never seems to have taken more than five days to write a play. April De Angelis describes a similar process, which is 'sort of surreal . . . like just putting your pen on paper and having something come out'. Other playwrights say it can take up to three or more years to arrive at a finished product. Christopher Hampton finds 'plays sort of marinate – they take their own time'. Many writers – Ann Jellicoe, Peter Gill and Kevin Elyot, for example – start with fragments, or images, which gradually take shape and form into something complete. Others start only when they know exactly what they are going to write. David Hare does not begin a play until he has a clear idea of the politics behind it. Simon Farquhar has to wait until he knows the characters so well that, 'When you write a line of dialogue where someone asks them a question, you know what they're going to answer.'

Some playwrights spend months planning and doing research, but Sebastian Barry calls that 'posh writing'; for him, 'as soon as you become rational, you're lost'. All of this, of course, is venturing into the mysterious inner world of imagination and creativity, and I was more than once reminded of some of the pronouncements of the Romantic poets, whose work I have studied and taught for many years. Few, if any, of the writers were able to answer a naive question like, 'Where do your ideas come from?' Terry Johnson has to wait for what he calls the car crash: 'two ideas, hitting each other head-on, and throwing you into a world in which you know immediately there's a dynamic.' Sebastian Barry spends 'a lot of the time waiting . . . It's like somebody else is doing something while I have to wait'. This was beginning to sound like Shelley, who wrote in 1821, 'Poetry is not like reasoning, a power to be exerted according to the determination of the will . . . the conscious portions of our natures are unprophetic either of its approach or its departure.'[4] Conor McPherson describes this sort of process well, if not in terms the poet would recognise:

> Suddenly it's in your brain. All these people sort of standing in your mind trying to tell you something, or trying to talk to each other, or something, and you're thinking, 'Who the fuck are these people?'

Generally, my opening question was, 'Can you remember the first time you ever went to the theatre?' Having been brought up in a world where everyone I knew was involved in some aspect of theatre, it was many years before it even occurred to me that there was any other way of life worth considering. But apart from David Edgar and Sebastian Barry, the writers came to theatre from a variety of non-theatrical backgrounds, and I was curious to know how and when they knew that this was something they wanted to be part of. A few people described a defining moment. For Louise Page, it was seeing *Noddy* at the age of three: 'I was captivated by having a car indoors, and the whole experience of indoors being out-doors.' Hanif Kureishi, taken as a child to the ballet by his mother and sister, 'fell in love with the darkness'. Timberlake Wertenbaker, whose mother took her to see a performance of Genet's *Deathwatch* when she was ten, described the 'shock of it, and the immediacy of it', which she believes made her a playwright. Several writers – Donald Howarth, Nicky Wright, David Edgar and others – started writing plays in order to direct one.

This question proved to be a sort of sociological survey of theatre-going experience, one that changed through time and was influenced by social class. Most of the writers of the older generation remembered being taken to pantomime as young children, though Arnold Wesker's family 'couldn't afford theatre, so we went to the cinema'. Both John Arden and Christopher Hampton described how, at public school, they had been hugely impressed by productions of Ibsen's *An Enemy of the People*. David Cregan was also 'overwhelmed by Ibsen' at the age of twelve. The importance of provincial repertory companies was clear, and some writers – Louise Page and Leo Butler, for instance – had been taken or allowed to go every week. People from working-class families may not have seen theatre at all: for anyone growing up in the sixties and seventies, television drama was often their first introduction to contemporary writing. The anthology series *Armchair Theatre* (1958–62), *The Wednesday Play* (1964–70), and *Play for Today* (1970–84) produced work by most of the important playwrights of their eras and had an important and formative impact on several writers, including Hanif Kureishi, Simon Stephens and Simon Farquhar.

The worthy attempts of Theatre in Education to interest and inspire generations of schoolchildren fell on stony ground for Ayub Khan Din, who was unimpressed by the six actors in clogs and black caps who visited his Salford school every year and sang songs about Arkwright and the spinning jenny. Roy Williams had a more positive experience, though, being amazed and intrigued at primary school by a man who turned up in a dress and sang songs with a guitar.

This led to the more metaphysical question of what theatre is all about. I didn't approach this successfully with many people, but when I did I was pleased with the answers. There seemed a recurring sense of theatre as 'a conjuring box . . . a magic place', as Snoo Wilson puts it. Terry Johnson has always felt a 'magical transition' walking through a pass door. Joe Penhall writes plays rather than novels because 'I think that the process from the page to the stage is like a chemical change of state.' And for Martin Crimp: 'The theatre is like a big musical instrument, a musical instrument that consists of the actors and the audience. And you have the chance to play it, and it's a fantastic instrument.'

Like, I imagine, most of the literary managers who came after me, I used to send out rejection letters which said something about the play not being 'Royal Court material'. At the time I must have thought I knew what that meant. Coming back after so long, I was curious to know whether those who select plays today had some kind of criterion in mind. When I asked how Ian Rickson saw his role as artistic director, he said: 'It is entirely inspired by the original statement made by your father, which is that the theatre should produce work that is original, contemporary and challenging.' Since the Royal Court today does indeed claim to be pursuing 'a policy still inspired by the first artistic director, George Devine',[5] I went back to some of the things my father had said. In 1960, four years after the English Stage Company began, he was interviewed in the *Daily Mail* about what he felt he had achieved so far, and what his original intentions had been. His answers seemed to me to be significant:

> I felt that the theatre *had* to take part in discussing *disturbing* things. The theatre should not be considered as something apart from life . . . I want the theatre to be continuously disturbing. I want people to ask questions. I want to make them anti-conformist . . . The main objective . . . was to keep this theatre going with plays which bear some vital relationship with life.[6]

I wondered whether the writers thought in this way about their own plays. Several did. For Richard Bean, to be oppositional and disturbing today is a great deal harder than it was in the fifties and sixties, because 'in the world of politics and big issues, everything is unbelievably mucky and complex and difficult, and that's what needs to be shown'. Also, as Joe Penhall points out, 'Occasionally I write plays that aren't intended to shift people's preconceptions, but just to entertain the audience, to entertain me.'

*

Of course the small collection of writers included here does not encompass everything the Royal Court has represented for half a century. David Edgar, who has always felt an outsider at the Court, offered me his overview of the whole period and his take on the Royal Court in general:

> Generation one is about the cultural consequences of democratisation and the war, so that's Osborne, Jimmy Porter, that's certainly the end of Wesker's *Roots*, that's Bond's *Saved*. The next lot, our lot, are reform versus revolution; then the women writers are about a search for identity; and then I think the brat pack – obviously it applies to some rather than others – are, 'Whatever happened to politics?' . . . The Royal Court has always been hip – it's always had its finger on the zeitgeist.

Max Stafford-Clark echoed this observation in May 2005, when I asked him what he considered his greatest achievement as artistic director had been: 'Obviously holding the mirror up to nature is the task if you run a new writing theatre, and holding the mirror up to society.' For David Edgar, 'our lot' are the writers who were the young politicos of the early 1970s – Edgar himself, David Hare, Snoo Wilson and Howard Brenton. These playwrights were the most dissatisfied with what they perceived as the Court's continuing resistance to the kind of political theatre they believed in. Indeed, the apparent failings of the present Royal Court caused both Edward Bond and Howard Barker to decline to be interviewed. Howard Barker, who has written about the failings of British 'humanist' or 'liberal' theatre,[7] described himself as 'deeply critical' and believes there was' always something anti-intellectual about the place'. For Bond, as he told me on a postcard, 'the present Royal Court is pernicious'. I wanted to know why, and wrote again. I got a long letter in reply, in which he explained some of the ways he felt the Court had failed:

> This is an age desperately in need of drama – it is like the Jacobean age, when the state invented a new God – or the age of the Greeks when the first enlightenment was threatened by the tyranny of Persia. We live in a world where cultures and creeds and markets are brutally thrust together – it is a kaleidoscope of chaos and violence. In such times humanness can renew itself only through drama. It is not to be expected that the state will understand this – drama must be autonomous. The Court's history makes it one of the few places where a new drama could be created. Instead it serves only as the

training ground for the soft fascism of Hollywood and TV . . .
I could not involve myself with the present Court – to give them a
play would be like asking a corpse to smell the flowers you brought
to its funeral.

I was sorry these two important writers would not talk to me. I did not
intend this book to be a eulogy. I wanted as wide a range of opinion as
possible, and hoped there would be contributions from people who were
critical as well as enthusiastic. But apart from David Hare and David
Edgar, who had relatively unhappy experiences at the Court in the 1970s,
when the kind of political theatre they wanted to write and promote was
not welcomed by the artistic directors, most playwrights spoke with
warmth about their experiences of working at the theatre.

For the writers whose plays were done in the early decades, the Royal
Court was the only place they could identify with because no other venues
existed (although, as Peter Gill puts it, the Royal Court in those days 'was
often a very bruising kind of place'). So it was interesting to hear the views
of more recent writers: many have experienced working at the National,
the Bush, the Royal Shakespeare Company and elsewhere. Generally, it
seems the Court has a special position as 'a touchstone of writing for the
theatre', as Martin Crimp expresses it (though he went on to say, 'I can't
say that it always is'). For Simon Stephens, the Court is unique for being
in dialogue with itself: 'the notion of what the Royal Court is, and what
it does, and what it ought to do, is discussed much more fervently and
much more heatedly . . . by people within and outside the institution' than
in other theatres. Above all, though, it's the way the theatre regards its
writers that is appreciated: 'They always treat your work with respect here,
even if they don't always do it' (April De Angelis). For Roy Williams, 'it
feels very communal. Every time I come here, it feels, and lives, and breathes,
like it's a writers' theatre.' Terry Johnson, who has been associated with
the Court for over twenty years, expressed it most positively: 'There's no
other space where the writer is the primary artist, and they feel it, and
know that it's genuinely felt by every department.'

I've asked many writers if there is such a thing as a Royal Court play,
and the answers have much in common. Ian Rickson's 'original, contemporary and challenging', seemed relevant, while another word much in
use is 'oppositional'. Simon Stephens uses the term 'transgression', and suggests Royal Court plays should be 'challenging in either form or content'.
Generally speaking, formal experiment is less in evidence at the Court than
intellectual, moral or ethical questioning: most of the writers responded

well to the idea of Royal Court plays shifting people's preconceptions. Politics, depending on who you listen to, have either been deplorably absent or, perhaps more convincingly, ubiquitously present. Roy Williams said: 'In a way I think all theatre is political. Even if I was to write a play and say, "This has nothing to do with politics," that act in itself is political.' In his unpublished autobiography, my father wrote that for him the theatre was 'a temple of ideas, and ideas so well expressed it may be called art'.[8] I toyed with the idea of describing the Royal Court as, if not a temple, at least a theatre of ideas, but, as the present literary manager Graham Whybrow pointed out to me, 'contemporary playwriting hasn't particularly attracted intellectuals in recent times'. Certainly the phrase has pretentious connotations and I now think it is not quite right. Royal Court plays have never been drearily worthy, or heavy with messages, but I would argue there is a seriousness of intent (which, happily, does not exclude comedy) that seems to persist through the eras.

This introduction should end with some wise thoughts about the future of the Royal Court. But, in truth, I don't feel much wiser or better equipped to make any judgements about this. It has been gratifying to find my father's memory held in such veneration there, though sometimes I find it peculiar to be treated reverentially there myself, like the daughter of some kind of secular saint, as he has been described. Of course I respect his initial vision, and perhaps even more so his tenacity in seeing it through in the face of so many difficulties, so much opposition and so little practical support from others. But for me he was just my dad: a good, kind, funny man, clever but not ferociously intellectual, practical and pragmatic, perceptive and thoughtful, but in the end simply a fallible human being. For others, he has clearly become a figurehead, someone whose ideals are there to be aspired to, whose words are still invoked to justify present policies at the Court, and perhaps that is right and proper.

It is sad that, as he wrote in the final weeks before he died, he felt he had 'utterly failed' in his desire to create 'a theatre that would be part of the intellectual life of the country'.[9] It seems to me that is exactly what the Royal Court has become. As Bill Gaskill says, George would have been astonished to find it is still in existence after half a century. But whether it will go on for another fifty years is impossible to predict, though there is no good reason why it should not. Unlike in my father's day, the theatre is now financially stable. Obviously the quality of the artistic director and the literary manager, and their ability to select plays that fulfil the double demands of artistic excellence and public acceptance, is crucial.

In a 'writers' theatre', the quality of the work submitted is always primary. As Ian Rickson says, 'The challenge to find good work continues. There may be more writers out there than in the 1960s, but there are also more outlets for new plays.' Certainly the theatre works harder than ever before to discover, promote and encourage new writing. Graham Whybrow believes that 'the theatre is responsible for creating a vibrant playwriting culture' and needs to be 'open, receptive, curious and creative in relation to existing and aspiring playwrights'. Clearly this philosophy lies behind the Young Writers' Programme, the International Programme, and the work behind the scenes on plays suitable for production 'subject to rewrite'.

So, of all the things I have learned, perhaps the most memorable and significant is the importance of the writers, and of having a theatre dedicated to their work. Ian Rickson puts it well:

> I begin from the premise that the creative act of writing a good play is little short of miraculous. Many people have managed to write poetry. A short story is achievable. Even the novel has a relative freedom to its form. But the construction of a piece of writing that dynamically detains people in a live space in real time is perhaps the most extraordinary creative achievement of all.

EDITING THE MATERIAL

I have tried to edit with as light a hand as possible, so that the writers' own voices are heard. Though I have removed some hesitations and repetitions along with any obvious digressions, I have interfered little with what they said. I have also left my own side of the conversations relatively intact. All the writers have had a chance to see and correct the original transcript of their interview.

At the beginning of each interview there is a list of the plays the writer has had performed at the Royal Court, and these also appear in a separate list of Writers' Works. The short list of further reading at the end contains books on the history of the Royal Court and on contemporary playwriting in general.

ACKNOWLEDGEMENTS

Peter Gill was the first person to suggest to me, many years ago, that I should do some kind of book about the Royal Court, and his support and encouragement were invaluable during the early stages of this project.

Donald Howarth has been there for me throughout and I can't thank him enough for his enthusiasm and for the many constructive discussions we have had. Ian Rickson has been unfailingly kind and supportive and I am grateful to Graham Whybrow for many valuable conversations as well as much practical help. I have also profited from interesting meetings with Bill Gaskill, Anthony Page and Max Stafford-Clark. Dinah Wood, at Faber, has been a most exemplary editor. I must thank Edge Hill College for their continued support, both financial and psychological. Finally, a Research Fellowship from the Leverhulme Foundation has enabled me to pursue the later stages of the work.

REFERENCES

1. George Devine, 'The Royal Court Theatre Scheme', unpublished MS, 1953.

2. *New Statesman and Nation*, 24 March 1956; *The Stage*, 25 July 1955; *Daily Telegraph*, 19 March 1956.

3. See her *Deadly Triplets: A Theatre Mystery and Journal* (Minneapolis: University of Minnesota Press, 1990).

4. P. B. Shelley, 'The Defence of Poetry' (1821).

5. Royal Court Theatre website: www.royalcourttheatre.com/about.asp?ArticleID=14

6. *Daily Mail*, 24 October 1960.

7. *Arguments for a Theatre* (Manchester: Manchester University Press, 1993).

8. Unpublished autobiographical fragment, quoted in Irving Wardle, *The Theatres of George Devine* (London: Cape, 1978).

9. Ibid.

Writers' Works

This list (and the list at the head of each interview) includes only plays that were performed at the Royal Court. They are listed by date of their first performance.

John Arden
The Waters of Babylon 1957
Live Like Pigs 1958
Serjeant Musgrave's Dance
   1959
The Happy Haven 1960

Ann Jellicoe
The Sport of My Mad Mother
   1958
The Knack 1962
Shelley 1965
The Rising Generation 1967
Two Jelliplays 1974

Arnold Wesker
Chicken Soup with Barley
   1958
Roots 1959
I'm Talking about Jerusalem
   1960
(these three plays forming
   'The Wesker Triology')
The Kitchen 1961
Chips with Everything 1962
Their Very Own and Golden
   City 1966
The Old Ones 1972

Donald Howarth
Lady on the Barometer 1958
Sugar in the Morning 1959
Ogodiveleftthegason 1967
Three Months Gone 1970

Peter Gill
The Sleepers' Den 1965
A Provincial Life 1966
Over Gardens Out 1969
Small Change 1976
The York Realist 2002

David Cregan
Miniatures 1965
The Dancers 1966
Transcending 1966
Three Men for Colverton 1966
The Houses by the Green 1968
A Comedy of the Changing
   Years 1969

Christopher Hampton
When Did You Last See
   My Mother? 1966
Total Eclipse 1968
The Philanthropist 1970
Savages 1973
Treats 1976

Nicholas Wright
Changing Lines 1968
The Gorky Brigade 1979

David Storey
The Restoration of Arnold
  Middleton 1967
In Celebration 1969
The Contractor 1969
Home 1970
The Changing Room 1971
Cromwell 1973
The Farm 1973
Life Class 1974
Mother's Day 1976

David Hare
What Happened to Blake
  1970
Slag 1971
Lay By (collaboration) 1971
England's Ireland
  (collaboration) 1972
Teeth 'n' Smiles 1975
Via Dolorosa 1998
My Zinc Bed 2000

Snoo Wilson
Lay By (collaboration) 1971
England's Ireland
  (collaboration) 1972
The Pleasure Principle 1973
The Glad Hand 1978
The Grass Widow 1983

David Edgar
England's Ireland
  (collaboration) 1972

State of Emergency 1972
A Fart for Europe
  (collaboration) 1973
Our Own People 1978
Mary Barnes 1979

Mustapha Matura
As Time Goes By 1971
Play Mas 1974
Black Slaves, White Chains
  1975
Rum an' Coca Cola 1976
More More 1978

Hanif Kureishi
Soaking the Heat 1976
Borderline 1981

Louise Page
Want Ad 1976
Salonika 1982
Falkland Sound 1983

Terry Johnson
Insignificance 1982
Cries from the Mammal House
  1984
Hysteria 1993
Hitchcock Blonde 2003
Piano/Forte 2006

Timberlake Wertenbaker
Abel's Sister 1984
The Grace of Mary Traverse
  1985
Our Country's Good 1988
Three Birds Alighting on
  a Field 1991
The Break of Day 1995
Credible Witness 2001

Martin Crimp
No One Sees the Video 1990
Getting Attention 1991
The Treatment 1993
Attempts on her Life 1997
The Country 2000
Face to the Wall 2002
Fewer Emergencies 2005

April De Angelis
Hush 1992
Wild East 2005

Joe Penhall
Some Voices 1994
Pale Horse 1995
Dumb Show 2004

Kevin Elyot
My Night with Reg 1994
Mouth to Mouth 2001
Forty Winks 2004

Sebastian Barry
The Steward of Christendom
  1995

Ayub Khan Din
East is East 1996
Last Dance at Dum Dum
  1999
Notes on Falling Leaves 2004

Conor McPherson
The Weir 1997
Dublin Carol 2000
Shining City 2004

Simon Stephens
Bluebird 1998
Herons 2001
Country Music 2004
Motortown 2006

Roy Williams
Lift Off 1999
Clubland 2001
Fallout 2003

Richard Bean
Toast 1999
Under the Whaleback 2003
Honeymoon Suite 2004
Harvest 2005

Leo Butler
Made of Stone 2000
Redundant 2001
Lucky Dog 2004

Lucy Prebble
The Sugar Syndrome 2003

Simon Farquhar
Rainbow Kiss 2006

John Arden

The Waters of Babylon 1957
Live Like Pigs 1958
Serjeant Musgrave's Dance 1959
The Happy Haven 1960

John Arden lives in Galway, and though I offered to go and see him, he didn't want a face-to-face interview, so I talked to him on the telephone. I remembered him well from when I was a child and it would have been good to see him again. He was one of the writers whom I knew from Bill Gaskill's Writers' Group, and I can remember at least one occasion when he and his wife Margaretta D'Arcy came to dinner at Lower Mall. His play *Serjeant Musgrave's Dance* made a huge impression on me, one I've never forgotten, and I was also taken with *Armstrong's Last Goodnight*, which I saw at Chichester in 1965. It took me a while to work out the technology for a telephone interview but we finally talked on 27 April 2005.

I'd like to start by asking you if you can remember your first experience of theatre.

When I was about four, my mother thought it would be a good idea to take me to see a production of *Alice in Wonderland* that was being put on by some children at the school. It must have been in the school hall, I think. I didn't understand the play – I was too young to have been taken – and I started screaming because I didn't like the way the curtain flapped when they closed it and opened it. Finally I think I had to be taken out, because every time they closed the scene by closing and opening the curtain, I began to cry. I remember most of the play – I remember them spilling the tea at the Mad Hatter's tea party, and I think I commented on that – I said, 'Why doesn't somebody come and clean it up?' But that was my first experience of theatre.

So it isn't a case of, oh, the first time I saw theatre I knew this was what I wanted to do with my life . . .

Well, that was true at a later stage. I didn't get to see very much theatre – I lived in a town that didn't have a theatre. Really I think in my earliest years the only theatre I saw was pantomimes, for which I would be taken to Sheffield or Leeds, where they had big theatre companies – which I enjoyed, but I wasn't all that mad about pantomimes. I'm just trying to think when I began to get really interested in plays as such. I think probably when we did little plays at boarding school, when I was about twelve years old. I really enjoyed taking part in acting, and sometimes inventing plays – they weren't all out of books. But later on, in my teenage years, I would go and see the repertory company in Sheffield, which put on fairly ordinary 1940s West End successes two years later – I saw some entertaining things there. I didn't get to see any classical theatre, I don't think, for a while. At my public school we had a visit once from a man who did Shakespeare as a one-man show. He presented, would you believe it, *Macbeth* and *The Taming of the Shrew* all by himself, very competently. We also had a visit from a touring company doing Ibsen's *Enemy of the People*. That was a good thing, I really enjoyed that – I must have been about seventeen, I think.

Funnily enough somebody else mentioned that play – obviously not the same production – I'm trying to think who it was – Christopher Hampton. He said to me that seeing that play had made a huge impression on him. Perhaps it's a particularly powerful play?

Well yes, it is. I think why it was powerful for me, apart from the fact that it's a good solid plot, of corruption being uncovered and so on, is that the last act, or the penultimate act, is a public meeting. And this was something that one had not seen, having only been taken to see West End comedies at the Sheffield Rep. In this production the company was including the whole auditorium as part of its scene, even the seats at the back of the gallery.

Yes – it must have made you see that other things were possible . . .

Yes, it opened up all sorts of possibilities that one hadn't thought about much.

But I know you started as an architect – did I read somewhere that you did some acting at Cambridge?

Not at Cambridge, no. I did three years as an architect at Cambridge, and then I had to do two years in Edinburgh to finish. I wrote a play that was put on by the students there, and I took part in it myself, and I also took part in a student production of *Romeo and Juliet*.

And did you ever think you might be an actor, or was it always writing?

I didn't really think I'd be an actor – I wasn't all that good. The reason I didn't do any acting at Cambridge was that the Marlowe Society had rejected me at an audition. And I thought, after that, that I couldn't be as good as I thought I was. I acted at school – I played Hamlet in my last year, but I didn't particularly want to be an actor, I thought I'd rather be a writer.

So writing was important to you, and at some point it became more important than architecture? How did that process happen?

Well, you see, I wrote two plays while I was a student. One was this play we put on in the college, another was a radio play, which won a prize from the BBC. Then I left Edinburgh and came to work in an architects' office in London. That would be 1955, the year before the Court opened. And I did come and see plays there. The architects' office was just round the corner from Sloane Square, and I was very much aware of the Royal Court. There was a play put on there shortly before George's company did its first production, an independent production by Wolf Mankowitz and Oscar Lewenstein, of Brecht's *The Threepenny Opera* – that was the first play I saw at the Court. And then after that, though I didn't see everything, I remember I was most impressed by *The Crucible*, and by *The Country Wife*. And then, because my radio play had won a prize, I got a letter from George, who was touting for writers at the time, asking me to send any scripts I might have that would do for the stage.

So they headhunted you.

They headhunted me. They didn't like the first play I sent them, but the second one was *The Waters of Babylon*, and that was done as a Sunday night. *The Waters of Babylon* I wrote while I was working in the architects' office, spending more time writing the play than doing my work, and then after that I saw George. He asked me to come round one evening to the theatre, and he offered me a job as a script reader, for which he was going to pay me. There were a lot of writers doing that at the time.

You probably weren't getting paid a lot of money for that.

No – but enough to keep me going and pay the bills at the time. It gave me a sense of actually getting something, just enough to give up architecture. Also they took out an option on my next play, which was *Live Like Pigs*.

And that didn't start as a Sunday night, did it – it went straight into the main theatre.

Yes. And Margaretta D'Arcy, whom I had just married, was in Anthony Page's acting group, which I think was a very important little group. I don't know how much you know about that.

Not much.

Well, under George's wing, he got together a small group of young actors who would work together on improvisational techniques, and all sorts of other fancy ideas that had come in from America, and could feed into the regular productions at the Court. So both of us were involved with the Court at that time.

I've read a story somewhere of you sitting in a performance of Live Like Pigs *and thinking, right, this is gritty realism – now I want to see something with a red coat. Is that right?*

Yes, I did, that is perfectly true. I'd always liked plays with gaudy costumes. I'd been in Edinburgh for two years and I used to go to the Edinburgh Festival, seeing plays of various sorts – this was when I was in the army, not when I was a student. And I remember there was a production by Tyrone Guthrie of the sixteenth-century *Three Estates* . . .

Oh – which you refer to later in Armstrong's Last Goodnight.

Yes. And then later, the next year, there was a production by George of Jonson's *Bartholomew Fair*, in the same place, in the Assembly Rooms. It was a big wide theatre, with a three-sided sort of Elizabethan stage. I was very impressed with both of those, and with the whole idea of pageantry as well as words, and non-naturalistic action, and so on, in both of them.

I was going to come on to that, actually, because that interests me a lot about your work. These days, plays always seem to be about people sitting in rooms talking to each other. I love to see things with a bit of history, and costumes, and songs, and so on.

But you see they can't afford the costumes and the large casts. It is a serious problem, but I don't know that it is an insuperable one.

At the Royal Court now, you rarely get a play with more than five people in it, which is sad.

I was thinking about your asking me about *Serjeant Musgrave*. What happened was that the folk singer Bert Lloyd was singing the songs in *Live Like Pigs,* and he had been talking to me about soldiers' ballads. I can't remember how that sprang up, but it did, and that also fed into my thinking at the time. *Live Like Pigs* was a totally grey play, grey and brown, as it needed to be. But I thought to myself, I wonder if I could do something a bit further on from that.

But it wasn't just to write a play with a bit more colour in it?

No – I wanted to write a play about the British army misconducting itself, as it had been doing in Cyprus. A lot of people had been very upset about that, and there had been quite a political stir in the previous year. I wanted to do something based on my feelings about that. Now the point was, most people would probably not have thought of putting it back into the nineteenth century, but because of these various influences on me I made that decision.

And looking at your plays since then, that appears to have been an on-going strand in your work – your plays appear to be about something that happened in the past but in fact there's always a contemporary relevance.

That is so, yes.

I know people argue a lot about Serjeant Musgrave – *is it a pacifist play? Is it advocating revolution? And so on. I read somewhere recently that you had moved from a pacifist position to an activist position and possibly then to a revolutionary position. Do you see yourself as having done that?*

Possibly, to an extent. But I'm getting back into more of a pacifist position. I'd rather not get involved in that argument. I'm really beginning to see – the only revolution I'd like to see at the moment is one that gets rid of Bush's 'new world order' – something more than slogans. But I'm not sure how we're going to do it. I'm certainly a kind of activist in that.

Somebody once called you Britain's Brecht. How do you feel about that?

I'm flattered. I don't really think I am – I think he's a different kind of writer. But I always thought well of Brecht. The first play of his that I saw was *The Threepenny Opera* at the Court, and then a year or so later the Berliner Ensemble came to London. I've seen a number of Brecht plays since. I think he's one of the great dramatists of the twentieth century. And just because the communist governments in Eastern Europe collapsed –

owing to their own internal contradictions, largely – this does not in my mind discredit Brecht, although a lot of people talk as if it does. He was never a servile party-line man, and I think there's great intellect there, and great dramatic talent.

And did you feel, having seen the Berliner Ensemble, that that was an influence on what you wrote?

Well, put it this way – I was already deciding that was how I wanted to write anyway. I remember I read an article by Kenneth Tynan a year or so before that – he'd been to Berlin and he was describing the work they did, and the type of production. I can't remember where this article was, probably the *Observer*. He gave a lengthy description of their *Mother Courage* production, and I thought, really, that sounds like the kind of play I would like to write, though without having seen it I didn't really know what it was. But it was exciting to me that there was a dramatist in Europe who was going in for the kind of work that did use history as well as modern realism.

So it struck a chord, really.

Yes.

Now, it's a sad fact that you don't write stage plays any more, do you?

I never wrote any more plays for the Court after *The Workhouse Donkey* in 1963, but I was writing them one after another (mostly with Margaretta D'Arcy) until the end of the 1970s. Much of the time we were working in Ireland and our own production of our *Non-Stop Connolly Show* in Dublin in 1975 realised most of the epic intentions that I think George would have wished to have implemented at the Court, had his board and its finances been other than they were. Our work was large-scale, political, analytical, poetic, etc., but impossible to have originated in the UK at that time, when there was an unspoken but very real climate of self-censorship about any theatre ventures touching on the Irish situation. Stuart Burge (when he was running the Court) did want to put on one of our other Irish plays, *The Ballygombeen Bequest,* but found it impossible, everyone was too timid. Since the end of the 1970s, it is true I have concentrated largely on radio plays. I had had a lot of trouble with the stage, with the relationship with directors, and companies and so on. And so I found it easier on the passions to work for radio. Although I've had some trouble with that, but not to the same extent.

Yes – because unlike some of the early Royal Court writers, you didn't have a director, did you, with whom you became associated?

That was one of the problems. I did very well with different people but I never stuck with one of them. George was directing *Live Like Pigs* and then he got ill in the middle and Anthony Page took over, and I think the production was somewhat spoiled by that – it left the actors a little bit floundering. Then Lindsay Anderson did very well with *Serjeant Musgrave*, but for some reason he didn't want, or wasn't able, to do my next play.

And didn't Bill Gaskill do one?

He did a couple – and then he directed *Armstrong's Last Goodnight* again at the Edinburgh Festival five years ago. There was a certain amount of continuity, but not like Arnold Wesker, who had everything done by John Dexter.

And you moved away from the Royal Court?

I wrote *The Workhouse Donkey* for the Royal Court, and Lindsay Anderson was going to direct it. I never quite knew what happened about that, there was some difficulty. And George farmed it out to do at Chichester. I don't know what the motivation was.

Was it not something to do with the sheer size of it?

I think it may have been. And also to do with the non-availability of Lindsay, who was off making a film somewhere. But I was presented with a *fait accompli*, which I was quite happy with. And then George died – what year did he die?

1966.

Yes – but he was ill for a while before that. And after that I didn't feel any attachment to the Court.

And you don't ever regret giving up theatre? You don't ever feel a pang, and wish that you could get back?

No, no pangs. Whenever I've had the chance to do a bit of theatre work I've done it, little pieces here and there for small groups in the UK or Ireland [many of them published under the heading of *Rough Theatre* in the Methuen volume of plays by Arden and D'Arcy]. Because they weren't produced in regular theatres, they may seem to conservatives to be inconsiderable, but they show I have never actually cut myself off from the stage, and that's the important thing. What I am really interested in, over and above the differences between theatre and radio studios, etc., is the opportunity to tell stories, and I've had that in abundance. I've written three novels, and two books of (not-so-short) stories, mostly dealing directly or indirectly with themes of theatre. I'm at work now on another collection of stories. I am at times a little nostalgic for George and his environment in Sloane Square but there were a lot of things that were not too happy about the Court. I mean – you never knew where you were, quite. If your play was a success they were all over you, and if it wasn't, it was as if you'd got some terrible contagious disease – nobody wanted to talk to you. One sort of detected a cold atmosphere about the place. I'm not talking about George – he was always very friendly – but a sort of atmosphere among the staff generally.

Sebastian Barry

The Steward of Christendom 1995

When I was making my first lists of people I wanted to interview, I had one rule – they had to have had at least two plays produced at the Royal Court. But I bent the rule for Sebastian Barry, who has had only one, the hugely successful *The Steward of Christendom*. He is one of the few writers I met who has done equally well as a novelist: his *A Long Long Way* was shortlisted for the Booker Prize in 2005. We met in the grand and beautiful surroundings of the Shelbourne Hotel, on St Stephen's Green in Dublin, in March 2005. We tried the tearoom but the background noise of the piano interfered with the recording equipment, so we ended up in the slightly less salubrious Horseshoe Bar. He told me that he had grown up in a house just across the square.

You lived in Dublin – were your family theatregoers?

Well, my mother, Joan O'Hara, was, and is, an Abbey Theatre actress.

So were you taken to see things when you were young?

I'm trying to think how young – but pretty young. We had a break and went to London for four years, as people did in those days, so I was a little Londoner for four years in the 1960s. Which was very helpful, actually. So when I'm in London, although I'm not an English person, I always do feel that part of me – there's a corner that is for ever – you know. And that's Hampstead. But then when we came back from Hampstead my mother rejoined the Abbey company, and then she started to bring me.

Do you have any memory of the first play you ever saw?

The thing I remember first – the only thing I remember – was her playing Yeats's Katherine ni Houlihan. And coming in with her – probably being driven in by my father, and then he would go on, probably to here, to the Horseshoe Bar – and Lily Shanley, who would be front of house in the

Abbey in those days, carefully bringing me to my seat – I might have been eight or something – and sitting me down. And then something started to happen fifty feet away from me. I wasn't quite sure what it was, in some way, but I realised after a while that it was my mother, but very, very old. And my first thought was, how was she going to get me home if she was now so old? I've talked about that before – but it never really left me. And there was also the experience of being brought backstage, and the sense of vanished companies, that I now think of, and Angela Newman sitting there, and saying to me, 'Oh, you're going to be a beautiful man when you grow up.' And just the largeness of the actors in the dressing rooms. Because you're never quite sure what size they are, and the dressing rooms make them look enormous – or maybe it's just because I'm eight. And a sense also of my mother being very quiet at home, and very obedient to my father's wishes, but in the theatre being completely in command.

So she was the leading actress at the Abbey.

She was, yes, she is. She's still alive, still working, at seventy-five. But as a child of eight – there she was, old. And then there's something about theatre, about turning off the lights. And instead of light being where you are, light's over this other place, which for an eight-year-old with no television in the house – it was putting the light from you to this other place, giving the light to those people, and you didn't have any light. And also sitting with the shadow when you're watching. Very curious for a child – if you were a Martian, even coming into the theatre would be very peculiar.

What was it like when you went backstage and she wasn't old any more?

I was relieved, that was the first thing. But I fully believed – and I don't think it was explained to me – that something had happened to her, and even at the end of plays now – indeed I remember always, at the end of *The Steward of Christendom* at the Court – I was absolutely certain, and it was absolutely true in a certain way, that – something to do with lighting as well – that Donal McCann's face was always changed – it wasn't Donal, something had changed him. But his old face would be back again when you went to the dressing room. So even at forty-nine, not at eight, I have a suspicion about the theatre, that there's something going on that good rational scepticism doesn't quite explain.

You wrote in the preface to your plays that when you saw Boss Grady's Boys *the actors had become those people.*

That's another similar moment. I would have been about thirty-three then. Not my first play, but my first proper play with a wonderful theatre – and that celestial casting that takes place. I don't know how it happens; casting directors can work as hard as they like, but there is a sort of divine influence sometimes, and in that play it was a man called Eamon Kelly, who came in to play Josey, and he'd been born a few fields away from the place I was writing about. He was a storyteller by tradition, and he just embodied the part in the most wonderful way. He wrote on the poster, I remember: 'Dear Sebastian, you turned Dublin's head.' And Jim Norton – how do these things happen? My mother had roomed with Colin Blakeley when she went over, I think, to do some early films, these lost films – and my mother indeed would have worshipped at the altar of your father, and the whole idea of the Court. But she'd stayed with Colin, and naturally we were very conscious of when he died – because he died so young. And I was writing plays then, and I was thinking it was very awkward because he was just the sort of man you'd want to be working with. But Jim Norton had been working with Colin Blakeley when he was very ill, and one night backstage – I think he knew he was dying – he said to Jim, 'Look, I've got three houses, beautiful cars, enough work for the next three years, and I'm not going to be able to enjoy any of that. So my advice is, if something wonderful comes up, do it, even if it's in the National Theatre of Mongolia, go and do it.' So then this little script came by Jim, *Boss Grady's Boys*, and he hadn't worked for a year. He was walking on the beach in LA or somewhere, reading it, and he remembered Colin's words and he came back to do it. That to me is how plays really start to work. If a play is a construct, and if there's a signal that the play gives out – it's no secret that not everybody wants to hear that signal, or can, or would bother with it. But if it is heard, it's like a sort of strange contraption of a radio, and the right actor hears the signal.

In your plays you are very clear about what the characters look like. Also, you use light so much, don't you? You play with light, and you tell the director how to do that, or you tell the director what you want and the director has to figure it out. They're very visual, aren't they?

Well, they're seen plays. Whatever that little space is at the back of your head – the difficulties arise, for me, when you're having to do a lot of drafts and things, because it means that you just haven't seen it on that twopenny-halfpenny stage at the back of your head. And you haven't heard them. And I don't see them as, you know, real people, I see them as actors in costume, which is for me hyper-real, it's another real. I don't see them as their original selves – that's not what I'm dealing with, it's certainly not what my head is doing, because I feel to a certain degree the theatre is an afterlife, and that it's a form of memory of things that never happened, but it is still a form of memory, and it's authenticated by the quality of its signal, rather than the quality of its truth.

Another thing you say in your preface is about being a child and wanting to tell stories about people you'd never met – because a lot of the plays are about your family.

Well, you know, it's an Irish family, and Irish families traditionally got very quiet about family members who didn't suit – whatever it might be, the way of thinking at the time, religious time and so on. For instance my grandfather, the painter, Matthew, he was a wonderful man, a gifted watercolourist and a supreme grandfather and I adored him, but long after he died, my father was at a funeral of one of the great aunts, and he for the first time heard the name, my father, of his own grandmother, Fanny Hawke. He'd never heard her name because his father had never mentioned her, because she had been a Protestant. So the name itself already suggests a calling out across a field. And Lizzie Finn was equally hidden, because she was the dark, dark secret of my great-grandmother, whom I didn't meet, she was in her nineties when I was small, and that was her mother. She had married Gibson – I don't know if his name was Robert, but one of the Castlemaines – and then something awful must have happened to them both, or to one of them, possibly to Lizzie, she may well have died. But the daughter was taken and given away to Gibson's batman, from when he'd been in the army, and she was brought up as Mary Donnelly. And she never would speak of it. She would go down to Athlone every year to draw some secret stipend – she was a very mysterious woman – and everyone thought she was illegitimate, but in fact they were married, in Christ Church, properly married, but she'd been given away. So therefore the story of Lizzie Finn was only accessed when my grandfather was looking for his mother's marriage certificate, and there it was. So they are all – well, not *Boss Grady's Boys*, though in some ways that play was a sort of secret history of myself and my brother, who's much younger than me – that's why Josey is so childlike in the play – there's a sort of shadow family thing there. And *Our Lady of Sligo* I knew only too much about, my mother's mother, because my mother talked about her excessively. And that made it a very difficult play to write, actually, because you're better off if you've got two little things to rub together, intimation.

So the process of writing . . . ?

You're asking me about writing plays, and I don't know – I'm writing a play now for Max Stafford-Clark, the fourth play, and I spend a lot of the time waiting, just waiting, and I'm often reminded – it's like somebody else is doing something while I have to wait. And I don't know who it is and I don't know where they're doing it. I have a third of it written. And a curious thing – you were talking about light – and I realised that for whatever reason, since I wrote those plays, I've stopped writing like that. Even my last play, which is still inside me, has very few stage directions. I think that's because I am critical of myself in some way, and I wonder why that is. Perhaps it's because at some level you slightly despair of the things you've seen being reproduced, because for some lighting designers that seems too easy, or too ordinary. They have to further metamorphose it or something. And this whole process of other things to do to a play, the lighting, or the set, out of politeness you say yes, but in the end you regret it, but you don't want to be curmudgeonly, or stubborn . . .

That is difficult, isn't it – you write a novel and give it to the publisher and it comes from you fairly unadulterated, but if you write a play you've got to give it to the director, the designer, the lighting person . . . so it's out of your hands. It's a risk.

Yes, and in some cases it might be sabotage. There's a kind of psychological sabotage that goes on in some plays, which can often be for the best of reasons. The theatre is so huge, people think they have to compromise. Ultimately that's not only distressing, it's disheartening, and furthermore it feeds into the way you approach it. So you say fine, if that's how it is, then you are going to have to do this work yourself, I simply won't do that work. And I think that is my failing, something I have to spruce up in the future.

That you sort of lose heart?

Yes. I still think it's very important. I just don't write it down.

Thinking of plays of yours I have read – Our Lady of Sligo seems to me to be a bit different from the earlier ones. You said it was more difficult to write – are you less satisfied with it?

It came after an enormous success. So the pressure was on. But it was only two or three years later, as my wife points out, and it was very successful. It was hard to write more for the reason that it was a frightening character, a sort of childhood bogeyman . . .

It's a very poignant play. Sad things happen in your plays but somehow one comes out uplifted, but that one, it left one feeling sad.

I've just been reading Synge's preface to *The Playboy of the Western World* (and this is the man who wrote *Riders to the Sea*, a fairly sad play) and he says that plays have to have joy in them. And I did feel a bit abashed.

I don't think many writers think like that now!

We don't! I wonder what changed?

So – let's get back to when you're eight years old. You go to the theatre, you see your mother – then after that going to the theatre becomes a regular thing?

Yes. And there was always somebody learning a script in the house. That's what my sister did with my mother – she was the script reader. And I couldn't do that, I don't know why – maybe I talked, or . . . didn't have the mechanism to do it. But then you're dealing with a house where the father is an architect and a poet, and your mother's an actress – and till a certain age you think all houses are like that, don't you?

Yes. I know I did.

And there are many drawbacks to that – your parents go out in the evenings, and the house is empty, and that's not so good. So, like you, I had the disappearing parents.

In your schooldays, was writing always what you wanted to do? You say your dad was a poet. Did you start as a poet?

No, I was apprenticed to my grandfather, as a painter. I think that's where all the stage directions come from.

So that's why your plays are so painterly – because they are – that's the way you present them.

Yes – and I think there was a period when I wrote those plays, from about 1986 to 1994 I suppose, where that age – thirty, thirty-one – that was part of being at ease in your skin, or happy, or so devoted, that your attention to it was complete, but you were vastly innocent at the same time. And then as you get older, moving out of the phases not only of the moon but of love, and having your children, and the darkening world – that whole thing – then you become more as if you were in a play yourself. You're no longer innocent of being in a play. That strange moment when you're forty and you wake up in the morning and realise you'll never be young. And you didn't know it the day before. I think that's the great change, you know, and that's what I'm trying to work out. And yet for me, that's the Royal Court, the Royal Court I knew. Because my mother acted at the Royal Court . . .

And did you go? Were you taken to see plays?

No – we went to the pantomime in London – or the *Nutcracker*. It would have been considered immensely grown up. But I mean the theatre is immensely grown up, that's the other important thing about it. And if you ask does it have a purpose, which as I said to you I don't know, it has something to do with offering, if not solace, then illumination to the difficulty of being in the world. That's how I'd define the purpose.

Yes. Though again I doubt that everybody would agree with that. My father said he believed plays should be disturbing. I think he meant some process that happens to you when you see a play that somehow shifts something somewhere – do you know what I mean?

I do, and I think it's something to do with . . . My father's farm in Greece lost the water supply, because there was a little earthquake, and the watercourse shifted somewhere underground. And a play in a way should do a little earthquake thing – nothing appears to have changed on the surface, except that the water has gone from the well. Or maybe the water's been put in the well. I mean I have seen stunned people after plays. I've also had the experience in recent years of seeing people enraged – enraging a whole town with a play, a country . . .

One of your own plays? Which one?

A play called *Hinterland*, which caused a terrible ruckus – and that's another form of disturbance. It's only now, three years later, that I begin to read the odd beautiful scholarly thing about it. It would almost make you cry, because it was what you actually felt yourself at the time, but you couldn't say anything. Now that wouldn't get you very far in the theatre. As I say, you start off with solace, but maybe you can only offer illumination. But it can also be repellent. And it also can be a failure. You've failed to illuminate. Beckett said, you can fail, but fail better next time, which is a way of thinking, a sort of sixties way. Of course there's a huge connection there with the Royal Court. I mean their devotion to Beckett probably allowed Beckett to continue to write.

I know my father was completely committed to Beckett.

And in a very serious and important way – he put his plays on, and allowed him in, probably half the time, to annoy everybody.

So you'd been writing for eight years – novels and poetry – before you wrote your first play. Did anything happen that made you decide to do that?

I was keeping away from theatre a bit, because my mother was a name and, like all families, we were a very complicated family, and that seemed like the wise thing to do. But then I met my wife, who's an actress, and she was working in the Abbey, and then she got a job on *Casualty*, which meant she had to go to Bristol for two weeks. I had read somewhere that if a play took longer than two weeks to write you were wasting your time. So I had two weeks – and sure I'd done it in ten days. So that was *Boss Grady's Boys*.

Pinter and Storey both say they sit down with a blank sheet of paper and have no structure, no intention. And Pinter says, I have no idea until I write the last line, and then I think, okay, that's the last line, I'm finished. But is that what it's like for you?

Well, actually I do believe that the structure of a play, whatever a play is, is an innate shape, a memory shape of something very proper and natural in the brain. So that it's not for no reason that it's the way it is. And I also think it pre-dates writing things down, and I think it predates *homo sapiens*, it predates *homo erectus* himself. I think it's so ancient – I think it's why it has that potency despite these dazzling technologies. In fact the more dazzling technology you bring to plays, even in the Victorian era, when Hans Christian Andersen was appalled by Edmund Kean's son's production, all glitzy and proper seas for *The Tempest*, you know, it was so incredible, and Dion Boucicault, who burned ships on the stage, and you know it kind of militates against the text. And I think that's why a lot of my stage directions have just drifted away and they've just become these enormous unplayable texts, really. Something I've got to stop doing! So that, you know, some creature a bit like us, a bit stooped, was allowing this thing to happen the way they marked the walls in the caves. They weren't thinking about painting, or art, or theatre, or mighty beings – they were just doing something like birdsong – like, as an expression of survival, or of 'We were here and this is what we were like,' or any of those things, or 'We are here and we are very afraid, and we are going to do this thing to become less afraid,' maybe that's what it is. And so when you're writing, that has to be – that is presupposed. Writing badly, for me, is when you disallow that fact, and you want it to have some technical book thing – posh writing, you know.

David Storey said that any time he tries to write according to some structure, some idea, it doesn't work.

You become chilled. That's what I call posh writing.

But you know a great many writers don't or can't write like Storey and Pinter.

I think that's what is interesting about the Irish theatre. Irish theatre is almost entirely composed of that sort of writing. And that's why it's so different to, say, English theatre. Not so much Scottish theatre. And some Russian plays are very Irish. I mean Chekhov – a very Irish playwright. Because they are a natural form. You know, in St Petersburg, when *The Seagull* was put on, he had fallen from his pedestal. His best friend said to him, 'We have to tell you we think this is deeply flawed.' He had simply followed his own inner *homo erectus*, with the river of his own thing running through it, which is what the words are. It's kind of like – after the waters come over the sand, and the tide's been left – very innate, very natural, extremely religious without religion, in the sense that you've got to believe it, although you can't see any proof. Because as soon as you become rational, you're lost. I mean, I often wonder why writers are elevated, because they are to all intents and purposes sort of benign madmen, and sometimes not so benign. This doesn't even have to be a good-hearted person, or a decent person, or an interesting person – it seems to be a kind of mortally afflicted person. Anyway, this is my difficulty now, in my present play, that I sort of know – I sort of knew at the beginning what it was about, and as soon as I started to write it I realised I did know what it was about and that is a fatal gate to come in at. I must not come in at that gate.

So what do you do, then?

Well, for instance, with this previous play, *Whistling Psyche* – this play is composed of what are essentially two monologues, or two women, who are in the same place, have met once in their lives, but they never speak on stage. And Claire Bloom and Kathryn Hunter played it, beautifully and brilliantly. But the play was harshly criticised for being non-theatrical . . .

Where was this done?

This was in April 2004, at the Almeida. And it was a rather wonderful thing, there was a magic attached to it, but I could see the objections. At the time, I remember starting that play, about a year and a half before, because it was about a person who is now quite heavily documented but wasn't when I began, an ancestor of mine, and doing it and thinking, well, because there's so much information about this person I must do this conventionally, whatever that is – but God forbid! And trying it every which way – I then sat down and did it and got incredibly excited and produced this – monstrosity. But whether it's an angel or a monster that you produce, it has to be the angel or the monster of your own blasted loins. And you never know quite what you've got. And then there's the mystery of the people who want to be involved, and the theatres that want to do it. And I have been blessed in that way. And you know, I'm here to tell you that maybe my sweetest experience in the theatre was in the Royal Court.

What a pity that you've only done one play there. Did they never commission another?

They did offer, yes. But I went recently to talk to them about a play – I described the plays I was thinking about and they didn't think any of them were very promising.

So where will the new play be done?

Who knows – who knows? Or if – if I ever get it done. Nothing is for sure. At the moment, it's just floating somewhere. But the Court is wonderful because – at a certain moment, 1992 I think it was, I had a play on at the Bush, *White Woman Street*, and I went to see Max Stafford-Clark, and it was a version of going to London to see the queen, or the king. I went up to his office, and he was on the phone to Edward Bond, so that was a good start, and we talked about this play, and he said, Yes, I think I will commission that. And I went down through the Court, and hurried out and ran out into the square, and nearly killed myself crossing the road, and onto the pavement, to find a phone box to phone my wife Alison, to say Max had commissioned a play. It was a really lovely thing. And we had talked passionately about the play. And then when I delivered the play, he was very nice, but he said, you know you talk so much better about your plays than when you write them! But you know Max – he was teasing. I didn't know Max very well and I was a bit shocked by that. But then he never, or seldom, praises his actors, for fear of putting them off. And this was the first draft of the play, and he was going to go on to the next draft, which is the big thing, really. Because that's the time to say no, when the first draft comes in. And what he was saying was, there was work to be done. He commissioned that idea in my head to allow me to do the work. So then I did the work, and delivered it, and he accepted it. But then Stephen Daldry took over, and Max was no longer in control of the theatre, and he started Out of Joint. And I knew Stephen was a bit wary. I had gone into the theatre and Max had shown me the beautiful auditorium, and I thought this is marvellous – four hundred seats – beautiful theatre, Shaw's theatre. Then Stephen said he would put it on, but Upstairs. I went up to see that and I thought, my God, it's a hut on the roof. But of course it's the most important hut on the most important roof in the London theatre. So that was okay – and he did write a letter saying why that was. He said, I want this play to be seen in all its glory – so that was fine. Then something happened – Max must have got very busy, or very overwhelmed by work – but there was a period when he said he didn't think he could direct it. So it went back to somebody in the Court, and somebody wrote to me, or to my agent, we feel this play is a bit static and we want to give it a rehearsed reading. And at this point I said to my agent, young as I was, and foolish, with two children, I said, 'Will you ask them to give it back?' Because my heart was being broken – as it is in these cases – and I think they said they would, which I don't know if it was a good or a bad thing. So then I rang Max and I said, 'Look Max, I know you can't do this play, but can you look after it? Because unless it's the lover of the play bringing it by the hand, its going to get into trouble.' So he said, 'Of course I will, I'll look after it.' The next thing I heard, he'd sent it to Donal McCann, and Donal had said yes, and then there was never any doubt. But even with Donal McCann it was going to be Upstairs at the Court. At the time it seemed a bit frustrating, but I see now it was also a question of care, and people were thinking. The only thing that is un-nerving about the Court, and I'm sure people have said this, is that every-one in the building has read the play. You can't get a cup of tea – in fact I don't think you can buy the *Evening Standard* outside – without the guy having read the play. And that was a new experience, but that is to its credit.

But you enjoyed the experience?

When I say it was a great experience, it was great because it was working there, and we had this most amazing cast. And yet, halfway through the rehearsals, I remember Stephen coming in – Stephen, you know, wears beautiful shirts. And he had a lovely yellow shirt on. So I asked him, did he have another shirt like that, and he said he did. I said, 'Well, if it goes into the main house, will you give me the other shirt?' And he said he would, probably feeling he would have no need to part with this shirt. And I asked Max afterwards, what did Stephen think? And he said, 'Well, I don't think he had great faith in the performance, so we're probably fixed where we are.' You know this is the lovely talk, it goes on all the time, and you think, Oh well, that's fine. But then this other thing happened, and took everybody by surprise, no one knew what was happening. The day we opened we were reviewed in the *Evening Standard*, and Stephen went down to get the paper and the paper man said, 'I think it's a good one, I think you'll be all right, Mr Daldry.' And I did glance at that review, and I went and phoned Ali again, and I said, something is happening. I knew it was happening. And the reviews that followed on, I did actually glance at them, I've never looked at them again – they were actually hair-raising, and when that happens you realise that something, maybe beyond anybody involved, everybody's faith, for some reason, adds up to this incredible thing. But this was the perfect experience in the theatre. To have had a play in London which had been well reviewed, which hadn't been booed out of the theatre. You know I don't think plays are successful or unsuccessful, I think they're either loved in some way or not. I mean you can love something ugly, you can love something just for its signal or for its strength. And I had that. A very bewildering and very wonderful thing. And you know at the Royal Court it was incredible, ten weeks, and there was never an empty seat. And Stephen said, if something happens, I will stand by this, and he did.

And did he give you the shirt?

He never gave me the shirt. I'm still waiting for the shirt.

And from your own point of view, which is the play that is closest to your heart?

Well, it is a series of seven plays, so even *Hinterland*, the latest play, hated and reviled in its moment of being put on, is part of that. And one of the reasons for that is because it is a play that is describing something irredeemable. A distressing possibility for me, as well as for everybody else. I think that group of plays, partly because it took so long, partly because it encompasses something, you know – my children's childhood – I feel it's the thing I did, in the world, to conceive of something, to intimate something, to have a sense of something, and then to end up doing it. And I didn't leave it unfinished.

But it's a curious thing to have written seven plays and to come out the other end so that the plays you write are no longer part of those seven plays.

And that is proving difficult. Because *Whistling Psyche*, although it's a possible ancestor, it's not quite a family play. And this one I'm writing definitely isn't. And I wonder about that. Also I've written four novels, one just coming out, two from about the time I started to write *The Steward*, and I don't want novels to take over, but I really am just waiting for the true signal. Because whatever it's for, ultimately, the fact remains that it can't be done except in the most . . . because it's total writing, theatre. It's too great a responsibility. It's good when you're younger, because you don't realise, but you are carrying the happiness of a lot of people, and maybe that is a little disabling as a thought. And actors are so brave, anyway – I mean I've put actors through hell. Especially with this last play, it's terrible what they had to go through. Maybe they're strong, resilient people, like the Irish soldiers in the First World War.

Richard Bean

Toast 1999
Under the Whaleback 2003
Honeymoon Suite 2004
Harvest 2005

Richard Bean came to playwriting comparatively late in life, having been a psychologist and a stand-up comedian. Both of those things have obviously fed into his plays, which are wonderfully funny as well as wholly serious in the issues they raise. When I talked to him in the Royal Court bar in April 2005, he'd recently finished working on *Harvest*, which was produced at the theatre the following September, to great acclaim.

Can you remember the first time you went to the theatre?

Well, yes and no. When I was growing up in Hull, we never went to pantomimes, never went to the cinema or anything like that. Art and culture were not part of the household that much. So the first time I went to the theatre would probably be to Hull Truck. I remember seeing some of the Beat poets. Roger McGough did a cabaret thing called the *The Masked Poet*, and I think that was the first time I went to the theatre, but even then it wasn't to see a play.

Did you get involved with theatre at school?

At primary school my only experience was having a lead in a sketch and forgetting my lines completely. So I avoided acting. You've got to remember that my first professional play was done when I was already forty-two, so I came to theatre very late. I don't think I went to the theatre for enjoyment until my thirties, really. In my twenties it was all punk rock and whatever – I'm the same age as Johnny Rotten, and punk was a huge movement then and I absolutely loved the energy and the politics of it, and got involved with that, though I wasn't a musician.

And then you were a stand-up comedian?

Yes – well, that was late as well.

You had a 'proper job' before all this?

Yes, I had lots of proper jobs. But I was doing stand-up when I was thirty-fourish. I only got involved in theatre because I took a room in a house, as a lodger, with an actor called Mark Brignal. Then I started going to theatre because he was in things, and his friends were in things. The first time I went to the National, where he was working at the time, he said, 'You must come along to the green room, come to the bar afterwards for a drink.' And while we were in there a big fight broke out, a big fist fight. So I thought, oh, theatre's a bit livelier than I'd imagined. But that was amazing, actually – backstage at the National, and there were tables going over. It was like the Wild West.

Between the actors?

Yes, a couple of actors kicked off. I think it was the cast of *Cinderella* – there must be a joke there somewhere.

So at some point during this period you thought, 'Oh, I'll have a go'? What made you suddenly decide to write a play?

I suppose in terms of theatre and performance, you've got to look at stand-up for me as an entrance to this business. Because then I started writing for radio, as a gag-writer, and I wrote a sketch show with a couple of other guys, called *Control Group Six*, which was quite successful – it was a bit like Royston Vasey, something like that. And then, of course, when you're doing that kind of work, you become less interested in the work you've been trained to do and you also have a different view of who you are. I remember doing stand-up, and if it went really well, I'd walk home and think, was that me? Have I become someone else? You can't conceive of ever doing that extremely difficult thing.

Where did you do the stand-up?

All around London, comedy venues – there's a photo of me on the Comedy Store wall still, I think. I had an agent, and I was doing the universities, going round.

And did you make a living?

Not really. I was an occupational psychologist, and I was working free-lance, charging £400 a day, so if I did three days of that a month I could survive. It was a mad lifestyle, really, but I was free, and I was kind of discovering who I was, reinventing myself, really.

And the first play you wrote was not done here, was it?

No. The first play I wrote was called *Of Rats and Men*, and it was done on the fringe in London, and on the fringe in Edinburgh. And then the BBC produced it as a radio play.

After the radio sketch show you thought you'd have a go at something a bit more . . .

Yes, but everything's been a bit fluky, really, nothing's been designed. I was trying to write for television, and a friend of mine said, Well, if you want to write for TV the best thing you can do is write a good play for the Bush. So I wrote *Toast*, and sent it to the Bush, and they weren't interested, but then the National Studio picked it up and got the Royal Court interested, so when it was done here it was a co-production. But I had no intention of writing for theatre, really, I just thought, what can I do? And I'd spent two years in this bakery so I thought, oh, I can write about those lads. And I think by then the biggest influence on my writing was David Storey, *The Changing Room*.

I could see that.

Yes, of course. So all those other plays I had seen before were completely irrelevant really. I went to see *The Changing Room* and I couldn't get the bloody thing out of my head. It was a funny experience, because at the time I saw it, when I sat in that audience, I was a bit bored. I saw the Royal Court's revival at the Duke of York's in 1996. I was actually a little bit bored watching it, but then for months afterwards I just couldn't get it out of my head. And I realised it was the sheer poetry of the thing, and that mix of poetry and naturalism, where you kind of believe that what's going on on stage is actually happening, but you know it isn't. It just astonished me. And I thought, oh, now I know how to write my bakery play. All those lads – I'd carried them around in my head for years, and I didn't know what to do with them. Because you can't show the bread production, it's too difficult. So I thought, oh, of course, you show them in the canteen. So if you ask when was the first time I went to the theatre, that was it really. Which was also interesting, because that would have been, I imagine, at the height of 'in-yer-face' theatre, and I remember that revival being really criticised by some of the in-yer-face writers, who were saying, 'We only went to see the bums, and what's all that naturalism about?' And saying how irrelevant it was. But because I'd never been to theatre, and knew nothing about it, I was just overcome by the twenty-two blokes on stage being real.

45

All your plays have real people in them, in different working environments.

Yes – Michael Billington said, 'Richard Bean must have had a hell of a life.' But I just researched them all, really.

And the trawlermen – they seem to recur in your plays. Did you know people who worked in that environment?

Yes. That's a whole community that you lived and breathed. They pop up in all the plays: I've got their voices in my head. I know how they would react to anything I said to them, or you said to them. And the new play I'm writing for here, *Harvest*, is again voices I've got in my head, which is East Yorkshire farmers. Because although I'm Hull, one hundred per cent, my family are from East Yorkshire, farming people, and we always went to visit relatives out on the farms. So the new play is East Yorkshire voices rather than Hull voices. I write them because they're easy to write, really, because I've got them there.

Let's talk about the process of writing. You say it's easy to write, but you also say you have to do research. How does a new play come into being? What's the initial thing that happens that makes you think, 'That could be a play'?

I think one thing for me is, I often want to be oppositional.

That word gets used here at the Court a lot. What do you take it to mean?

Well, if you take any subject – let's say anything in the political spectrum – I mean, my play *The God Botherers* is about aid workers. If you take a subject like aid workers, there's a general consensus amongst the theatre village, a certain view . . . I think it's pointless to watch an anti-war play, when the whole audience is anti-war already.

My father said, in 1960, 'I want the theatre to be continuously disturbing. I want people to ask questions. I want to make them anti-conformist.' Is that the kind of thing you mean?

Yes, but this is more difficult, this is more complex. Because, of course, when your dad was putting on oppositional plays, there was a hierarchy, so the oppositional thing would be, privilege is a bad thing, what we need is egalitarianism, what we need is education for all, what we need is non-discrimination against women. But now we've got all those things, you've got to find new things to oppose, and they're out there – the orthodoxies are all out there. Take *The God Botherers* – the orthodoxy there is: aid work to Africa is a good thing, we need to give Africa more money, we need to send white, educated people over there, teach them how to live their lives, whatever. And I wrote that play saying: look how aid work destroys, how it is contaminating and destructive. And in many ways, though it's not the whole story, that's the oppositional point. I mean things have changed politically. The concept of ideology – right-wing or left-wing – is now such a no-brainer that it's nonsense. I mean take Castro, for instance – is he left-wing or is he right-wing? He's obviously a fascist. The whole idea that an ideology can be presented to the public that will educate them and raise their awareness is patronising and nonsensical. The truth, and this is much more interesting, is that in the world of politics and big issues, everything is unbelievably mucky and complex and difficult, and that's what needs to be shown. That's the obligation. *The God Botherers* is not against aid work, it's just saying look, this is the thing that happens – people go out there with Western values, they muck up the local culture, the local culture responds, and then you've got this turmoil. Am I being too intense?

No – I love it. I'm wanting people to talk about exactly those kinds of things. Lately there's been Debbie Tucker Green's Stoning Mary, *and* My Name Is Rachel Corrie, *and I'm wondering what political theatre can be now. You're right – everything is messy and difficult and complicated, so people are less likely to write political plays because they don't know where they stand.*

Because they can't take one polemic, yes. I think it's a legitimate thing to present the complexities. There's a danger with political theatre. Take the current vogue for Tribunal plays. The tenor of all those things is anti-establishment. But the one called *Justifying War* – about the scientist who committed suicide – well, it was an anti-war project. But the guy who killed himself was for the war, and that seems to get missed. And it's that kind of complexity that a playwright can bring out.

But now you're saying this in a general way, and you've talked about The God Botherers, *but what about your other plays? Do you think all your plays are political?*

No, not at all. I mean there are political elements in them, I suppose – I think political in the sense that they've got to be about the human condition in the end, and that's obviously a political thing. The only overtly political play is *The God Botherers*. In *The Mentalists*, which is a two-hander, one bloke's a right-winger and one's a left-winger.

47

So – you say you've been carrying those blokes around in your head for twenty years, but why were they worth putting on the stage? What was it you wanted to say about them?

That's a good point. One of the reasons why I work with Richard Wilson as a director is that he has got this commitment to putting on stage the lives of those who are not normally represented. So he was very attracted to putting the shipworkers, the trawlermen, on stage. There's also this strange kind of Hull thing with me. You can't get to Hull, and why would you want to go there anyway? We're the forgotten city – nobody likes us, but we don't care. But one of the wonderful things about growing up in Hull is the dry sense of humour. The men and the women are all comedians, but they don't laugh. They just have this extraordinary dry irony about everything, about their lives, in fact. So they don't call the Job Centre the Job Centre, they call it the Joke Shop. It's just that kind of, how do we get through life when it's this difficult? The oxygen of my family life, growing up, is that laughter. And growing up with that, you want to write it. You just want to write those lines that your uncles used to say.

Giving voices to people, yes. I think that is sometimes thought of in perhaps a rather narrow way, and just applied to ethnic minorities.

Yes – well, the people of Hull, and Yorkshiremen, tend to think of themselves as an ethnic minority, though probably in a rather superior way. There's a terrible arrogance about Yorkshiremen. But the new play, about a Yorkshire factory farm, you could say is about people who are ignored, or taken for granted. They feed the nation, and they get abused by central government and the meat-eating public, who just want cheaper meat, and who put them out of business. So in that sense it's a political play in representing that. I go back to Yorkshire, and I meet these relatives of mine, and they've worked hard all their lives, and they've got nothing. For the pig farm play I interviewed a kind of half-uncle of mine, who'd been a pig farmer for about forty years. They went out of business, and now they're scratching around. And I said, 'Well, you're sixty now, what did you think you'd be doing when you were this age?' And he said, 'Well, when everything was going well, we thought we'd be in the Bahamas at this age.' And he's working as a clerk in a lorry depot now. And that's all because of political changes, and the politicians of this country having no interest in little groups of people who keep the country going. Like the fishermen – a small group of people, three thousand people, signed away one day in Iceland without a thought. And the Icelandic government offered a long-term deal to the British that would have kept the fishermen going, and they just signed it away. A Labour government as well. That's what I mean by complexity.

And you're just interested in people's lives, as well.

Yes. I sat on my half-uncle's sofa, and his knees are shot through, because pigs always charge your knees, and he's got a bad hip. I mean, I couldn't work a week in a pig farm, never mind forty years. And basically he's been ignored by the wave of global politics that's just swept his life aside and made it irrelevant. There's no point in producing pork in England when you can do it cheaper in Europe, because the legislation's different. And the government don't seem to be aware of that. So I like to represent those people. And the other thing is, there was a time when people wrote plays about kings – and queens, but mostly kings. Then earlier in the twentieth century there was the standard play about middle-class people. And then the working-class heroes came forward, thanks to your dad and this theatre. So it's just a continuation of a tradition, I suppose. Of course, the Royal Court's accused of being involved in the tourist industry – the middle classes of London come to see how the working classes of Hull live – but I'm from Hull, and I'm not going to not put my own people on stage. Because I value them as much as anybody else.

Tell me what the process of writing a play is like. Is it easy, difficult – how long does it take? What do you do? Do you always have to go around talking to people or does it sometimes come straight out of your head?

Sometimes it does. But less and less so. I suppose in a way I'm always attracted to something I know a bit about. For instance, this week I'm trying to finish a cricket play. All my life I've played cricket, so I'm writing a cricket play. And obviously I don't have to go to the library or the internet for anything – I've played cricket for thirty years at a very poor level, and I just wanted to show a game. And I can do it very quickly. I will write a play in two weeks or three weeks, and it will be finished. But I'm writing another play about the European Parliament, which is a farce, set in a Strasbourg hotel, a classic farce, doors, men in cupboards. And I know very little about the European Parliament so I had to go to Brussels, and I'm researching it. I've got literature in my bag here which I'm reading on the tube. It's taken me a year, and I've done one draft in that time. But that's also because it's a farce, and a farce is more difficult because it's a machine, and you're building an engine.

49

What about Honeymoon Suite – *was that difficult to write?*

No, it was quite easy, really.

Although it has quite a complicated structure.

Yes, but there was no research in that. The dominating thing is the structure of the play, and once I'd hit on that – which I'm not claiming to be
original – but once I'd decided to do the three acts simultaneously, everything else was easy. There was no research in the characters, I knew who
they would be. They're very typical Hull voices. And it was interesting
when John Alderton wanted to do that part – he described it, when he
read it, as putting on an old cardigan. Because he's from Hull, and he just
knew those voices. Especially the male, the very low self-image of the
male, which is such a common thing in Hull now, because all the jobs
have gone. So that was in my head; I just got that out quite quickly.

And are you writing to commissions a lot?

Yes. I don't really like to write for commissions, but what I haven't had is
a commercial success, because that's more and more difficult now. And in
terms of the structure of theatre that's a big issue for us younger playwrights. I say younger – I mean I'm older, because I started when I was
forty-two. But even if you have a hit – *Under the Whaleback* was a critical
success and a box-office success, though in a hundred-seat theatre that
doesn't really count; but there's never even been a phone call about it:
'Can we do that in the West End?' You'd think after that somebody would
be interested in your work. But just one theatre, a fringe theatre in Australia has done it, and that's it. Apart from Hull Truck, who were a dead
cert to do it, of course. But your older guys you've been talking to, if they
had a hit here, they'd expect a life from it, and beyond. So I think that's a
difficult thing, that the West End is not supporting new writing in the way
that they used to.

*Now supposing you have a commission from the Royal Court and one
from the National, would they be different kinds of play that you'd write?*

Yes, you do write with the theatre in mind as you're doing it.

*But how does that operate? Is it purely about the stage, or is it the avail-
ability of a larger cast, or what?*

On cast size, yes. You're limited in many theatres to four or five, maybe six
characters. The Royal Court and the National don't limit you but you would

be more conscious of cast size for the Court than the National. I've got a play I'm writing for the National, a commission, and cast size won't be a problem. But the staging of it might be. You'd think, God, I'm supposed to write this for the Olivier, so you wouldn't write the kind of play where you had four characters and they each had an equal dramatic arc. You'd need a big male (usually male) central character to dominate that. So you'd write a hierarchical play, with a larger cast.

But you wouldn't be thinking of the content, or the message, as being particularly different?

Well, I think for a Royal Court play I would want to annoy the audience a bit more, challenge them.

More than you would for somewhere else? That's a kind of agenda for the Royal Court?

Only an agenda that I give myself; no one gives it to me. You get a sense with the Royal Court that there are some sacred cows, and I think in an ideal world you want to take those sacred cows and show them to the audience for what they really are. Something that motivates me is to challenge, to do that oppositional thing with a Royal Court audience.

Okay. But you are also involved with this group called the Monsterists. Do you want to tell me about that?

Well, it's basically about writers of our generation being given permission to write big plays for big stages. We think of ourselves as the black box generation – me and Roy Williams have been very lucky, because we're allowed on the main stage here, for instance. But there are many writers up and down the country who are writing for the studio theatres around the back of the main theatre where a dead playwright is on the main stage. So a lot of it is about dead playwrights and living playwrights. And the second thing is about big plays, large casts, big production budgets, stars, big directors. That's the main campaign. It's not to do with the Royal Court really – the Royal Court is a writers' theatre, and lots of theatres are not, they're artistic directors' theatres.

So it's not so much an aesthetic thing – it's a campaign on behalf of those people who are shunted off into tiny venues.

Yes, mainly.

I went to see Tristan and Iseult *at the National recently, which I thought was fabulous. There was lots of music and dance and spectacle, and I found myself wishing more theatre was like that. So I wondered if your Monsterists idea was a desire to be given the scope to do something like that?*

Well, yes. When you're given a commission, you have a cup of coffee with the artistic director, and he'll show you the black box theatre with one hundred seats, and he'll say, 'Well, we can afford five characters.' And that's it, and you write that, and that's your living. That's your job. And the bigger theatres, theatres that have got six hundred seats or more, main stage, and a hundred-seater studio, will be spending their government grants on doing expensive Chekhovs, Gogols, whatever, and the living writers will be in the studio. The star directors – I don't want to slander these people, but in the hierarchy of directors, the star directors won't do new plays. I mean here they do, obviously, because it's a new play theatre, but elsewhere they won't. So we want the star directors, we want the stars, we want the budget to do that. I mean a set budget for Upstairs here is about seven or eight thousand pounds – again I'm using this theatre because I know it – main stage will be thirty-five, forty, fifty thousand. We want the resources put into the living writers. Part of it is that we can't earn a living – that's the other thing. You can only earn a living if you get plays produced on big stages. You can't earn a living from studio writing. But that's a minor thing, a living – or is it? It's the chief thing, but you can't mention it, because it's perceived to denigrate your argument, but it's a true thing as well. That's why so many writers do television and film.

I'm quite surprised by how many of the people I've talked to recently do that.

I don't.

Could you say overall that there are one or more things that you think your plays are actually about – is there something going on under all these things that you want to say?

I guess for me it's about the human condition, it's about the individual in the context initially of a group of people, often a work situation, and then the imperatives of a wider context, say society. If you take *Under the Whaleback*, the central character is Cassidy (though many people would think the central character was Darrell) – you'd look at that character and say, where does this man get his values from? There's that fishing culture, machismo, drinking – all the family values, they're all big family men. Then there's society, their role in society – oh, they feed the nation. Well, how does the nation treat them? 'Oh, sod off, we'll get our fish from somewhere else.' So there's always that continuum. Again, with the pig farmers – there'll be the pig farmer as an individual (in this case a woman), then her immediate group, her family, it's a family farm, and in the context of society – what does she do? She feeds the nation – how does the nation treat her? With contempt.

They all feed the nation – the bread people in Toast *feed the nation too!*

Yes – so it might be food. The director Paul Miller says there's only one consistent thing in Richard Bean's plays, that a man has a pee at some point. I hadn't really looked at that. It was the thing my mother didn't like in *Mr England*.

What does your mother think in general about your plays?

I think the most telling thing is that she keeps a scrapbook with all the reviews, and when I go home she shows me if there've been any new ones. I was looking at it recently – and Nicholas de Jongh hated *Honeymoon Suite*, so I'd never read the review, because my agent rings me up and says don't read that one, because I get too upset. But there it was in my mum's scrapbook, all pasted up there, and it's all diatribe. She's proud that I'm in the papers – I could have robbed a bank and been on the front page and she'd have pasted it up.

Is there any sense in which you feel you are a Royal Court playwright? Do you feel any loyalty to this theatre?

I feel loyal to the Royal Court, but also to the National. A lot of it is to do with individuals – Ian Rickson, Graham Whybrow, but also Jack Bradley at the National, and also Hull Truck. Do I think of myself as a Royal Court playwright? Other people may see me as such. I suppose the Royal Court has opened all the doors for me.

Leo Butler

Made of Stone 2000
Redundant 2001
Lucky Dog 2004

Lucy Prebble

The Sugar Syndrome 2003

When I wanted to talk to some of the newer writers, I thought first of Lucy Prebble. The George Devine Award committee in 2004 – the first one I had been on – was absolutely unanimous in choosing her play, *The Sugar Syndrome*, as that year's winner. I'd met Lucy at the award presentation and was looking forward to talking to her about her work. When I turned up for the interview, in the Royal Court bar, in January 2005, she was sitting with another young playwright, Leo Butler, whom I'd met recently when I saw his play *Lucky Dog* in the Theatre Upstairs. It seemed too good a chance to miss, so I talked to both of them.

Leo – can you remember your first experience of theatre?

LEO I guess my first experience was at school – a nativity play. And the different shows we'd do there – *Snow White and the Seven Dwarfs*, *Charlie and the Chocolate Factory* . . . And since we lived in Sheffield my parents took me to see lots of plays at the Crucible – and not just for kids. I saw *Macbeth*, and *A Streetcar Named Desire*, and *Who's Afraid of Virginia Woolf?* when I was very young. A lot of it went over my head, but it was a good experience.

But did it kind of grab you then and there? Did you think, wow, this is what I want to do?

LEO Yes, absolutely – I absolutely loved it. I got involved with a youth theatre, the Sheffield Youth Theatre, and by that time I was writing anyway, little short stories. I had a pile of notebooks, with a story in each of them. And in the youth theatre we did some Eastern types of theatre, we took some Japanese tales and adapted them, and then we did Shake-speare. So from age eleven to fifteen I was acting in plays like *The Merchant of Venice* and *The Tempest* – playing Shylock at fourteen. And I was writing these stories. And the director of the youth theatre, Meg Jepson, said, Well, you should keep this up – because I'd shown her all these things – and when we next do a show you should write a monologue to present, so I did. She always encouraged me – she said you must always keep writing. So from a very early age I was thrown into it.

You saw yourself as being part of it all, very early?

LEO Yes. And I hated school, I was always in trouble at school, but when it came to the youth theatre I was absolutely committed – that was my education, really.

And what about you, Lucy – the first memory of theatre?

LUCY Well, the first memory I have is of going to musicals. My parents weren't particularly avid theatregoers, but they would always go up to London, and take the children, if there was a big new musical on. So I have memories of seeing things like *42nd Street*, and big new musicals in the West End, and being absolutely aghast and amazed by the whole artistry and the flamboyance of it, which was really my falling in love with theatre. And even today I think it's seeing people do things that take your breath away and that you recognise you could never do yourself, which is really incredible. So it was musicals that I went to see when I was growing up. And then I acted at school. I was at an all-girls' school for most of my formative years, and we would do a lot of Shakespeare. And because I was quite a broad-shouldered young lady, I would always play the men, which in Shakespeare means you get all the best parts. So I remember playing Jaques when I was fourteen, and playing Hamlet, which was great in a way, because when I got into theatre myself later on, I didn't see any divide between male and female parts. I was so used to playing them all myself anyway. But also I was the youngest of three children, and my elder brother and sister were very academic, and good at school, and good at all sorts of things – my sister was a great cook, and used to paint – and I think when you're the youngest you have to find your own niche. So I think an element of it for me was, well, no one else in our family can do that – acting or writing or whatever – so that'll be what I go towards. I think that psychologically you try to find something that's yours, and for me it was writing.

So you were also writing?

LUCY Yes, but terrible stuff . . .

But they were plays?

LUCY Not really – short stories, that rings a bell. There'd be a comic that I was really into, or a television series, and I would write little stories based on the characters in those – create my own stories for them. And I also kept my own awful diaries that were full of emotional angst – of course a lot of teenagers do that, but I was very committed to it, and I wrote in it every day. But not until I was much, much older did it ever occur to me to write dialogue. It just didn't occur to me at that age.

So when did you think of writing dialogue?

LUCY Well, not until university. What happened with me was, I just fell very much in love with a guy who was on my English literature course. I was besotted, and he was very active in the university theatre productions, which I'd never been really interested in. I wasn't particularly interested in extra-curricular things, other than going out, really, like a lot of students. But I was completely besotted with him, and he used to do a lot of acting. In a bar one day I overheard him say that he'd like to direct something, something new, and I said, 'Oh, I've got loads of ideas for stuff.' And he went, 'Oh really?' And I said, 'Oh yes, loads, loads.' And then of course I actually had to do it, because he got quite interested in that – he said, 'Oh, okay, why don't you write me something and we'll see if I want to direct it next term?' And so that was the very first time I ever tried to do it – to get a man!

And how was it when you started writing?

LUCY It was very, very hard. I still find it a really difficult process. But because there were people there who said, 'Come on, write it, we want to put it on,' I had to do it.

You had a commission!

LUCY Yes, basically, I had a commission. Based on – I want this guy to fancy me so it'd better be good. The best commission ever!

And was it any good? I mean how did it come out? Did it come out okay?

LUCY Yes – it was a one-act play, and it actually ended up getting into the National Student Drama Festival, which was being held in Scarborough. It went along to that, and it was selected, and it ended up winning the new writing award there. And it wasn't until that happened that I'd ever considered that I had some sort of professional capacity for writing, or that I could in any way do it. So it was a success at university – all the students came to see it.

And when you say it was hard – what was hard about it? Did you have an idea what it was going to be about before you started?

LUCY Yes, I had an idea what it was going to be about, I had a subject.

What was it about?

LUCY Well, it was about management consultants – it sounds so dull! But I had a lot of friends – and my brother, too – who'd left university, and had gone into very high-flying positions in the City. It was very interesting to watch these people who'd been quite truant, or left-wing, or whatever, taking high paid jobs, and watching the changes that happened to their characters. So it was about graduates who'd taken jobs in a management consultants' firm, and one of them, a guy, gets testicular cancer during his year there. It was about his experience of coming to terms with that, and what he wants to do with his life – when he finds he's mortal. So it was based on my friends' experiences, and that was the basic idea. I mean I read it now and I'm embarrassed, but generally I'm embarrassed by stuff I've written three weeks ago.

So it was difficult to – what?

LUCY To make it good. I don't know what Leo thinks, but I was at university and I'd been taught a very analytical way of looking at texts, and taking them apart. And when you've been trained in that way, and you come to try and be creative yourself, every line is incredibly difficult, because all you do is look at it and take it apart, and think, oh, that's so weak . . . and so it's getting past that, and having to say to yourself, well, just don't think about it, just do it.

So what about you, Leo, was it difficult for you to write? Let's go back a bit – we've got you to where you were with the youth theatre – what happened after that?

LEO Apart from Shakespeare, I was influenced a lot by *Monty Python* and by Charlie Chaplin, and Laurel and Hardy. So I began writing a lot of sketches that were put on at school. They were really just slapstick, very silly, but the rest of the school liked them. Then when I was fifteen, sixteen, I did a Performance Arts BTech, and there I was much more interested in acting.

Did you want to be an actor at that point?

LEO I guess I wanted to do everything! I remember directing David Mamet's *Sexual Perversity in Chicago* and thinking, well, I think I'll direct, I'll write and direct and act in all my own shows. But then, gradually, at that time I started reading a lot more contemporary plays. I remember reading a lot of Joe Orton, early Edward Bond and Caryl Churchill, and thinking, oh, wow, this is a completely new approach to writing. And it gave me confidence to write the things that I was interested in writing about. I realised that it was possible to do this in a new way, in a way that was exciting, that didn't feel classical. But it was only later that I got into analysing the text. Analysing plays too much can be quite destructive, because writing has to be so instinctive and organic, rather than coming from an academic point of view.

So do you have a parallel with Lucy – the first full-length play?

LEO Well, the first full-length play I wrote, when I was about fifteen or sixteen years old, was a science-fiction epic.

LUCY Wow! You don't see enough of them!

LEO It was about a hundred and fifty pages long, a huge two-act play, about a brave new world – comic, full of extremes, all about revolutionaries taking control from the Prime Controller, with huge giraffe heads that got eaten on stage, and people injecting themselves with these fluids that got delivered to the doorstep.

LUCY Sounds great!

LEO You look back and read it and think it was bloody awful. But you can also see the freedom of expression I'm always trying to tap back into, because you can get locked into a certain type of writing, or start thinking, well, what makes a Royal Court play? Is it social realism, is it political theatre? You just have to wipe all that away and think, well, it can be anything.

LUCY You have that when you're younger, don't you? You have no references. So you think, well, there's no reason at all why I can't do that, whereas now you go, oh well, no one really does that.

So what happened then?

LEO I moved down to London, and I went to a drama school, Rose Bruford. I did a three-year writing course there, a BA in playwriting. I think they've stopped it now. When I was there, there was a lot of politics going on, both tutors and students were getting kicked out or leaving, which upset the balance rather. I left in my second year.

Because you didn't think it was much good?

LEO I didn't learn anything. And we were promised that we would have our plays performed and they weren't performed. I gave the tutors a play I'd written and they completely failed me for it but, when we put it on, the audience loved it. Then the tutors started saying, 'Oh no, we were wrong.' And a couple of my friends got thrown out for various reasons – and I wasn't learning anything, and I was probably smoking too much dope – and so I thought quite arrogantly, 'Oh well, I don't need this place, I can do it on my own.'

I don't see how you can teach people to write plays. Perhaps you can teach them the basics . . .

LEO Some tips, I suppose.

LUCY Dominic Dromgoole puts it rather nicely. He says it's like teaching people how to have sex – there should be an element there that's more . . .

LEO I think there's a danger that you get to a place where the imagination can be shut down, or censored. If people are saying, 'This is the way to write, you have to have this many beats in an act' – you can't write like that. So I left the drama school and I spent about five or six years doing odd jobs and signing on – and I kept writing plays, and sending them out to agents and different theatres, and to the Royal Court. Over six years I had lots of rejections, as well as some positive feedback. It was a hard time to stay committed. But I had made a contact with Willy Russell, who really liked my work. He was like my mentor for several years, and he helped me get a grant from the Peggy Ramsay Foundation – he didn't have to do it, but he did it because he believed in the work. So I thank God that he was around to support me when I was in the wilderness.

Because otherwise you must feel so lost, without anybody believing in you.

LEO Yes, completely. I used to do little readings of my own plays at home. A lot of my friends were actors, so I'd get them together and do a reading – basically starting from scratch. Then I got a job ushering at the Royal Court in 1999, and through that I learned about the Young Writers' Programme. I sent them a couple of my plays, and they came back saying, yes, this work is very exciting, we're very interested. So they put me on a ten-week writing course with Nicola Baldwin tutoring, and then I did a course with Hanif Kureishi – and it really inspired me. I was writing new stuff, like I hadn't written before – it really opened some creative doors. I was still ushering in the year 2000, and in the autumn of that year it was the Young Writers' Festival. I submitted three plays, one old play and two new plays. Then, I remember, I was ushering for the final show of that summer, downstairs, and Ian Rickson came to find me. He said, 'Did you write *Made of Stone*? Because we're really impressed with this play. So I thought, oh my God, finally!

What a wonderful story.

LEO It was fantastic. I was ushering in the summer, and in the autumn I had my first play on, in the Young Writers' Festival. And it completely changed my life.

So Lucy – back to you. You'd written this play and it had won a prize, and you were still at university – which university?

LUCY Sheffield. I was taking my finals so I left it for a while – and then I got a letter from the Personal Managers' Association, where I'd won the prize. They said, as part of your prize you can do some work experience in a literary office, which turned out to be at the Bush. So I thought, great, I'll leave university and I'll have somewhere to go for a couple of months. It was a wonderfully shambolic experience because I turned up at the Bush and the person who'd agreed to take me on for this work experience had gone on holiday and no one else knew anything about it. So everyone went, what? I was terribly embarrassed, but it turned out fine. I did a lot of administrative stuff, and a lot of reading for the Bush, and that was very, very useful, because I read an awful lot of scripts from the slush pile, not sent in by agents but by ordinary people. And that was really useful, because you either read something that's really good, and think, wow, or you read something that's rather bad and you think, well, someone's taken the trouble to write this and send it in, and I know I could do better, so why aren't I having a go? Which is equally inspiring for someone who's not very experienced. So that started all those kinds of thoughts in my head, and after the couple of months at the Bush I thought, why not give it a go? I'll temp for a month to get some money together, live with my parents, and I'll try to write a full-length play, rather than another one-act play. So I spent two months writing the play and at the same time I did the writers' course, which Leo was talking about – my tutor was Simon Stephens. That was very inspiring. And the play that I wrote was *The Sugar Syndrome*. I handed that to Simon and he gave it to Graham Whybrow, and people started saying, 'You know what, I think there's quite a good idea here.' Now in the meantime I'd applied for lots of jobs. I come from a very untheatrical background, so I never really believed anything would come of it. One of the jobs I applied for was at the National Theatre, as an assistant to the directors, and I ended up getting that job. So all this time when the play was going through the literary office here, I was working as a secretary at the National Theatre. And during that time the Court decided to put the play on Upstairs. So I was running back and forth between the National Theatre and here, going to auditions and rehearsals, and then going back and putting my filing hat on and doing the filing, which was quite an interesting contrast. It was brilliant, though, because I met so many fascinating people, so many great writers who were all working at the National Theatre, who all had very kind words for me. And it was after *The Sugar Syndrome* did quite well, and I had an agent, and people started coming to talk to me about doing other stuff, that I had to leave the National, because I couldn't keep on with the job and keep going with this writing thing that had suddenly emerged. I made the decision quite sadly, because I really loved the job. But it seems to have turned out okay so far.

So what was it like, writing The Sugar Syndrome *in two months? I mean, you said writing the first one was really difficult – was it difficult with the second one too?*

LUCY Yes. I'm coming to terms with the fact that I find it so difficult. I'm deeply jealous of writers who say, 'Well, I incubate an idea for a while and then I sit down and write it in two weeks.' I understand that, because I think it's a brilliant way of working, but I've never been able to work like that. I find every page an absolute trauma, and I blame myself for being too analytical. I read it and think, this is terrible, it's just like that other writer . . . I don't know really what made me go on writing. I think it was partly doing the course here. Because every week Simon would say, I want to see something from all of you by the end of January or whatever, and I'd say to myself, well, I must go on. I've got to prove to myself, either by failing or succeeding, what my path in life is going to be. If I hadn't managed to do it, I probably would have gone, fine, I'll go off and do something else – and been perfectly happy doing it.

So where did that idea come from, for The Sugar Syndrome?

LUCY Well, I wanted to write about something that I hadn't seen done that well before. Principally the thought was – I'd lived with a girl with a very severe eating disorder while I was at university, and one of the things I felt was never represented very well was the sense of humour and the intelligence of women and men who suffer from eating disorders. I thought, it's always portrayed quite two-dimensionally. So are paedophiles, who are represented on the front pages of red-tops as monsters – at the time it was a big thing, with celebrities being accused and so on – so I thought, okay, wouldn't it be interesting if I wrote something where the guy who is supposed to be the monster was actually quite nice, and the girl who was supposed to be the victim was actually quite funny and intelligent. And so that was the basis of it.

Well, that was what I liked so much about the play – that it overturned one's preconceptions.

LUCY Yes – it was challenging preconceptions, which was good.

Do you think that's what plays are supposed to do? Make people think?

LEO Yes, I think it's really important to show people different perspectives, and challenge ideas, whether that is the war in Iraq or a very personal relationship. The different perspective in *The Sugar Syndrome* is the tenderness of that relationship, which really struck me. It was great, because you got such warmth from the characters, but you could never quite escape the cruelty of that character.

So I want to know – you say a university course in playwriting was no use, but the Royal Court writers' programme was useful – so why is that? What goes on there?

LEO On one hand, going to see plays – mostly at the Royal Court – you get free tickets. But of course when I was ushering I saw several plays many times – I saw Conor McPherson's *The Weir* about thirty times, which was very inspiring. But in the Young Writers' Programme, it was mostly analysing different plays from the Royal Court canon, and also just being forced to write.

LUCY Yes. You're set an exercise every week.

So that would be what? A passage of dialogue, something like that?

LUCY Yes.

LEO A short monologue, or . . .

LUCY Simon Stephens was very good at setting you a vague but helpful premise – something like a dialogue, but one in which one person has a higher status, or knows something that would affect the other person and can't tell them. It sounds very simple, but those are the kind of things you wouldn't do for yourself. It's like working for an exam – you never do the test paper because you think, oh no, I don't want to. But if someone says, come on, we're going to do this, it really forces your brain to work, and you may well produce something which is exciting to you, that you wouldn't necessarily do on your own, because you get – I get very bored with my own work. And then when you come every week, and you read it out to people, and they say, oh this is quite funny, or something, it's a huge help.

LEO Also I think when you're just sitting at home on your own, it can be a temptation to take ten pages of work you've done and just go over and over it, and rewrite it. But coming here every week you're forced to come up with something new every time, and that does get the creative muscles working.

LUCY The other thing which was always important to me on a more practical level was seeing people who earned a living, successful or not, through writing. I didn't know anybody, not my family or friends, who'd ever done that. So to come somewhere like this, where Simon says, 'Well, I write plays, and that's how I earn money, and I occasionally write for television' – you go, wow, that's pretty amazing. That was a real shift for me. Also it's great to be sitting around with lots of other people, some of whom are really committed to being writers. Otherwise you feel so lonely and isolated, whereas if you spend time with other people then you get very motivated. You think, well, they can do it – and you might disagree with something they said, but you go home and you – I mean *schadenfreude* has something to do with it. You go, well, I didn't like their play very much, I could do much better than that. Again you have none of those factors if you're just doing it on your own.

LEO Yes, I think that's the key to the whole thing – just having other people around you – otherwise it's such a solitary thing. Writing professionally now, that's one thing you can miss. You savour the times when you come down and meet Lucy, or Simon, or David Eldridge – everybody's going through the same turmoil! And I think you need that.

So, Leo, after Made of Stone – *what happened after that?*

LEO After that I was put on attachment at the Royal Court, and given a weekly wage (which was fantastic), and given a little office, a little writer's room – I was holed up in there . . .

And expected to write!

LEO Yeah. And because I was being paid, and had the focus, I wrote a play called *Redundant*, very quickly – I wrote it in about two weeks. I would stop overnight at the Court, in the office, and leave in the morning, and I wrote this play – I wasn't rushed, but it came in a continuous flow.

And was it a pleasure to do that?

LEO It was brilliant. And the interesting thing was, I think the process was quite unconscious. I'd had a central character in my head for a while but I hadn't known what to do with her – and then I just had an image of her sitting on the edge of her bed with snow falling outside the window. I used that as the central image to work towards. I knew that would be the final image of the play, and it just happened very, very quickly. I gave the first draft to Graham, and Ian, to read – and then I began to hear things. People were saying, 'I read your play and I really liked it.' Then the next thing I knew, I got a phone call one weekend saying I'd won the George Devine award for *Redundant*. Then I worked for the next couple of months quite closely with Dominic Cooke on redrafts of the play, and then at the ceremony for the George Devine Award Ian announced that it would be on Downstairs, in the autumn. So from ushering, in the space of a year I'd had a play Upstairs and a play Downstairs, which was great. Unfortunately we opened on 12 September 2001, and I'd written a line in the play where the grandmother says, 'Someone should bomb this bloody country – Saddam Hussein or Bin Laden or somebody – teach us how to suffer.' We kept the line in for a couple of nights and then we cut it, because it was just detracting from the main play. But it was a strange time to be having a play down in the main house, just after 11 September, because whatever the play was saying personally and politically, it was dwarfed by the events of the time. It was a difficult time to open. But it was a glorious first year of professional writing. Following that I wrote a play called *Devotion*, which toured schools in 2002, and in the meantime I wrote a piece for TV, and then I was commissioned again for the Royal Court. But I think after a year of having two plays here, and the award, that the expectations – not so much of the people here, but my own expectations of myself – I had to battle through that. I had to force myself to stop writing, and really take some time to think what it was I wanted to write next. So the next play, *Lucky Dog*, even though when I actually got the idea it only took a couple of weeks to write it, took me a good year to feel . . .

To get yourself into the position where you could start?

LEO Yes. I was writing every day – pages and pages of material – and it was getting too complicated and messy. Then I got a very simple idea and I thought, yes, actually I can go with this, I can move with it. It feels very interesting somehow.

And how did that come, the idea for Lucky Dog? *Was it based on people you knew, or people you'd observed?*

LEO Well, I guess my work always begins with an image. In *Redundant* it was Lucy on the bed with snow, with *Made of Stone* it was two brothers at the graveside, and with *Lucky Dog* it was a woman barking at her husband, sort of circling and growling and barking at the husband, and I knew I wanted to do something with this. Then I was thinking of the idea of parents having to rediscover themselves after the children had left home, that process of rediscovery – and playing with the idea of the family dog being such a symbol of unity. But I guess the defining moments were having the woman barking and the image of Christmas – the couple sat at the Christmas table with their Christmas hats on and it all being very empty and silent, but with tension bubbling under the surface. I guess eventually it's having the confidence to think you don't have to have huge plot twists, huge melodramatic moments – the plays that I love, seemingly nothing can be happening on stage but in fact everything is happening on stage.

So Lucy – after The Sugar Syndrome, *what happens now? You're writing two plays?*

LUCY Yes – one for here and one for the National Theatre. Which is very exciting because they are the two places I feel most strongly about.

And both of those came out of winning the award?

LUCY They both came out of *The Sugar Syndrome*, the reactions to that. Graham and Ian got me into the office the day before the press night, and commissioned me – because they wanted to make it very clear that they were commissioning because they really liked my play, not because of whatever happened on the press night, which was very gratifying and very encouraging. And at the National Theatre – I was still working there at the time, every day – Nick Hytner commissioned me the day after he came here to see it. He just came in and said, 'You and me and Jack [Bradley, the literary manager] need to have a talk,' and they commissioned me the next day. That was quite phenomenal, because it was based on people's honest reactions to my writing, which is always very nice. So that's what I'm trying to write at the moment.

And have you got deadlines for those?

LUCY Yeah – they've gone.

So how do commissions work? They say, we'd like to have something by such-and-such a date if possible?

LEO With the Court it's really quite open – they say, whenever the play's ready.

So – one is going better than the other?

LUCY Yes – the National Theatre one.

And you're trying to work on them both simultaneously?

LUCY Not really. I wrote a first draft for the Court and I finished it about a month ago and gave it to Graham Whybrow – but I've fallen out of love with it. I'm not convinced it does what I want it to do.

And what does he think?

LUCY Graham's a very good literary manager – he does what all great literary managers do, in my opinion, which is to try to make your play as much like the play you wanted to write as possible. So what will happen is, I'll be in a meeting with him, and I'll say, I really want a play that does this, and has that in it, and I know that this doesn't yet do this. Graham tries to get you towards where you want it to be. So he's not sitting there in judgement saying, 'This is no good, you know it's no good.'

So how does he do that? Is it possible to say?

LUCY I would really describe it as a mixture of psychoanalysis and being a barrister. Graham will spend some of the time asking you what it is you want from the play, how you feel its going, getting a sense of it – and he will allow you to be very open about it, how you feel it's going. He knows where he wants to get you, very much like a barrister asking leading questions in a court. He's pushing you towards saying, look, I need to do another rewrite, or this play isn't working – so he's very gently making you say what he already knows, which is a very good way of operating.

Yes . . . as long as what he already knows is right, and that you feel it's right. I mean are there occasions when you think, no, he's got that wrong?

LUCY There have been for me, yes.

And have you had that experience of working on a play here too, Leo?

LEO Yes, sitting down with a first draft and Graham going through it very thoroughly, and asking, what's this bit about then? What's happening here? So without his imposing his own ideas, just sort of working through . . .

Just clarifying? Bringing out what's there already, or what perhaps he wants to be there but isn't there?

LEO Yes – so I might say, yes, I cheated in this moment, I put in a link . . . In a sense it's like creative therapy. I've never felt anything's been imposed.

I wonder if other theatres and other literary managers or directors work like that, or whether it's fairly unusual to have somebody working so closely with writers on plays?

LUCY It depends entirely on the writer. I know from working at the National that there are certain writers who, if they hand in a draft, that's the play. So it depends on who the writer is and what their attitude is. It may be a very big successful writer who simply doesn't negotiate. But I've found from my own experience that if you are getting feedback you mustn't just say, Oh yes, okay, like a desperately anxious-to-please schoolchild, and go and make the changes. Even though it may be tempting.

So that one is in a state of limbo?

LUCY Well, yes.

And the National Theatre one you've only embarked on fairly recently?

LUCY Yes. I wanted to make sure Jack knew I was working on it, and that the idea was bearing some fruit, and I've become absolutely obsessed and fascinated with it. And the difficulty with writing, as Leo was saying, is that you've got to work on what you're really interested in at the time, because you don't know how long that will last. So the idea for me has really just taken off, and I'm going, oh, wouldn't that be great – I could do this – and so I've suddenly switched a bit towards it.

And this raises an interesting question: do you write a different sort of play for the National from the kind you'd write for the Royal Court? Does it feel different to be writing for the National Theatre? Is there any sense of, this is a Royal Court play, this is definitely not a Royal Court play?

LEO I think in the nineties there was a sort of myth created of what a Royal Court play is. In-yer-face drama. I imagine it changes, every ten years or so.

Well, yes, I think it changes a lot. I think looking back as I'm doing over fifty years, you can identify the decades by the sort of thing that's going on. But being in the here-and-now is more difficult. I mean, what is a Royal Court play in the new millennium? Do we know that yet?

LEO My feeling is that the Royal Court is in a state of transition. And judging from the variety of work that's been on – anything from Debbie Tucker Green's *Stoning Mary* to Terry Johnson's *Hitchcock Blonde*, from *The Sugar Syndrome* to *Lucky Dog* – they're all very different kinds of work. And I think that's how it should be. But it's only in perspective, when you see what's been successful, or infamous if you like, that you can get an idea . . .

LUCY What's quite interesting about going to script meetings here, which we've both done . . .

You both read plays for the theatre now?

LUCY Yes. And after hearing Graham and Ian's feedback on plays, actually if I wrote a play now, which in terms of its subject matter or style people might consider a Royal Court play, I'd be much more inclined to give it to the National Theatre, and the other way round. Because I know, having been in those offices in those sorts of places, that actually they're dying for those sorts of plays. The last thing a theatre ever wants to be is a cliché of itself. And Nick Hytner is always going, 'Well, this isn't the sort of play we normally get, so I'm going to read it.' So one goes, oh, okay, so these notions are created not by the people running these theatres, but from the kind of stuff that people write for them. So I'd be much more inclined to do that – which again makes a whole mockery of it in a way. I'd love to write a historical drama for the Royal Court, I'd love to write a sex play for the National Theatre.

LEO I think – what we were talking about earlier – I think there's always an element of challenge in a Royal Court play. Either in what it's saying, or just formally, in the structure.

Another difficult question, for both of you. Is there one thing, one recurring idea, that your plays are about?

LUCY That's a very interesting question – I think most writers always write the same play. It's a question of psychology. We're often supposed to be trying to recreate situations from our families in later life, and that's why you often end up in relationships that are with similar sorts of people, even if they're negative and bad for you. There's definitely a truth to that in writing, in that you're emotionally trying to solve something, albeit unconsciously, or even consciously – sometimes I'm writing something and I think, oh yes, I'm recreating the same sort of relationship that so-and-so and so-and-so had in *The Sugar Syndrome*. And when you notice that, you sometimes feel a little bit wary. But I believe that yes, there is a retelling underneath an awful lot of plays by the same author, which is what's interesting about them. Somebody like Kevin Elyot gets pilloried about it from the critics, but you see, with some older writers, like Arthur Miller or Tennessee Williams, that's what makes them artists, because you can link all their great works. It's whatever the critic decides on the day, as far as that's concerned. But I would say that mostly it's true.

LEO I think you can see that with Caryl Churchill, for instance. All her themes are very different, but they somehow all come from the same universe – there's a distinctive style, or voice, or perspective, somehow. And somebody like Beckett – each play is unique, but there's an incredible likeness in some way. I think for me – I've only just started – but for me the only theme is really myself.

David Cregan

For some reason I never met David Cregan during his glorious period in the 1960s when seven of his plays were produced at the Royal Court over four years. I clearly remember the first one, *Miniatures*, which had two historic Sunday-night performances with a cast that included my father and Lindsay Anderson. I'd met David a few times at the George Devine Award presentation, but our interview, at the British Library café in June 2005, was the first time we'd had a proper conversation.

Can you remember the first time you ever went to the theatre?

Yes. It was with my father, and it was to see a pantomime at the Buxton Opera House, in about 1936 – *Red Riding Hood*, I think. And I remember saying afterwards to my father, 'How did you know that was going to happen there?' Thinking I'd seen something that really happened. I was about five or six.

So you thought you'd just happened on an event.

Yes. That we'd all gone there, and somehow it had happened for us. And then I kept on going to the theatre, and he explained that you could see it again. It was rather a strange old touring company, and I did indeed see the pantomime about four years later and it was the same pantomime, in the same theatre. But we used to go to the theatre in Buxton – I went quite soon after that. The Old Vic came up, before the war, and they did *The Merchant of Venice*, and I remember seeing the man slip the portrait into the leaded casket, which spoiled the surprise. That's all I remember, really. Diana Wynyard played Portia. Then we used to go to the repertory company during the war – there was a little theatre next door to the Opera, staffed by people who were too old or too sick to be called up. And they played every Aldwych farce, and every thriller of the time, like *Ladies in Retirement* and *Rope*, and things like that. And every week I saw one of these things. And at the end of the war, the company changed, people got added to it – Gwen Watford, and Patrick Cargill. But also there came through at some stage, when I was about twelve, Jean Forbes Robertson playing *Hedda Gabler* – I think it was the only part she could remember, she was pretty alcoholic. And I was completely overwhelmed by Ibsen then. So it was the two things, the farces and Ibsen, which really stuck with me. It was not so much the farcical situations, but the breathtaking ludicrousness of farce, which I suppose morphed into absurdity.

So was there a moment when you thought, theatre's what I want to do?

Well yes, though I can't remember at exactly what stage. I can't have been more than ten when I was rather ill at home. I went to a little prep school in the town, and while I was away one of the teachers – a very magnetic, probably rather evil teacher – wrote a version of *Troilus and Cressida* for us all to do. I didn't recognise it as *Troilus and Cressida* at the time. And he couldn't get anybody to play Thersites. So I came back and I said I'd do it. I had been in plays before that, but on this occasion I thought, this is fun, but I could write this better. So I went away instantly, and within a few days I wrote a version of *Jason and the Golden Fleece*, which lasted two minutes. We performed it under a great bar in the gym, and I brought some sheets from home, which we nailed across – and I was delighted, years later, to go to the Berliner Ensemble and find that they also used sheets! So we performed this play, and it was over in two or three minutes, and the headmaster had been delayed by a phone call and had missed it, so he said would we do it again, which we did. And from then on I never stopped. I just kept writing.

And you did English at university?

I'm a slow reader, and I knew I wasn't going to read all the things I needed to read unless I studied English at university. I would just be a hollow shell. And so I read enthusiastically. And quite by chance my supervisor – I was at Cambridge – was a specialist on Ibsen. He'd just written a book called *Ibsen's Dramatic Method*, which was the first one to take account of Ibsen's stagecraft. His name was John Northam – he's just died.

Funnily enough, two other people – John Arden and Christopher Hampton – both told me it was Ibsen who first started them off, though it was with another play, An Enemy of the People. *Both of them had seen it at school and said they were absolutely bowled over by the way the audience is included.*

He's such a powerful writer. I remember when I was twelve, I made my mother take me to all the Ibsen plays that we could find. She adored Ibsen too, but she was a very strait-laced lady and she thought that *Ghosts* was the most evil play she'd ever seen.

I saw Hedda Gabler *when I was about twelve because my dad was in it, at the Lyric Hammersmith, with Peggy Ashcroft.*

I remember that production well. Anyway, I had a problem with my loyalty to Ibsen because, when I was at university, it was the first time I'd ever seen a Chekhov play – *Uncle Vanya*, an amateur production by Peter Hall, who was still at university himself. And I was swept away by this and I thought, but it doesn't have all the clever structure that Ibsen has, and all the intellectual language, and yet I loved it tremendously. So I've always had this problem, that I really love Chekhov more than Ibsen, but Ibsen draws me tremendously strongly, because architecture in plays – not just his architecture – has always fascinated me. The shapes of plays, the possibility of changing the shapes, as John Arden said to you. So that was my first experience of theatre.

So you were writing plays at university?

I was much more flippant than John Arden – I was a Footlight at Cambridge, with Jonathan Miller and so on, and I was writing scabrous lyrics and silly sketches. But they always had a serious undertone for those who could listen to them. And that's how I've always found myself, that I was entertaining. I had an interesting discussion with your father, when he was in *Miniatures*. It was only done twice, on two Sunday nights. The first Sunday night was a great success because he was in it, and Lindsay Anderson was in it, and Nicol Williamson, Roddy Maude Roxby and Graham Crowden – the theatre was packed. And everybody roared with laughter, which surprised me. Donald Howarth had rung me up to say they'd read the script, and they'd decided to do it as a Sunday night, and I was thrilled – I was still a schoolmaster. And then he ended up by saying, 'I just have to tell you it's one of the funniest plays I've ever read,' and then he rang off. And I went through with tears in my eyes to my wife, and I said, 'I don't think it is funny, I didn't mean it to be funny.'

How extraordinary!

And it was funny, of course – the first night was terribly funny, amazingly funny. The second performance was less funny, and George said, 'Oh, they're taking it a different way.' And I said, 'Well, I never thought it was a funny play.' And he said, 'Oh, David, it is a funny play, but they're not laughing, because they're holding back. If you listen, they go through three laughs and then they laugh on the fourth one, very largely.' So after that I always wrote seriously. If I wrote humorously it never worked, but if I wrote seriously it always turned out to be funny, or if I let that instinct go. But it was strange. I don't know if I've ever told Donald about that particular experience. He edited the play, told me what to take out and what to leave in – he was very wise.

I am really interested to hear that, because there is a myth that in the early days the play was treated with such reverence that nobody ever made any changes. The play was a sacred object and no one ever edited it. But you are telling me it's not true.

No, it's not true. Donald would say, 'It won't work if you do this or that,' and we would take it out. And so did Jane Howell, who I also worked with.

So tell me how you started writing.

After university I went to America, to teach, and I wrote a novel, which was published by Hutchinson under an imprint called New Authors. I'm trying to buy up all the copies and burn them. I hate it, though it was quite well reviewed. I went on teaching for a couple of years, English and Drama, and I put on quite a few plays at school. Then I taught part time and concentrated on writing, and I sent a first draft of a play to Keith Johnstone. He wrote back and said he wasn't going to do the play but he did like the way I'd written it, and would I join his writers' group. So I joined it – and I think the only person who went on from it to write was Edward Bond. We used to do a lot of improvisation, and mask work, and wherever I was I'd come home for that Wednesday evening with Keith. And I wrote three plays, of which *Miniatures* was one. This was in the mid-1960s, and *Miniatures* was 1965. That was after three years of work, and the release of those mask classes was what did it for me. So *Miniatures* was going into the main bill, but I'd presented them with another play by then, so it didn't go into the main bill. I'd written a short one-act play called *The Dancers*, and someone, I can't remember who, rang up and said, 'We think we'll do a short Ionesco play along with *The Dancers*.' So I said to Ailsa, 'They say they're going to do an Ionesco play,' and she said, 'Are you going to let them?' So I sat down and wrote *Transcending*, in three days. And *Transcending* was the success, though *The Dancers* has now been abbreviated and has been very successfully done elsewhere. *Three Men for Colverton* followed, which I loved – Desmond O'Donovan directed it, or sort of stood in front of it. Then I did a play which was rather an exercise in commedia work, called *The Houses by the Green*, which I now don't think much of, and which sort of went down the pan. And then Nicky Wright asked me to write a play, the opening play, for the Theatre Upstairs, which was never published. It suffered from the hands of Michael Bogdanov, who was the only director I've ever quarrelled with. It was called *A Comedy of the Changing Years*. It was a play about the rise of the Thatcher generation, although that generation didn't exist in those days. It involved an impoverished farming family who produced a schoolteaching offspring who shopped at Heals, interspersed with a sort of comic version of the last days of Hitler – the ten days in the bunker. Bill had given me an introduction to the Berliner Ensemble – I'd been to Berlin to see the company and was so impressed by it. *Days of the Commune, Coriolane* – I went to rehearsals and it was wonderful. And I'd been reading Trevor-Roper's *The Last Days of Hitler* and I thought I would use six actors and a lot of hats. However, Michael Bogdanov directed six chairs, which could be turned into crosses, or swastikas, or railway carriages, and he never paid much attention to the actors. They used to come to me for advice, and I still felt I was too much of a tyro to explain what I wanted. It was one of those occasions which sometimes happen with directors, when you use a word like 'funny', or 'serious', and they mean different things, and you don't know until too late. You can only try and translate what you're saying into something they can understand. That was 1969 – and at the same time *Miniatures* was televised by Granada and performed up North. And then I moved away from the Royal Court and they never asked me back. But I was always able to continue as a full-time writer. I wrote about twelve plays for TV, and a lot for radio – and I've done a lot of plays for Stratford East, pantomimes. Most of my work now is done at the Orange Tree in Richmond. I love the theatre in the round. Sam Walters has fallen in love with my style, and I think he's done thirteen of my plays.

So what's the process of writing like?

It's rather like what I suppose happens when people get pregnant. You don't quite know what's happening at first, and this goes on for quite a long time, just with a certain uncertainty in one's mind. And then it comes out with a blank piece of paper, and the problem is you've got to write someone's name. And it very often starts as A, or B. But there are two things that affect it. Sometimes I've heard something, a conversation, or a phrase of some sort which is slightly memorable, and that seems to be the inception of it. And the second thing is, the shape appears at some stage – a shape, or increasingly, less shape than music, the sound of it – I suppose all that work in radio affected me in some way. I think I take the word 'play' to mean what it says, and so write playfully. I often think 'playful' is typified by those little white farms sitting on Lake District hillsides, grinning and yet at the same time dangerous. Friendly, yet somehow sheer, secret, laughing to themselves. Peggy Ramsay once said to me, 'Most writers are ninety per cent adult and ten per cent child; in you the proportions are reversed.' When speaking of music I think of the surprising bits of Mozart and when thinking of architecture it's the unquantifiable sense of proportion that goes with looking from room to room which only works in very special places, the ones I love to live in, like our French cottage, where there isn't much, but what there is hums quietly and persistently with loud bits coming as a surprise. But the last letter my tutor wrote to me – we still communicated right till close to his death – I sent him a copy of three of my plays that had been published by Oberon, and he said two things. First of all, that the plays said very much with very little – I always was very abbreviated. What affected me about Beckett was the brevity of his sentences, but before I'd ever seen Beckett I always wrote briefly. And the second thing he said was, 'Your style is increasingly musical; it's like chamber music, in the shorter plays.' I've also written three community plays, one eighteen years ago, and one five years ago, and last week one finished in Tonbridge – huge casts, in different places.

So you're starting from a different place for a play like that?

It is difficult to get started. You have to know the place and walk the streets, and then you have to twist it for your own point of view, but you also want to advance your craft in some way or other. It always looks peculiar to the people who are doing it – it's only when they are putting it together at the end that they see the point, and I always enjoy that moment. I wait for it.

But is writing itself a pleasure?

Oh yes, but like most pleasures it's difficult. It's absorbing, rather than anything else. The bits you really enjoy having done you can't remember, or I can't. I come away from a day that's been extremely good, and I can't remember the process, though I enjoy reading what I've written.

Is that because on those days it's sort of written itself?

Yes – you've got your mind going so that . . . it's like when you've learned to ride a bicycle, suddenly it goes without your having to concentrate on it. It's a wonderful thing – the mystery of it. It's beguiling.

I think that's really what fascinates me – that whatever plays people write, this mysterious thing comes from God knows where.

I've been lucky because we were always able to live; my wife always worked, so I've been able to write.

So when you begin, you just think, 'I'll write a play about a school . . .'

Yes – with *Miniatures* I was teaching in a school, and there was someone there who really irritated me, so I put him in the play – the part that was played by Roddy Maude Roxby. Jane Birkin was also in it, her first part.

Do you feel any sadness or regret that your fantastic four or five years as a Royal Court writer didn't lead to a continuing relationship?

I do have a sense of regret that you can't find any of my plays anywhere, because I've written a great many, and most of them are published, but most are not done. I'm not a name that springs to anybody's lips. I rather think that, although I am disappointed not to be recognised in some more public way than I am, there is a certain compensation in not having the crushing expectations that must accompany great fame. Or rather, perhaps, there is a certain shyness in me, fear even, that prefers to work, or experiment, perversely – and to my chagrin – out of the limelight. I admire the plays of Robert Holman, who has a similar way of going about things, I think. And when critics do write about what I have done, they come up with the most astonishing piffle, ascribing influences in schoolmasterish ways that make one feel a breathlessly impatient teenager all over again.

Isn't that funny?

Well, it is, but I think the style in which I write is possibly unfashionable. I don't mean it's old-fashioned, but I'm always aware of the importance of what is not said. I'm not overt in my plays, but plays are more overt these days. I mean I'm not opposed to that, it's wonderful, but I'm not overt.

So if I said to a group of students, 'Can we say that there is an underlying theme in David Cregan's plays?' what would it be?

Well, I was thinking about this only the other day. There is a particular tension in my plays – a lot of them are about people who are anxious to preserve their home in some way. I don't mean just the house they live in, but the immensely conservative instinct to be safe – in their beliefs and so on. And the opposite, which is to be adventurous, and socially expansive, and so on. So the plays often typify those struggles, but again it's not overt.

And it's not a deliberate thing, presumably – it just comes out?

Yes, but it does come out. So that theme is frequently there, but I think there are others, which I haven't yet discovered. There is a play of mine called *Poor Tom*, that was done by the Contact Theatre originally, which is about an absolute scoundrel, a ne'er-do-well, living in a house in Manchester which is going to be sold, and he kills the landlord and pretends to be him. It is a comic piece but you can't fit the story into contemporary theatre, which is why the plays are not done. There is a certain elegance about them, too, which is not very popular. I don't mean there to be – I think ugliness is very important in the theatre, and they are ugly sometimes, but they are ugly in an elegant sort of way. I can't help that.

Is there any one play that you feel proudest of?

Yes – the one I wrote for Dartington, *The Land of Palms*, about a group of hippies contesting an oasis with a group of mercenaries.

What about your Royal Court plays?

Well I always liked *Three Men for Colverton* very much. Bill Gaskill said once that of all the plays that were done under his management, *Colverton* was the one he'd like to have done again, which surprised me. I think it was because it was very diverse. I like the Orange Tree plays very much, but they are very concentrated. The Orange Tree audience is rather literary, grey-haired, not very exciting. The last play I did there was about people lamenting the past – an anti-war play. I like quite a lot of them.

So the last question: why do you write plays rather than novels or other forms?

I'm utterly fascinated by the build-up power of dialogue, the way that it advances. I'm fascinated by actors, who I think are a much maligned group of people. I often find colleagues who say, 'Oh, actors are so bad,' but I think actors are wonderful. You can give them very little to go on and they will build the character enormously, and build the progress through the play, and they will make it happen. And I can't do the same thing with prose, which I don't think I do very well, so there's no point in doing it. I discovered that with my novel. I could do the bit where she says, 'Come and see me,' before she lies back on the sofa. It was the bit where she lies back on the sofa that I could never do.

Martin Crimp

Martin Crimp and I appeared destined never to meet – we seemed to take it in turns to cancel appointments. But we finally managed it at the end of May 2005, and talked on the blue sofa at the back of the Royal Court bar, in the little area that used to be the Sloane Square ladies' public lavatory. I enjoyed meeting him, and I am grateful to him for suggesting an improved title for this book. He asked me to point out that he has written about his relationship to theatre in the introductions to his collected plays: *Plays One* (2000) and *Plays Two* (2005), published by Faber and Faber.

So, can you remember the first time you went to the theatre?

Well, that's strange, because you see, for me, that was the Royal Court. I was brought up in a little town in Yorkshire, where there wasn't a professional theatre, so being involved in plays at school, and reading them, was my only experience of theatre when I was growing up. My first experience of professional theatre was here, in 1974. It was Beckett's *Not I*.

What a place to start!

Well, it was a very good place to start, because Beckett was a writer whom I hugely admired. So I suppose it was exactly the kind of theatre experience that you should have, because it was completely unexpected. I didn't know what this play was, or what to expect. And that was followed by *Statements After an Arrest Under the Immorality Act* by Athol Fugard, which I can remember seeing. I can see the stage, but I don't really remember what happened in that play. It was about adultery between people of different skin colours. But the Beckett play was extraordinary, and it stuck in my mind.

And how old were you?

I was either eighteen or nineteen.

So at school you knew drama on the page but not on the stage?

Well, I knew it on the stage through doing it. I was involved with productions, especially of Ionesco, whom I adored. That was one reason I was so keen to work with Simon McBurney on *The Chairs*, which was a co-production between Theatre de Complicité and the Royal Court. Stephen Daldry brought it about, as the producer. Because I wanted to pay a homage to Ionesco, a writer I had so admired when I was adolescent. Because it's strange, you know, the writers like that, Ionesco, Beckett, they appeal to the adolescent for reasons you don't really understand until you're much older. There appears to be a nihilism about those writers, which isn't in fact the case. So that was why it was one of my pleasant Royal Court experiences when my short play, *Face to the Wall*, was presented here in 2002, because that was an eighteen-minute play, and ever since I was eighteen or nineteen years old I'd had the ambition to write a short play for this theatre. This makes me look very sentimental, which in fact is not the case.

At what point did you start thinking you wanted to be involved with the theatre in some way or other?

Someone else who has said this more beautifully than I ever could is Peter Handke. I don't know if this theatre's ever done any of his work, I don't think so, which is a great omission. Peter Handke wrote a wonderful book called *The Afternoon of a Writer*, and on the first page he describes how it wasn't until he found himself unable to write for a time that he gave himself the name writer, and realised that that was what he was. Because I think for people like me, who just write because they feel compelled to, or because that's what they love doing – you don't think of it as a profession until the moment you have difficulty. And when you run into difficulty, that's when you realise that is what you are. And that's quite a shock. So I can't say I had the ambition to be a writer, because it was a sort of given, for me.

So all your growing-up years, you were writing? At school?

Yes.

And plays?

Yes, I did write plays. It's probably best not to discuss them, but I did.

At what point did you think, 'Now I'm going to start sending my plays around'? That must have been a conscious decision.

Yes, it was a decision. But I didn't realise that I would be a playwright.

What did you think you would be?

I still think and believe that – I'm not fifty yet – I'm going to write prose instead. That's what I began doing, and very sensibly it was turned down by publishers, when I was in my early twenties. And they were absolutely right to say no, I think. So playwriting filled the vacuum.

So many playwrights I've talked to have said, 'I couldn't possibly write prose, I can only write dialogue.'

I love it – but perhaps that's because it's a little holiday from playwriting. Because both those collected *Plays* of mine have little introductions, which are not really introductions, they're little bits of prose . . .

Indeed they are!

And I enjoyed writing those so much. But that's the amateur's pleasure.

They're so good – a little bit of extra enjoyment to have from the book.

Yes – so there's extra pleasure there, at moments when the theatre does not give you pleasure.

Come on then, describe the process of getting to the point of writing a play . . .

Okay, we can do this very rapidly. I was fortunate, I suppose, to have been nurtured by two organisations, BBC Radio through the 1980s, and also the Orange Tree Theatre, which was on my doorstep, also in the 1980s, where Sam Walters embraced all my work and put it on. That was fantastic, and that's the thing that's really hard to find now. It's hard to find in this building, because there is so much competition – we've generated this culture of new writing, so there is fierce competition for all the slots. So writers will find themselves being rejected even if they have commissions. I was very lucky – Sam Walters just put all my work on, and it varied in quality, I suppose. That was a great thing, and I learned a lot. But at a certain point you just want to look over the hill, and see what's over the horizon. And it was towards the beginning of the 1990s that I got involved with this theatre, and that was a decade of involvement.

And what was the first play that was done here?

The first play that interested them was a play about child abuse, called *Getting Attention*. It had a reading here, but it wasn't produced here, it was produced at the West Yorkshire Playhouse. But then that production played for a while in the Theatre Upstairs, in 1991. And on the strength of that play the theatre commissioned me, and I suppose I developed a kind of Royal Court commission addiction during the 1990s, which produced some work that I'm proud of, including *Attempts on her Life*, which was directed by Tim Albery.

And that was done Upstairs?

Well, it was done on the mezzanine, really, that's how you should describe it, for the Royal Court in the Circle Space at the New Ambassadors, a two-hundred seater amphitheatre space. So it was not in a studio space. It was a rather good space, really. It was a very good operation, I think, to leave the Royal Court and leave the institution of the Royal Court, an exciting time of de-institutionalising. And then *The Country*, which Katie Mitchell directed here in 2000 – those pieces of work were very important to me, and for me, if we're talking about horizons. They enabled me to see over the UK horizon, if you like, which is another important thing.

And when you see over the UK horizon . . .? You see Europe?

Yes, in my case I see Europe.

Because I was reading what Dominic Dromgoole says about you – he's actually very funny about the European thing, that you are seen as a kind of European writer. Why do you think your work is taken up over there?

There are two answers, a pretentious one and a flippant one. I prefer the flippant one, which is that being embraced by many cultures isn't a guarantee of quality, because you only have to think of McDonald's. So when it says on the back of the book, 'translated into nineteen languages', I think, well, okay, so is Big Mac, I'm sure. But the pretentious one – I suppose it's not really pretentious – is to do with my models. When I think about what I read, it's not necessarily simply UK work, so maybe there is something in me from those other writers, I don't know.

The book is to be called Fifty Years of Royal Court Writers. *But do you feel like a Royal Court writer? You may not want to be labelled as that.*

'Fifty Years of Writing at the Royal Court' sounds better. I mean *Fifty Years of Royal Court Writers* has a sort of dying fall. And also you don't have the label. It's just a suggestion.

It's rather good, actually.

84

I would agree! So – I have an ambiguous attitude to all institutions. I don't like belonging and yet I do belong. I don't know if I'm unusual as a writer in that a variety of artistic directors have remained interested in my work. There has been Max, and there was Stephen, and there has been Ian. And where there is interest, there is a reciprocal interest to produce work. On the other hand I have played in other places. So somewhere like the Young Vic, that produced my adaptation of *Le Misanthrope* and then recently a co-production of *Cruel and Tender*, facilitates (horrible word) a kind of playfulness in my work. I take this building very seriously, and I don't know why that would be.

Are you saying that if you had a commission from here and one from the National Theatre you would write a Royal Court play and a National Theatre play?

No, I don't think that's true, actually. But I don't think I'd want to be commissioned in that way at the moment. I think you've found me at a particular moment because that's not what I want – I don't want the label. I would like to think of the Royal Court as a touchstone of writing for the theatre. But I don't know, I can't say that it always is. And it works both ways, doesn't it, because the artistic director has to have the integrity to act as a touchstone, and the writers also have to produce the work for that to happen. So there's a lot of flowing between what people produce and what people encourage.

Does your work come under the umbrella of what they call 'in-yer-face' theatre?

No, not really. In that particular book, I'm a footnote – I'm an appendix. It was really strange – I mean it's easier for me just to speak anecdotally about it – how odd it was for me to receive books, translations, into Czech, or something, and to find it was three British playwrights, Sarah Kane, Mark Ravenhill and myself. So we formed this little cluster for a time. But I'm not in their generation.

I have enjoyed reading your plays enormously but I don't know how to classify them. I can't really say what they're like.

No, I can't really say what they're like, either.

So talk to me about the actual process – what's it like? How does it start, where do the ideas come from? What happens to you when it's time to write a new play?

What happens to me . . . [*Long pause.*] Well, you can see what happens to me – this is what's happening to me. I can be specific about some things, and I can be specific about some things in relation to the Royal Court. So, for example, a play like *Attempts on her Life* is a kind of anti-play, if you like. I'd been writing little bits like this for ages, and then saying, no, no, this isn't a play. But then – I suppose it was at a point during the 1990s, when I felt that the work here was very conservative, formally – I thought, well, why not, why shouldn't this be a play? Isn't this the kind of thing that the Royal Court, should be dealing with? So in a sense, knowing that I owed this theatre a play empowered me, but it was finished as an oppositional gesture which then fortunately, and very beautifully, the theatre embraced. Because they saw this was important and they said yes, we want to do this, we want to find a way of doing it. And Stephen Daldry very brilliantly pointed me towards a director – because I didn't know Tim Albery's work – who knew exactly how to deal with it.

So it had been in existence as fragments, is that what you're saying?

Yes. But this is the case with many pieces of work. That they're . . .

They don't spring out fully formed?

Very rarely. Only if they're seven or eight pages long. In fact the Royal Court is about to do a piece in the autumn called *Fewer Emergencies*, which is actually a triptych of three plays of which *Face to the Wall* is in the middle. And that was a piece that I wrote in a day – it's just eight pages long. But this is a very rare and wonderful experience. Very rare.

And normally bits come and you see how they fit together over time? Or do you have a general idea of what it's going to be? I mean, about Dealing with Clair – *did you think, 'I want to write a play about an estate agent who disappears'?*

Not at all, no. There were certain relationships that I'd written and certain images that I'd written, and they were in search of a narrative. And the estate agent narrative allowed me to complete the play in a coherent way. So my writing tends to be pieces that are looking for a home, and for me it's always hard to find a home. In *Attempts on her Life* the concept was Anne – that was the unifying feature.

So it's quite a long-drawn-out process from conception to birth?

It is a long-drawn-out process, but that's par for the course, and I think you can make too much of that. There are some very funny things written by Roland Barthes about writers and their struggles, and that this was an invention – I'm not sure I agree with this – a sort of Flaubertian invention of the nineteenth century. Though of course Virgil was said to take a lot of trouble, and polish away . . . I suppose it's an inheritance of modernism, as well, isn't it, the desire to polish and hone and give things very sharp edges, which is something I always aim to do. I suppose I always aim to create something that is crystalline, if you like, in structure. It's quite good sometimes to be pushed away from that, but I come back to that.

And if a bunch of people, as maybe they already are, are sitting in a university, studying the plays of Martin Crimp . . .

Yes, they are, they're sitting in that university.

And if they had a teacher, like me, who was saying, 'Now you've read a play which is about an estate agent, and you've read another play which is about child abuse and so on – but what is he really trying to say in these plays?' . . .

Well – um – I believe that writers have ideas. It's very clear. And some people make this very explicit. I mean, Edward Bond, for instance, will tell you exactly what the ideas are and how he intends to explicate them in his play. Though if I understand Edward Bond correctly, I find a strange kind of empathy there, because what he seems to be saying is that he does not want to set down ideas, he wants to make something inside people come alive through his writing, which is not quite the same thing, is it? And I don't know what that would be. But when writing works, you, the writer, feel slightly more alive. And writing is a way of making something that satisfies you. But I wouldn't want to give it a psychoanalytical rationale, really. I mean in one sense it's a way of reconciling yourself to the world, but then many things we do are that – you could say that everything is, isn't it, so that's not very specific. And obviously there's a very strong satirical element to my work, that's very clear, very very clear. So I don't need to describe or explain that. And for me, now, it's interesting to try and ditch that habit, as in a play like *The Country*, or as in a play like *Cruel and Tender*, and move away from the scoring of satirical points.

So you're actually pushing yourself past your own boundaries, in a sense.

Yes – I wouldn't want to put it that way myself, but that's always what you're trying to do, isn't it? So yes, I'm aware of that satirical impulse, and that there are other ways of using it, or other places to go.

87

You said you imagined yourself stopping writing plays and writing a novel – is that going to be a conscious decision, to stop?

I have no idea. It's just an ambition. I mean, it's important to have ambitions, isn't it? And that's why I talked at the beginning about the nature of institutions, and the fear of institutions. And of becoming institutionalised. That's why it's wonderful to be embraced by a building that remains important in our cultural life, but there's a part of me that always resists that – which is kind of ironic, isn't it, for someone who is embraced.

Apart from the obvious difference between writing dialogue and writing prose, also, with a novel, there's nothing between you and the reader. When you write a play the whole thing moves out of your hands and becomes bigger than itself. And hopefully that's a good thing.

Yes, I agree with that. And I've been very fortunate in that I've had a number of excellent relationships with directors. I think I'm really lucky, actually. And it's true, if that relationship is good it will bring something to the text you haven't seen. That's one of the good things about writing for the theatre, to see what the director, and what actors, can bring to a text. I think it can take quite a while to let go; and to surrender, in that sense, and to learn that what's happening emotionally on stage may be as important, or more important, than getting words right. You have to learn to let go about things like that, obviously.

I was talking to Conor McPherson recently and he said that he prefers to direct his own plays – he prefers to keep control of his original vision.

Yes. I feel more comfortable talking about this kind of thing because I have very strong views about it. One of the reasons for writing *Attempts on her Life* was my knowledge about the Beckett estate's control of his work, which for me is a negative aspect of his inheritance. Because I had seen Deborah Warner's production of *Footfalls*, which was a fantastic production. But she was prevented, by his estate, from taking the play on tour because she had split the play between two levels in the production – for this reason – and I thought this was anti-art. Because theatre art is about collaboration, and writing a text which then can be taken, and used. When you first produce a play, you want to be involved, and close to what happens. Or at least you want to provide some insights if people wish to have them. But for that to go on and on, to be so prescriptive, seems wrong. So I originally had some stage directions in *Attempts on her Life*, and I removed almost all of them – I think I have two now. Because

I wanted it to be a completely open text. I feel very strongly that directors can contribute and I suppose two that I've worked with who have brought that home to me very much are Katie Mitchell and Luc Bondy. Bondy is the most extraordinary director. He, for example, has a way of making your play glow. He makes it glow. There are many directors in Germany whom British writers are afraid of, because they impose a concept on a play. That isn't a good thing. But someone like Bondy simply opens up the play, makes it more human, and that's a very special gift. It's really interesting to see on stage something that you couldn't have predicted, but that is still absolutely your play, rather than something that you couldn't have predicted that is a travesty of your play. Because that doesn't often, or always, happen.

I suppose in a sense one thinks that's what should happen – that if theatre is going to work it should be more than the sum of its parts.

Yes, that is true. I mean this is all quite a vexed debate. Because one of the reasons there are very powerful directors on the continent is because they have a lot more time and money, and this tends to mean that writing itself is a marginal activity. Because of the power-based directors. In other countries, I've witnessed people who have eight or twelve weeks' rehearsal and at the end there is no difference from what might be produced here in four weeks' rehearsal. If, on the other hand, that time is spent constructively and creatively, it does give a chance to produce work of a quality that is not possible here. However, if you look at the eighteenth century, they were just whacking them up, producing plays very quickly for just a handful of performances. But times have changed.

So, I think one of the things I started out wanting to know was – I was brought up in the theatre, and I never thought there was anything but the theatre, it was just what people did. But now I want to ask, what's theatre for? But that's like saying, what's art for? Also I have this thing my father said – 'Plays should be disturbing' – he wants people to walk out of the theatre thinking.

There were two questions there. Why theatre, and what does the writer think? What is unique to theatre is that the performance is about the relationship of the play to the audience. It's a relationship that involves a group of people, so there's a sort of tension there, which I think you are conscious of in writing. Obviously the writing of silence, since Chekhov, has become a defined thing in the theatre. And you don't write silence unless you are aware of the audience, because otherwise the silence doesn't mean anything. The silence in a play is about the relationship between the actors on stage and the audience, and this is a very special and particular thing – the acknowledgement of that silence. I can't talk about intentions, but what I can say, following on from that, is that the theatre is like a big musical instrument, a musical instrument that consists of the actors and the audience. And you have the chance to play it, and it's a fantastic instrument. That's what you're doing, when you write for the theatre, you're playing this musical instrument. And following on from that, for me the theatre is also the acid test of language, the test of the language we use every day, and it exposes it, enriches it, or reveals it. That, I suppose, is why I'm still addicted to theatre despite these desires to write prose. Because it's when you hear words spoken that they are truly tested, and that for me is what's always going on. I'm testing these words, and that is my musical instrument. I'm testing the words. And the other part of the instrument is the audience – they are hearing the words, and they are testing the words themselves. So that's what's happening, I think – it's about testing the words. That makes sense, doesn't it?

Yes it does. David Hare has written in an essay that a play is what happens in the air between the stage and the audience, which is a bit like what you are saying, but not exactly.

Yes – it's also about a relationship, isn't it. But I wouldn't put the point quite so equidistant between the audience and the stage. I think the point is closer to the stage, closer to the words. But my relationship to the theatre is really explored in those short texts, the introductions to my collected plays. And if you wanted to say anything about me and my relationship to the theatre, that's what you should quote, or footnote. It's something that I have had to sit back and think before I write. Because just as I realise that theatre is a test of language, I'm also aware that an interview is a test of language. And I don't have as much time to consider these words.

April De Angelis

Hush 1992
Wild East 2005

Although April De Angelis has only had two plays done at the Court, she has been involved with the theatre in other ways. She has taught on the Young Writers' Programme – Joe Penhall was taught by her and describes her as being 'adorably encouraging' – and has travelled overseas as part of the team involved with workshops organised by Elyse Dodgson and the International Programme. I met April in the Royal Court bar on 28 January 2005. It was about an hour before the opening of her play *Wild East*. The bar was full when we started the interview and even fuller by the time we finished, so there was a huge amount of background noise – talking and laughing and clinking of glasses. The venue was not ideal, and certainly the timing could have been better. April was apprehensive about how the play was going to be received, and we started by talking about it.

When I started writing this play, *Wild East*, I was actually doing something else, writing another play. Then I suddenly started writing this play, and I wrote it in a matter of weeks and it wasn't thought out beforehand. I didn't say to myself, come on, you've got to write this. I just sort of followed my instinct. And I gave it to the Royal Court in March – I'd started it in January, so it hadn't taken very long, I'd spent about five weeks writing it. So I sent it and I said, 'Look, I've done this thing and you can tell me to stop, because I don't really know what I think of it' – I still don't know what I think of it now. But I got a kind of hint from them that they were really interested. And being a writer, you smell blood, and you think, okay, if they're going to do it, I'm going to carry on with it. So that's what I did, and that's why it's on. But I sit back now and I think, what did I do? Why did I do *that*? But then again – well, it's an experiment. I'm just that sort of writer. I think I'm always going to be experimenting – I'm never going to do anything properly.

So how did it all start? Can you remember your first experience of theatre?

I can, because I've thought about it. My mum took me to see a pantomime with Jimmy Tarbuck in it – I think it was *Aladdin*. We weren't a family that normally went to the theatre.

And where was this going on? Where did you live?

We lived – actually with my grandmother and my mother – in Shepherd's Bush. So this was the first time, and I remember being really disappointed, because at one point everything stopped, and they said to the audience, 'Now put up your hand if you want a doll.' They got about fifteen children on the stage, all lined up, and they gave them a doll. And I can remember thinking, this is terrible! I was really certain that it was wrong, and I didn't know why. But I felt sure that it was wrong, because everything had stopped, and I didn't like it. I was thinking, what did it mean? What was the point of it? I had quite a strong reaction. And I remember that, and it is interesting, because there was no reason to know, to have an opinion, really, because I'd never been to the theatre before. So that was my first experience. I didn't go to the theatre again until I was about fifteen when I went to see Marlene Dietrich in a theatre in Wimbledon. I'd wanted to go because we used to watch her old films. She was absolutely amazing – she was about seventy and she looked brilliant. She sang songs and did a bit of smoky talk. But before that I'd done lots of school plays, and that was how I got to know theatre.

And you became an actress?

Yes, I was an actress. I used to get the parts when I was at school, and I loved it. I was never interested in going to watch theatre, I just wanted to be in it. Then I went to Sussex University and did an English degree, and after that I went to East Fifteen for a year, for a diploma in acting. And I did act for a bit. But I didn't like being an actress, for what it meant your life was like, and I really wasn't good enough, because I didn't want to be that sort of person. I think I was changing. I mean you watch real actors, and they're in their element. And if you're not in your element, it takes a while for you to realise it.

Obviously you weren't yet thinking of yourself as a playwright, but did you write stuff when you were a teenager?

No, I didn't. But I used to read a lot and that led me on to reading plays, because I used to hear words like Pinter, and I'd think, who's Pinter? I'll read that. I was quite determined to know all that, to have read everything.

Then I wrote something at university, because the university drama society said they were going to put on plays by students. So I thought, I'm going to do that, then. So I did, I wrote a play, and it went to Edinburgh.

What was the play about?

It was a sort of classic eighties play. There were two characters, a woman and her reflection, and this woman had beaten her own child. Then there was a doctor, and it was a sort of dialogue between the three of them. It was probably nutty.

So of all the things you could have written a play about, why did you choose that?

I don't know. Nobody knows these things. But I'd seen a play someone had written, an adaptation I think of a story by Ian McEwan, where a dummy comes to life. And the dummy was a woman, and you had an hour of the play and then three minutes where the dummy comes to life. And I remember being really cross about it and thinking, 'Well, that's really silly – I'm going to write a play where the woman speaks.' So that was it really, it was written in reaction, and that's quite a good way to write, in reaction.

You do seem to have always been interested in writing about women.

I think I still am, really.

So you decided rather arbitrarily to write this play for Edinburgh – but what was the process like? Did you enjoy it?

Well, it was sort of surreal. I was at university and I think I was writing it at night. It was like just putting your pen on paper and having something come out – that's just what it was like.

You didn't have a clear idea of what it was you were going to write?

No, I never do.

You're a writer of the David Storey school!

Well, I think my problem as a writer is that I'm torn between the two. I understand the necessity for structure, I love structure, but at the same time I just love putting the pen on the paper and doing that thing. Which I did for *Wild East*. But there's a strange mixture of strengths and weaknesses with that kind of writing.

This morning I talked to Kevin Elyot, and he said it takes him two years to write a play. He said, 'I'll do a collage. I'll write one bit and then I'll write another little bit, and this might go on for ages – then I'll fit them all together.'

I have written like that, but not for this play. Sometimes you write in a collage and sometimes you write from the beginning. It's very strange. But they all have their strengths and weaknesses.

But you do enjoy it, whichever you're doing? Or do you find it painful?

Well, I do enjoy it. But then I worry about the fact that it's not me just doing it for my own pleasure – it's my job. There's always that aspect.

And also you may have got a commission.

Yes. And all these frictions sort of rub together – it's a fascinating process. But also you wonder if you have pursued the right idea. Because you're looking for an idea to unlock you, that's what you're doing.

And where does it start from?

It starts from something that interests you. And if you can see it clearly, if it seems straightforward and simple to you, and you think that's right, that's probably a good idea. If you can see how it can be done, that's what a good idea is. But you're not in a rational world, and you can be beguiled by an idea.

Have you had experiences with directors who've attempted to make you modify your plays, to make you change them?

Yes, sometimes I have – they do change. Max Stafford-Clark, for example, when we were working on *A Laughing Matter*, was always saying, 'What you have to do is to write convincingly. You've got this Dr Johnson but your Dr Johnson's not convincing.' I said okay, fine. And you have to work on the intellectual argument. Other times people may say to you, there's a beat missing here, or the journey of this character needs clarifying. It's a shortcut – you may really know it but it helps if people say.

So you don't mind that.

Oh no – I really love it. It's collaborative, and that's what should happen.

But you've never worked on what we think of as the Joint Stock method with Max?

I actually never have, no, not the actual experience of taking an idea raw –
I wouldn't mind doing that but I just never have.

When you wrote Playhouse Creatures, *or* A Laughing Matter, *you must
have done a lot of research.*

Yes, I did, of course. But funnily enough, when I did *Playhouse Creatures*
in the early nineties, there wasn't actually that much material. It was sort
of a hidden area. I had to go to the Fawcett Library, and read these books
from the 1950s, which had a very paternal tone to them. They were written by men, all about these jolly women on the stage, and you were reading
between the lines to write the play. So you couldn't research it that much.
But for *Laughing Matter* there was a lot of research. It felt a bit
overwhelming. Because to do Dr Johnson you had to read his work – and
then you'd think, my God! And then Garrick's life didn't seem naturally
dramatic, despite his being an actor.

But it was your decision to write about these people?

Well, Max wanted an eighteenth-century play to be coupled with a contemporary play. That's what we were given. So I started out reading eighteenth-
century plays, and the only one I liked was *She Stoops to Conquer*. Then
I discovered there was a story of that play not being put on by Garrick,
and I thought, perhaps there's a play there – putting these two together. So
it happened like that.

*Each one of your plays has a different subject, of course, but could you
say overall that there's one thing you're saying? Can you say, 'Well, this is
what my plays are about'?*

There is, actually. I knew you were going to ask that question. I've always
thought it was a weakness if you don't know what that is. I think in some
way they're about the parent-child relationship. It could be expressed in
social terms – it could be authority versus the young person, or the powerless versus the powerful. Essentially, what's done to the person who's
innocent. I don't really want that to be my subject because I don't actually
think it's very interesting, but I think it is my subject.

*My father said: 'I want the theatre to be continuously disturbing. I want
people to ask questions. I want to make them anti-conformist.' In other
words, plays are supposed to nudge at your preconceptions. Do you think
that's right?*

Yes, I do. You want some shift to take place. That's what's needed for it to be theatrical The very nature of the theatrical is the fact that it's doing things before your eyes – kind of tugging at your perceptions and doing it in a material way, before your eyes.

I think that's really interesting. That's true. Perhaps this is getting at something it's difficult to ask people, though I try to ask it in the way of saying, why theatre, why not other kinds of writing? Because, after all, novels are supposed to change the way you think too, aren't they?

They do, but it's a different kind of medium. I'm thinking about Sarah Kane's *Blasted* – it starts realistically, but when the soldier comes through the wall, suddenly you realise you're in a completely different kind of world, and it happens intellectually, physically, emotionally, with fear and pity, as Aristotle says, all in one moment. You could spend hours talking about that moment, but with the acting it's done in a couple of seconds. That's the theatre, isn't it?

I think you're right. Now, this is only the second play you've had done at the Court – the first was Hush – *and you've had plays produced in lots of other places. So did you have a certain feeling about the Court when you started to write, as a place you'd like to have your work done, or had it lost that kind of cachet?*

I wrote that first play when I was at university, and I'd never even heard of the Royal Court. I knew about it when I got back to London, because I went to see Caryl Churchill's plays, and I used to be overwhelmed: it was such an awe-inspiring kind of place. But I think that when you start writing, you realise that without the Royal Court it'd be devastating. It's so emotionally necessary for a writer to know that they have this home, right in the centre, that is so respected and so exciting. They always treat your work with respect here, even if they don't always do it. So even if you're writing for the National – of course they do new writing too – you're aware that the real home of new writing is the Royal Court.

And if you are commissioned at much the same time to write a play for the Court and a play for the National, do they naturally turn out to be different kinds of plays?

Well, funnily enough I had a commission for the National and I was supposed to write it this year. But I started doodling, and I wrote this play, *Wild East*, instead, and I thought, well, the National wouldn't want this play, I'll send it to the Royal Court. The Royal Court has a sense of freedom about it. Do you know what I mean? A no-limits sort of thing. The National had said to me, 'We want an ensemble play for a large cast,' and that's their right, of course.

But is it more than just to do with the size of the company? Is it to do with the content as well?

I think it is. The Royal Court wants you to take risks – makes you feel there are no boundaries – it's great. It's incredibly important. People sometimes say that, in this era of technology, we don't need the theatre. But it constantly reinvents itself, and it does offer something through its form – people still seem to want it.

They seem to want it more now, in a sense, than they did fifty years ago. The Court in the old days had a huge struggle to get audiences – whereas now . . .

Well, there is a buzz about the place. I love the theatre myself, just socially. I love the idea that I'm part of an audience that has a particular relationship with this particular event. And it's ephemeral, it's not going to be there for ever. Also I love actors. I go to rehearsals every day, and I need to because they ask me all the time what things mean. And I always remember this, that the first thing the parents did after the Dunblane massacre was, they went to the theatre together. That was the first thing they did as a group. They went to see *Evita*. They wanted to go out together and they couldn't imagine going anywhere else. It was somehow a human-sized event. And the fact that you share that respect for others in the audience, and for the actors – it's very civilised.

David Edgar

England's Ireland
  (collaboration) 1972
State of Emergency 1972

A Fart for Europe
  (collaboration) 1973
Our Own People 1978
Mary Barnes 1979

The Everyman Bistro in Liverpool was very busy at lunchtime on 14 May 2005 when I met David Edgar. He'd come to Liverpool to run a playwriting workshop. I was looking forward to meeting him – several people I'd talked to had said how much they owed him as a teacher, and he is obviously an important figure as a writer of plays and of theatre commentary. But I was rather apprehensive, too, as I always am when I meet someone so declaredly political – I was afraid he would be a fierce Marxist and make me feel woolly and liberal. But I needn't have worried. He was very kind and friendly (as well as very tall) and we had an enjoyable lunch.

In an essay of yours I read recently, you say you have never had a full-length play put on at the Royal Court Theatre. So Mary Barnes *came in from somewhere else . . .*

I've never had a full-length play *produced* by the Royal Court.

Apart from plays that went on Upstairs? What about A Fart for Europe?

A Fart for Europe was the only play I've written directly for the Court. It was written with Howard Brenton, it lasted forty-five minutes, and the most subtle and elegant thing about it was its title. It was our response to Britain's entry into Europe. *Our Own People* was a tour, and *Mary Barnes* was a transfer. I mention that because it was both turned down by the Royal Court, and then given too short a run by the Royal Court. So its relationship to the Royal Court was tense.

And yet it was the second most successful production that year in terms of box office and attendance.

That was a point I made. I remember Oscar Lewenstein fighting through the queue to see *Our Own People*, Upstairs, a queue for returns, as he explained to me that nobody would come and see a play about psychiatrists in London.

I read it the other day and I thought it was a really interesting play. I could not see anything in it that would make somebody at the Royal Court say they didn't want it.

By that time they'd done Howard Brenton's *Magnificence* and David Hare's *Teeth 'n' Smiles* – but there was certainly a sense in which the early 1970s was probably the only period when then Royal Court was not on the right boat. It was still dominated by great writers like Storey and so on, but Oscar really didn't have any sympathy with the New Left, the post-1968 Left – he had no sympathy with the sort of anarchist side of that. There's an anecdote which illustrates that, to do with *England's Ireland*, which was written on the Gary Gilmore principle. When Gilmore was executed in Utah by a firing squad, in 1977, as is traditional with a firing squad one of the bullets was blank, but nobody knew which one it was. So no one in the firing squad knew if they had killed a man, because they might have had the blank bullet. Similarly the principle of *England's Ireland*, as with *Lay By*, which preceded it, was deniability – that we could all deny having been responsible for the most outrageous things in it. And *England's Ireland* contained two quite different scenes. One was a rather solemn out-front scene at the end, a descant on getting 'back to normal' (one of the best lines was 'Is Jack Lynch normal?') – it was very presentational. Then was another scene, more than a scene, a whole sequence, which expressed the experience of the internment and torture of republicans, and the incarceration of republicans, in terms of the arrest, persecution and trial, the flagellation, persecution and crucifixion of Christ. The last line of the sequence, which ended the first act, was Tim Curry appearing with the beret and the dark glasses and the machine gun, as it were over the jail from which he has flown, saying, 'O ye of little faith, I have come into my kingdom.' As you can imagine, Oscar Lewenstein took me aside, and said, 'David, I really like the bits you did, like that bit at the end about whether Jack Lynch is normal, but why couldn't you have stopped Howard and Snoo writing that awful religious scene which was so over the top?' Now, David Hare and Howard Brenton and Snoo Wilson had written the presentational bit at the end, and the crucifixion bit actually, because I was well brought up in a good Protestant school and know my Bible, was written by me and Howard. Of course it's a syndrome with group writing that you can start writing like everybody else. I liked Oscar Lewenstein very much, partly because he was an old communist and I could speak that language more than a lot of other people, but I don't think the Royal Court really caught up with what was going on at that time.

It's certainly the messiest and hardest period to get your head round, looking at it retrospectively.

I think that the theatre finally caught up when Max Stafford-Clark took over. Max really started off the women dramatists. He realised that was happening, and that's what he did.

I've talked to both David and Snoo about the collaborative writing of Lay By, *and that story gets told a lot, with variations. But how did you actually set about writing* England's Ireland *collaboratively?*

I was a journalist in Bradford, and Chris Parr (who was Fellow in Theatre at Bradford University) had this rather obvious idea that instead of doing endless productions of Edward Albee's *The Zoo Story*, he would engage young writers to write plays for students, and pay them about £50 a time. And so he did the Brenton Trilogy, he did lots of John Grillo plays, Richard Crane plays, and various people who've been forgotten, and then me. So I did a lot of plays for him. And so Howard was involved, and he invited me to join the *England's Ireland* group. I wasn't part of its conception. But I left journalism on a Thursday in early 1972, and on the Friday I went down to Pembrokeshire, and that evening walked into a house consisting of six other unhealthy-looking men, and a female secretary. David Hare had booked the house, and he'd given up on trying to explain what we were doing. So he'd described us as a walking party. Now the house was owned by the pub opposite. So you can imagine – seven guys and one girl, in a house, claiming to be a walking party, never going out, occasionally coming out and kicking a ball about – and this was all about twenty miles from Tenby, which is a good place for connections to Cork. And had the police been called, and they'd invaded, they would have found detailed street maps of Belfast and Londonderry – so the fact that we weren't all arrested was very lucky. So we split up into twos and threes and we wrote a lot of scenes. We were only there for a week – we wrote some other scenes later on. Then David and Snoo, who directed it, basically put it together. But it was, you know, 'What do you want to write about?' But as you can imagine, though I'd written a few short plays, and had them done, that was at quite a low level. So actually to be working with those people like that – it was a baptism of fire, but I would recommend it to anybody. My first seven days as a professional playwright were writing with Howard Brenton, Snoo Wilson and David Hare.

Does that play ever get revived?

Not only does it not get revived, but it seems the script is missing. I've got a sort of first draft, but the last section starts, 'Scenes in a mess', so that was an early stage.

And how did it go down at the Royal Court?

I don't remember – David will tell you. The original plan was to do theatres all round the country, and suddenly theatres, as soon as they got wind of what it was about, or what its tone was, started finding that they had to overhaul their central heating, or whatever. But I can't remember what the relationship with the Court was, all I know is that Oscar didn't like it.

Tell me a little bit about your theatrical family.

My parents were actor/stage managers, and my aunt worked for Barry Jackson. She went to Stratford as his production manager and then came back to Birmingham Rep. So she was running the theatre throughout my childhood – she retired when I was fourteen or fifteen. I first went there, to see *Beauty and the Beast,* when I was nearly four, and had to be taken out of the theatre because I screamed the place down when the Beast came in.

So it was absolutely part of your life when you were growing up.

Yes. I don't know when I first went to the Royal Court, but I do know that most of the Royal Court plays I saw first at Birmingham. So I remember very well seeing *The Knack, Look Back in Anger, The Caretaker* – but at the Rep. That is the repertory tradition, that, for example, a successful play like Joe Penhall's *Blue/Orange* would be done – except that now it wouldn't be. The fact that the reps are no longer doing the contemporary is one of my bugbears – theatre writing of the past thirty years is the uninvited guest of the current theatre repertoire. Obviously I've got a personal interest in that because I'm part of it. But though I saw most of my theatre in Birmingham, I did see some things in London – I saw Brook's *Lear,* I saw *Marat/Sade,* I saw the World Theatre Seasons, and obviously by that stage I must have been going to the Royal Court.

And did you think all your life that you wanted to be in the theatre?

Always. At first I wanted to be an actor. The family joke is that my mother came to see me play Miss Prism at school, and said, 'Well, it's not going to be acting, is it, dear?' Very unfair on her, but probably not unfair on my performance. So I read drama at Manchester University, and by the time I did that I wanted to be a director.

So, like several people I've talked to, you started writing plays so someone would let you direct them.

Or indeed act in them, absolutely. Then my second year at university was 1968, so there were obviously a lot more interesting things going on than studying Shakespeare. So though I completed my course, and got a degree, really in my second two years at university I wasn't very interested in drama. I edited the student newspaper, I got very involved in student politics, I was chair of the Socialist Society, which was the basic university revolutionary grouping. Oh, the other thing was, I went to the Round-house in the summer of 1969, to the Living Theatre, and I was absolutely knocked out by that. I think actually that was something that persuaded me theatre was worth going into. Of course that was the period when censorship had ended, and you suddenly got, in addition to all the stuff that was done in Britain, all this stuff that came from abroad. And then I got a job on the *Bradford Telegraph*, which I think was a much more important three years for me than my three years at university – educatively it wasn't so important, but politically and personally it was. Chris Parr started doing my plays, and gradually I came to a point as a result of several things. *England's Ireland* was one, but other things happened that year, one of which was a residency with Max Stafford-Clark at the Traverse, which meant I couldn't carry on being a journalist, so I decided to take the plunge. It was a period of great fecundity, the early 1970s – the effect of the abolition of censorship was that there were lots of small theatres putting on plays. So my joke was that in the early 1970s it was possible to write a play for five actors, lasting under an hour, so terrible that no one would put it on, but it was very difficult. And I failed to write such a play. So all of my stuff – silly jokey political farces, really – got put on, and it was a wonderful period, a good experience. Then I submitted stuff to the Royal Court that got turned down, I think probably in most cases rightly. And then *Excuses Excuses* was commissioned by the Court, but Charles Marowitz ended up doing it at the Open Space. I think that was commissioned and not done by the Court. But certainly for all these various and weird reasons I ended up not being a Royal Court writer.

But then you started to be a success elsewhere.

Yes. The other big thing that happened was my experience with *Destiny*. The play had been turned down by everybody. It was too big for the Royal Court even then. It was written initially for Nottingham and they turned it down, it was rewritten for Birmingham and they decided not to do it, and it was turned down by the RSC. But then the director Ron Daniels took it to Trevor Nunn and said, 'You've got to do this,' and it was done at The Other Place and then at the Aldwych.

Strange that no one wanted it – it's a very powerful play.

Yes. I genuinely don't know why that play got turned down as much as it did. I do understand why Nottingham turned the first draft down, because it was a bit of a mess, but by the time I'd done it properly . . . So Trevor Nunn said, 'Right, I'll do it in The Other Place.' So it was done there, and then it transferred to the Aldwych. That was the beginning of the long period when, with the exception of *Mary Barnes*, all the plays I was writing for conventional stages, as opposed to touring, were for the RSC.

So your relations with the Court were always rather troubled!

Certainly in the 1970s we were quite aggressive, and denunciatory, especially of the first generation of Royal Court writers, in a way that the present generation are not. I mean writers like Penhall and so on are absolutely charming to the old buffers – really nice and respectful. The idea of any of us being nice and respectful to Wesker and so on, at the time! But at the Court in the beginning there was I think that Romantic nineteenth-century sense of the writer as the expression of the holy muse, and I think what has happened in theatre as well as everywhere else over the last forty years is a very gradual shift from things being run in the interests of the producers to things being run in the interests of the consumer. Teaching playwriting could not have happened in the old tradition of the Royal Court Theatre because, as people like Alan Plater still say today, what writers do is they express themselves, and it's all in there, they're born with it. And what playwrights do is protect their self-expression from the various forces that combine to undermine it and destroy it and stamp it down – notably critics, directors and actors. So I think we've got much more open to the idea that dramatic structure has rules, that actually the way you write plays is not entirely an internal matter – it may be largely an internal matter, but it's also about the plays you've seen, and the society in which you live. That's one thing, and the other is that you do have to pay some attention to what the audience is wanting to see. Now I think that's gone far too far the other way, and I think what we now have to do is absolutely reassert producer power. But I think we were the cusp generation that gently began to call into question that original idea – and it was partly because we were all libertarian lefties. Now it wasn't entirely true – because the Theatre Writers' Union, which I helped to found with several of the other usual suspects, was about serving writer power. But nonetheless I think we did accept that directors and designers and actors were artists too, in a way that some of the first generation didn't accept and never have.

But now, at the Court, they work all the time with writers. They sit with somebody for many hours if necessary, thrashing out how to make something which looks promising, better.

And I must say I think that has produced better work, or more consistent work. But there's another reason for it: the virtue development produces is clarity. Clarity is the central virtue of narrative. It's difficult to say, as a compliment, the narrative was unclear. You could say lots of things were held back. But on the other hand, clarity isn't particularly a virtue, say, in character. Actually complexity, interest, surprise – all those things are values of character. But because of the shift from producer to consumer, while paradoxically all the postmodernists have been telling us narrative is dead, what's actually happening in the marketplace is that there's been a sort of Gadarene rush back to it in the narrative arts, which include novels, and even television and film, and even narrative visual art, like Tracey Emin. I've just done a two-week workshop on my new play, and – I knew this was going to happen – we spent two weeks saying, is what's happening here clear to the audience? As opposed to: is this character interesting? Is this complex? Is this surprising, will this knock them back in their seats? Is this play sufficiently critical of late capitalism? Now all these things are the questions you would have been asking in the 1970s. My play *Destiny* was about a by-election, but the by-election was a clothes-line, really, on which you hang what you want to do. I call it the clarity versus colour battle. I think what the Court does, with writers, is that it sits them down and says, what are you trying to say and is it clear?

Do you go to the Royal Court now? What is your take on it?

Obviously the current view is that the Court has got sort of mired in elegant, ninety-minute slice-of-life plays. One of my projects on the train back tomorrow is to read April De Angelis' *Wild East*, which looks very interesting. But clearly the sort of ninety-minute, elegant, incident-based play like that one, and in another sense the Kevin Elyot *Forty Winks*, which I saw – people now think that's what the Royal Court is doing, and obviously Rickson's stout defence of the short play in the *Guardian* recently is actually not denying that. As far as the ninety-minute play is concerned, I think Michael Billington's analysis has got a point. A play of that length doesn't give lots of arguments, and asides, because it doesn't have time to do that. It presents something to you and is sort of self-consciously and deliberately saying, 'Well, we don't have an answer to it.'

Well, your own plays, at least the early ones, are full of all sorts of things, songs, and spectacle.

Yes – I moved rather away from that on to a slightly more realistic mode later on – and oddly enough, I've moved back a bit. But I believe in writing big plays, about public issues, which are about debating the relationship between how we operate as human beings and how the world works.

But the Royal Court really has never been the sort of political theatre you would have liked, though it's always been left-wing.

It's strange – it's always resisted it in a way. The big Howard Brenton political plays aren't done at the Royal Court, or if they are done at the Royal Court, like *Magnificence*, it's sort of grudgingly. But I have a kind of model of the history of the Court, which says, generation one is about the cultural consequences of democratisation and the war, so that's Osborne, Jimmy Porter, that's certainly the end of Wesker's *Roots*, that's Bond's *Saved*. The next lot, our lot, are reform versus revolution; then the women writers are about a search for identity; and then I think the brat pack – obviously it applies to some rather than others – are, 'Whatever happened to politics?' Mark Ravenhill writes about people who can't see past next Thursday or back past last Tuesday, but he doesn't like it. It's an elegy. And so is Sarah Kane's work. The Royal Court has always been hip – it's always had its finger on the zeitgeist – so in a way it's always been more culturally up to the minute, which paradoxically has made it less politically up to the minute. Maybe that may account for that resistance to my kind of writing, because I'm the stopped clock of British theatre. At the point where everybody says political theatre is dead, I'm still producing it. So I just carry on, and occasionally political theatre comes back into fashion, and there I am again. Not that I've not had all my work done, I'm pleased to say. So I think that it's true – you can probably read more about what the culture is in what the Court's currently doing than you can in what the National is currently doing. The Court has one hand in the National, and one hand in the Bush, really, doesn't it?

Kevin Elyot

My Night with Reg 1994
Mouth to Mouth 2001
Forty Winks 2004

I saw Kevin Elyot's play *Forty Winks* at the Court in 2004 and liked it very much. We met for the interview in the very civilised Covent Garden Hotel at the end of January 2005. He obviously has good taste – while several of the writers were impressed with the iPod I was using to record the interviews, Kevin admired the pretty beaded bag in which I carry it about. I was also pleased to hear that one of his important early influences had been the acting of David Warner, who had been a good friend of mine years ago.

You started out as an actor, didn't you?

Yes, I did. And I did it for about twenty years.

Before you even thought of writing plays?

No. I wrote my first play for the Bush, *Coming Clean*, in 1982, halfway through my acting career. And then during the 1980s I intermittently wrote and intermittently acted. But after *My Night with Reg* I gave up acting.

So you think of yourself as purely a writer now.

Yes. And it's a great relief.

So – can you remember the first time you went to the theatre?

I used to be taken by my parents to places like the Birmingham Hippodrome, as a little kid, to see variety shows. Also to the Alexandra Theatre, and to see things at the Rep – this was at quite an early age – and also tours of companies like Sadler's Wells. And I remember my first trip to Stratford, I think in 1961, to see *Richard III*, with Eric Porter and Christopher Plummer. And also seeing Vanessa Redgrave in *As You Like It*. So as it was only a bus ride away, I started a kind of love affair with Stratford.

So was there any point where you were absolutely smitten by theatre?

I don't remember exactly when it was, but I do know that was what I wanted to do, from quite an early age. I was a choirboy, too, in Birmingham, at a church called St Peter's, and afterwards at Birmingham Cathedral. The church ritual might have somehow influenced my thinking. So – all these things. But you never really know where it comes from; because my sister in fact is an agent, but my parents and relatives have nothing whatever to do with theatre. You do wonder where it comes from.

And you went to drama school?

No, I didn't. I went to Bristol University to read drama, and then went straight in.

And did you get lots of work?

Yes, but I never felt I was really satisfied with acting. I never quite got the opportunities I wanted. But then writing seemed to fall into my lap, somehow.

How did that happen?

Simon Stokes at the Bush suggested that I try my hand at writing. Quite casually. I was working there – I did quite a few productions as an actor.

How interesting. So was he just suggesting that in a sort of blanket way, to lots of people?

I don't know why it all came about. But then I thought, why not?

At university I suppose you're just forced to write . . .

I wrote at school. At university not necessarily, I don't think so. So I wrote *Coming Clean* for the Bush, and then Peggy Ramsay took me on.

So what happened to make you move on to the Royal Court? Did they seize hold of you at some point?

No, it didn't happen like that. I got this idea for *My Night with Reg* – I got the title about ten years before I wrote it – and I eventually got commissioned by Jenny Topper at Hampstead, when she started to run that theatre. So we developed it for a short while there, and then finally she passed on it.

I bet she kicked herself for that afterwards.

Yes – and so my agent sent it to Stephen Daldry and Max Stafford-Clark. It was just at the time when Stephen was taking over. And they wanted it. So it was never rewritten or developed by the Court, it was presented as a fait accompli. They brought in Roger Michell, the director, and that was that. I submitted my next play to the National and they accepted it, but I didn't know who I wanted to direct it. Trevor Nunn suggested Ian Rickson, who at that time wasn't artistic director at the Court. So I went to see his production of *The Weir*, which was having its first run at the Ambassador's, and I was very impressed by that. And so we met – and that's how Ian and I got together. And then he got offered the Court. Next I wrote *Mouth to Mouth,* which I offered straight away to Ian at the Court, because I felt it was the right thing to do rather than the National. Then I wrote *Forty Winks*, which I thought was rather more a Royal Court play than a National play.

Well, that's an interesting idea . . .

But in a sense I don't feel I am attached to any theatre particularly.

Yes – that seems to be the thing now. When you talk to the earlier writers, Arnold Wesker, Ann Jellicoe, there is no question that they felt themselves to be Royal Court writers. But now it's very difficult for playwrights – why should they identify themselves with one place or another, because there are so many places that they can go? But it's interesting that you thought Forty Winks *was more of a Royal Court play. What do you think made it a Royal Court play?*

Well – that I find really hard to answer.

I read an interview yesterday with April De Angelis about the play that's opening there, Wild East. *She said she had sent it to the Court rather than the National because it had a smaller cast, only three people. But that is rather a basic thing, and that can't be true of* Forty Winks. *That had big set changes and a relatively large cast for the Royal Court.*

Yes, in many ways I'm now wondering whether maybe *Forty Winks* should have gone to the National for that very reason! Because Hildegard Bechtler designed a very ambitious set . . .

Did that bother you? When I saw it, it was a preview, and the set changes were very long.

They never got much shorter.

But I thought it was rather good, really, sitting in the dark and listening to music and noises – I found it evocative and interesting. You could sit and ponder a bit, and then you got the next bit. I thought that was okay, but I know there were people who didn't like it. I suppose you could say to hell with them, what does it matter?

I think the whole thing about Katie Mitchell, the director, is that she has a very bold vision. I was really quite excited about working with her on *Forty Winks*. And the very fact that she made no apology, although she was aware that these scene changes had to get shorter – and they were shorter by the time it got into the run, but not that much shorter – in fact she made something of them. So you almost had something like a radio play, with lots of little clues in what you're hearing. I thought, why not? People are so used to . . .

Well, I'm glad you say that. Because I liked them, and I didn't know how to defend my liking for them.

It's amazing even these days how people resist newish ideas. And some of the critics really had their guns targeted on *Forty Winks*. Katie had said from the start, 'This is really going to divide people, this play and what we're doing.' I'd thought, surely not, because I'd always had quite an easy ride, but she was right – some of them were quite cruel. But, arrogantly perhaps, I think that's a reflection on them rather than on Katie and myself, because I do think there was an awful lot of talent up on that stage, and not only with the actors, and Katie herself, but Hildegard, and Paule Constable, who is the most fantastic lighting designer, and Gareth Fry, the sound designer. I mean, there was an array of talent there, and for that not to be totally appreciated really grieves me. Because you never get a second bite of the cherry in this business with a new play. And these people, they'll write some slightly spiteful review, and then the next day they'll have moved on to something else, but the damage has been done. Something that should be addressed is the ability within the budgets of places like the Court to back up projects with really efficient marketing, because it's such a competitive business. There's so much going on every day in London, and things just sink without trace if you're not really careful. I think they should try to sort that out – it's money really, and how you use that money. There were enough good reviews that could have been splattered all over the place, but they simply don't have the money, and when you've taken about two years to write something, it's just out of proportion.

Let's get back to your writing. Does it always take you two years to write plays?

Since *My Night with Reg* there has tended to be a three-year gap between plays and each one does seem to take about two years to write.

So what on earth goes on for those two years?

Well, I'm writing other things as well . . .

Okay. But how does it happen that an idea for a play comes along? Is it always the same process? Does something happen that sparks it off?

It might be a moment that intrigues me, or – it can start off in the oddest way. And really it makes me sound a bit capricious and maybe rather shallow because, while some playwrights might sit down to write a play about Guantanamo, or the Health Service, I tend to write a play because I want to see two people doing a tango, or want to hear a piece of music in juxtaposition to something else. And then gradually you put pieces together over a length of time, and shape something out of it.

So it starts off with fragments?

Yes.

Funnily enough Peter Gill told me that's how he writes. It's fascinating talking to different writers, because, for example I was talking to David Hare yesterday and he told me that he has to know what the politics are. If he doesn't have a political idea he can't write a play.

Making a play is fiendishly difficult. We all have our different methods.

But in any case you've got many extremes. David Storey starts with a blank piece of paper. He has no idea – he says if he has a sort of concept that he's driving towards at the beginning, the play doesn't work as well. But this idea of starting with bits and pieces, a sort of collage that gradually builds up – you're not totally alone in that. So you're not somebody who sits down and forces yourself to write every day – just when the mood takes you. But when you're commissioned, that's working to a deadline. How do you find that?

Well, I do it, I'm never late. But I worry a lot. I think that's how I function. Under stress really, which is very bad for the health.

In the end, do you think, looking back over the work you've done since the 1980s, obviously your plays tell different stories, but could you say there's one thing your plays are actually about? One thing that you return to again and again? Something you want to say?

I don't think that's for the writer to say, really. When you become too self-analytical – I become superstitious about it, as if I might lose the trick. But it seems to me, having written about five original plays, that there are certain things that do recur, without my necessarily sitting down consciously to write about them.

I think that's what's interesting . . .

And it's all to do with an obsession – they're all obsessive, really – about the passing of time, and about mortality, and missing the moment of something. There's that sequence in *Forty Winks* when Diana says, 'It's now that matters, isn't it? Now. This moment. And even this is already a memory.' And that's the sort of thing that obviously exercises me quite a lot. But then again if I sat down to write a play deliberately about that, it would probably be something very dull.

Well, quite. Because that's something obviously fundamental, which is going to be there whether you deliberately put it there or not. It seems to me a lot of yearning goes on in your plays.

I think you're right.

I mean not just unrequited love – but it's connected with what you've just said really. It's very obvious in My Night with Reg, *isn't it, where this poor guy has been living for God knows how many years on this moment where something could have happened but didn't.*

You should read *The Day I Stood Still*!

I shall! Is that the one that was done at the National? Donald Howarth told me that at the end of that the tears were just pouring down his face.

That's very good to hear in a way – but it did seem to have an effect on people, that play. Ian Rickson did an extremely beautiful production.

How many times have you worked with Ian?

Just twice, that and *Mouth to Mouth*.

And have you felt on the whole well served by directors?

Oh yes. I've been very fortunate.

It's obvious, when you talk to some playwrights, that they've had at least one very unhappy experience: obviously a director can make or break a play.

Obviously. And I'm not saying that it's always been comfortable, or enormously friendly, but that viewing the work, the end product, I've been extremely well served. But going back to writing, and what one does, I know the Court does all kinds of groups and so on: I've always avoided that. Because again I've felt that once I start being analysed, I worry that I'll lose something, which is ridiculous, maybe, but that's the way I do it.

But I suppose there's a case in which a play might land on someone's desk and they might say well, this play is great but I'm not so sure about Act Three, so will you rewrite Act Three? At which point you could say, no, fuck off, I don't want to rewrite Act Three. Has that ever happened to you?

Yes, but there's a difference between teaching someone to write a play and – I mean, I do rewrite, don't get me wrong. And we discuss some scene or moment, and even sometimes at rehearsals if I see a scene or moment doesn't work, I'll rewrite it. But with that I can't make a generalisation. And also, doing screenplays you're always rewriting, and that's fine as long as it's specific. It's not that I've got a closed mind. I think it's earlier on that I worry about it; when you've got something, it's more secure. Because it's a very fragile process, and I think it would be foolish to pretend that it's not. Another thing that interests me is when you get some people saying you should be writing big plays for big stages on big issues – well, of course you could, but I don't think you can force it. And seeing a play about a big issue might not be the most theatrically exciting thing you could see, whereas something that I thought was terrifically good last year was Conor McPherson's *Shining City*. That was a wonderful play, absolutely wonderful. And there were little moments in that that I thought were stunning and quite profound and transcendent. And yet, what is it about? It's not about the nature of world politics or anything – it's a ghost story really.

Isn't it shocking, really, to think anything else? Why can't a play be just about thoughts and feelings?

Us just having a cup of coffee could touch on something much more resonant than seeing someone bestriding the stage like a colossus. I'm not saying that it necessarily would, but it has that potential. And it's how you do it rather than what you're doing, I think. That's what I have to keep reminding myself – that it's finding the moment, or the moments, to make an audience really . . .

This kind of answers a question I've been thinking about – something my dad said in 1960. He said he thought plays should be in some way disturbing. Of course a play can be disturbing in many ways, but I think he meant it should make you think. It doesn't really matter what about – it could be about some major political issue or it could be about some rather more nebulous internal state. It's true of any art form, I suppose.

I think that's very true, and I've always thought that – and I do think theatre is the most important forum to push the boundaries a bit. If there's just one sequence in an evening where an audience is made to think twice, to feel uncomfortable – not for the shock value necessarily, but just so you're not preaching to the converted, or allowing complacency to set in. I think that's what's exciting about theatre.

Just nudging at people's preconceptions a bit. So would you say that there is anybody or anything that has influenced the way you write or the way you think about writing?

It sounds so predictable, but I read a book when I was at school about Shakespeare's dramatic imagery that was a revelation to me, that opened a door that I didn't even know existed. I think that was a great influence. And Chekhov. And Peter Stein's *Summerfolk* at the Lyttelton in the 1970s. And Peter Brook's *Dream*, and David Warner's Hamlet. Things like this. I could go on.

Simon Farquhar

Rainbow Kiss 2006

I met Simon Farquhar for the first time at the presentation of the George Devine Award in May 2005. His play, which was then memorably if rather inelegantly called *Fuck Off*, had been submitted for the award by his agent. No one had heard of him – not surprisingly, considering he had never had a professional production – but the play impressed everyone on the committee. In the event it was a runner-up rather than the winner, but I was very pleased to hear, the following August, that the play had been taken up by the Royal Court for a production in 2006. So he became my last interviewee. We met in the Royal Court bar, and as we settled down to talk he told me that, among other things, he was working on a book on the history of the BBC's *Play for Today*, which he had watched avidly in his early years.

So it all began with you watching Play for Today!

That's right.

Where did you live? In Scotland?

Originally. Then I was packed off to school in England, which I hated. I'm not from a theatrical family or anything like that; my dad was a police-man, my big brother's a prison officer. I don't know why, but something must have grabbed me early on, and I remember 'Play for Today' was a big thing, even when I was too young to understand it. It really had a big impact on me, especially Jim Allen things, like *The Spongers*, or Trevor Griffiths' *Comedians*, Colin Welland's stuff, and John Hopkins'. And big-gest of all, was the Scottish drama that came out of the seventies, because at that time you just didn't hear anything like that on television. When you saw things set on rainy streets in Greenock – though that was the other side of Scotland from where I was from – it just seemed like . . . and then it all seemed to suddenly stop. And I was always good at English, it was the only thing I was good at at school, but briefly I wanted to be an actor. I think everyone who's interested in theatre wants to do that first – no one has childhood ambitions to be a director. But you find your way by trial and error.

Did you do much drama at school?

There wasn't really the opportunity to do it, and I was terribly unsure of myself. Certainly when I was tiny the first thing I wanted to do was write, and used to all the time. But when I went to university I did English, and I got involved with the drama society there.

What university was this?

Aberdeen. But after I graduated I auditioned for a play in Edinburgh, and got a part in that, and went down there for three weeks. It was the Edinburgh Festival. And one night, in a pub, I was talking about my schooldays, which were pretty horrific. I went to a public school, and it was absolutely dreadful, a bit like *Scum* with posh accents. Everyone else's parents were very middle-class, merchant bankers or whatever, and I was completely out of my depth. I was talking about this and everyone was very interested, and someone said, 'You should write a play about it.' I'd written some short stories, but I hadn't taken it very seriously. So I wrote this play – and there used to be a festival in Aberdeen where you could put on one-act plays, so I put on *Speech Day*, and it had a bit of an impact. The next year I did another one, *I Do Solemnly Declare*, which got published, and then the third year I did one called *Childhood Haunts*, that got a little local award. I thought then that I was ready to take on the world! So I came to London – and realised that it didn't mean anything.

What year was this?

The third play was done in 1998. I came to London, and nothing really happened. What I always wanted to do was write for telly, and it just became clear that that wasn't going to happen, not least because that sort of television is dead now.

You were sending things in and nothing was happening?

I don't think I was even sending things in after a while, because I just realised it was hopeless. Most people think the way writers start off is, you write a play, you send it somewhere, and people say, yes, we like this, and they just do it. And of course that doesn't happen in real life. And yet so far in my career that's exactly what has happened, with this play and with my radio play! So I had two or three years in which nothing happened. I had so many false starts, something almost going to happen and then not, and I began to hear all these appalling depressing stories about how things go into development for ages, if you're lucky. And then I went home for the weekend, to the north-east of Scotland, and while I was there I was literally just sitting on the seafront when I had this idea for a radio play. I'd been hearing that radio was slightly easier to break into. So I wrote this play, *Candy Floss Kisses*, basically in an afternoon, and I just had a feeling – I don't know where it came from – that it had something that everything I'd done before didn't quite have. I showed it to a friend and he said, 'I think this has got something, I think you should send it off.' So I sent it all round the BBC, and every producer turned it down. It was too Scottish, was what one producer said, but the Scottish people didn't seem to want it either. Then I sent it to the BBC New Writing initiative, a joke of a department, and they said, 'Yes, it's good, but we've done other things like it . . .' and I nearly gave up. Then eventually it fell into the hands of Martin Jarvis. He read it and loved it and said he'd like to do it. So he then had to take it to the BBC – they didn't realise they'd already turned it down – and he fought and fought, because I was an unknown, and got it commissioned. I owe him everything for that. So that got me an agent. And once I'd got an agent I thought I'd tackle a stage play. Because although television was the first thing I'd got interested in, theatre was what really excited me by now, from when I did plays when I was a student, and when I started going to theatre. That's what I loved. I loved the pauses, and the work that you, as an audience member, do yourself there, and I loved the immediate reaction something gets. So I wrote a stage play, *Spin the Bottle*, and my agent read it and liked it but nothing really came of it. The Soho Theatre read it, and they liked it, and said would I come in and have a chat. So they said, 'We like it, but we don't want to do it. But could you write something else?' And they were at that time doing the Verity Bargate Award – it had been open for a few months but it only had about two weeks to go before the closing date. So they said, 'Could you write something to enter for that?' I'd just finished a second radio play, *Elevenses with Twiggy*, and I was shattered, but at the same time I was taking up any kind of opportunity that presented itself, however vague. So I wrote *Fuck Off* in ten days, and sent it off. It didn't win the Verity Bargate but they liked it, and asked me to do a rewrite. And I was like, well, what do you want me to change? There seems to be this culture of, you must do a second draft, it's a knee-jerk reaction. And then my agent sent it to the George Devine Award – and the rest is history. The change of title to *Rainbow Kiss* was nothing to do with prudishness. There was a lot of talk about it, and really *Fuck Off* was precisely what was apt for the play considering its themes. But Graham Whybrow pointed out that though the Court had in the past produced two plays with the 'f-word' in the title, that was where his concern lay: he feared that it would look a bit nineties, and people might pigeonhole it in their minds before they'd even seen it. And I thought that if it was going to keep people away then of course I should change it. *Rainbow Kiss* was always the title I had in reserve.

You haven't done a rewrite – it's as you first wrote it, in ten days?

Yes, that's right. I don't know if that's a good thing or not. I should say that although it was written in ten days, I'd had the idea for several months, and I'd been noting stuff down. I was just about ready to start writing, but I probably wrote it quicker than I would have done other-wise. I really went hell for leather on it. And then, when I came for the interview here with Graham Whybrow, I had no idea what was going to happen. I mean, I knew the Royal Court history backwards, and I'd always dreamed of having a play done here. But when I came here, and sat in this room full of folders with names like Ted Whitehead and John Osborne on them, all the mystique about the Royal Court and all the reputation it has felt justified. Because what they seemed to be interested in was the play, not how good I looked on paper as a writer.

So you started to like drama because of television, but did you ever go to the theatre when you were a kid?

The first thing I ever saw in the West End was *The Secret of Sherlock Holmes*, with Jeremy Brett and Edward Hardwick, which was fabulous. It was a great introduction to theatre because it was actually not too much of a leap from telly for me. I can remember seeing the sweat and grease-paint pouring down Jeremy Brett's face, and he was so fabulously theatrical as well. It all seemed so exciting. But the atmosphere of it was extraordi-nary. It was just peculiar.

How old were you when you saw that?

About sixteen or seventeen. But it was just the silences, and the tension – and I've always liked that thing that happens in the theatre, when some-thing is obviously an illusion but you're swept up by it, you're caught.

I saw a great *King Lear* at the Barbican soon after that with John Wood and Ralph Fiennes and Norman Rodway. I remember some of the other things that made a big impact on me were plays like Mark Ravenhill's *Shopping and Fucking* – that made a big impact on me, it really blew me away. I didn't actually think it was that great a play, but it had a heck of an impact.

Did you see that here?

No, I saw it at the Richmond Theatre, on the very last leg of its tour. I really missed that whole nineties thing; I was stuck up in Scotland. Irvine Welsh's *Trainspotting* made it up there – I was right in Edinburgh when all that was happening. I went to see the stage play of that and I didn't like it at all. I was really bored in Scotland with seeing the only thing you'd ever see there, apart from the commercial stuff, which was these sort of angst plays. There was a real trend in the nineties for a particular style of acting that was really confrontational and in-your-face. It was a little bit too self-consciously cool, rather like the movie of *Trainspotting*, which bored me because there wasn't a great deal of storytelling. I love story-telling. I saw Conor McPherson's *Shining City* last year – it was one of the best nights you could ever have in the theatre – it was amazing. And the storytelling . . . people suddenly opening up. Like that beautiful moment in Christopher Hampton's *The Philanthropist* when Philip tells the story about the tramp who cleans his car, a magical moment. Maybe that's why storytelling seems to crop up a lot in my stuff. I've always liked that, it just brings it back to the basics of what theatre should be.

Yes – I've only read one of your plays, but it's full of stories.

A lot of that, I think, is because I'm really interested in male bonding. And male bonding sort of gets mistaken for being something to do with blokes getting together and watching football and getting drunk. That's male partying, it's not male bonding. Male bonding is when a guy has had his heart broken and his mate comes round. It's an incredibly tender thing, and it only happens between males in private, when they say things to each other. I mean sometimes they'll say things like, 'Don't worry, I've got some really good porn I can give you, that'll sort you out.' But there's a real sweetness to that, though it doesn't get shown. I don't know, I'm not a girl, but the way it's shown in films and plays is that if a girl gets dumped, all her mates say, 'Don't worry, all men are bastards.' It's quite a sort of defiant thing. Whereas blokes can really go to pieces, and guys really comfort each other. It's a fallacy to say that blokes don't cry – they may keep their tears back in front of women, but not in front of each other, believe me.

I wonder if that's always been true?

It probably hasn't, actually. But what strikes me is that blokes always tell stories to each other to make each other feel better. I remember something I read at school, by John Wesley – he said that the beauty of a great psalm is when the heart and the mind are in accord. And I think that's just the same for any kind of writing or drama: it's when you think, that's exactly how I feel but I couldn't have put it so well. It reminds you you're not alone in feeling a certain way. So in the play the storytelling is always offered as a comfort, it's offered along with a drink, for that reason. It's a Scottish thing, perhaps. We're a hard-luck nation – we're resilient, but misfortune or lack of opportunities are our identity, and drinking and out-misfortuning each other are parts of Scottish life. Stories also put our situation in perspective. That was one of the main things I was interested in. And *Rainbow Kiss* was really born out of living in Aberdeen for nine years – I'm not from Aberdeen itself but I lived there for nine years, and I've fallen in and out of love with the city throughout my life. But I was quite shocked when I went back there recently to find how changed the city is. To the outsider it may have changed for the better, because it's been poshed up a lot, but whereas in the late eighties and early nineties you saw a lot of old guys drunk on street corners who'd lost their jobs under Thatcher, who are all dead now, on the street corners now are young kids on heroin. They're everywhere and they're very prominent, because it's a small town. But everyone in Aberdeen has something in common, which is that they're in a fairly remote and unexciting city, so people do strike up a kind of camaraderie in the place, and some people do live fairly desperate lives there. When I say unexciting, I find it a very interesting city, but not even a fan of it like me would ever call it exciting.

One thing that interests me is the process of writing. You've jumped in on that one in the sense that you said the idea came to you and you wrote it in ten days – is that typical?

Well, yes. In fact looking back, apart from that one radio play, which came pretty much off the top of my head, every single time it starts the same way. It'll just start with an idea, which will come from wherever ideas come from.

And what kind of an idea is it – a story, an image?

Could be anything – a story, an image, or a theme. But from there I will just start noting things down. And my mind will just focus on it. And then for a month, or two months, maybe three at the most, I'll jot things down all the time – bits of dialogue, ideas – and then, by the end of it, I'll think, right, now it's time to start writing. I never start writing until I know the characters inside out. Because basically once I do, it's like tuning into a radio station and writing down what I hear, like dictation. But until I know where the characters went to school, and which desk they sat at, I can't start it. If you know them that well, when you write a line of dialogue where someone asks them a question, you know what they're going to answer. You can't pause and think, oh, what would he do in this situation? You have to know them like they're your best friend or something.

How do you get to know them that well? They just appear in your head?

Well, to give an example – the next radio play I've written, *Elevenses with Twiggy*, which is one of the things I'm most proud of, that came out of wanting to do something about the sixties. I'd seen a documentary about design in the sixties, and it was really interesting and exciting, and I loved all the music from that era. And one of the icons of that era was Twiggy, who, even though I was a seventies child, I sort of associated with my childhood. I suppose I thought of London in the sixties, and Scotland in the sixties, the contrast, and I thought that when I was a kid, in the early seventies, in a tiny fishing village in the north-east of Scotland, the papers didn't arrive till the afternoon, and the pubs closed at nine o'clock at night – all sorts of ridiculous things. And I thought the sixties would have been great if you'd had a lot of money and lived on the King's Road, but they would have been lousy if you'd lived in the north-east of Scotland. And I had this idea about these two brothers who win one of these competitions, you know, a date with a celebrity, and they come to London to get away from this awful existence they've got, and they meet Twiggy. But then I thought more and more about these two brothers, and I thought, why would they be doing this? Well, one of them must be a dreamer, and the other one is really unhappy – and it just built up until I had pages and pages of dialogue, and ideas, and things I wanted to get into it. And then it was just a case of sitting down and making it make sense. I'll note down and note down until it's time to start writing.

But do you actually use those notes when you start writing?

Oh yes – though it's actually quite bizarre how much you can retain in your head as you go along. But although they're all there beside me to refer to, I can't go from A to Z referring to those too meticulously. I have to just drive, just hear it as if it's actually happening, like you're driving a car and the map is beside you but you've kind of got the gist of the route in your head. That way you get a better sense of pacing and knowing what you've kept people informed of and so on, by sort of playing it out in your head from start to finish and writing it out as you go without constructing it all too slowly.

I know you said this one got written in ten days, but would you normally expect to go back and do a lot of revising?

What I do, and I always do the same thing, is I write longhand – I can't write on a computer because my typing is not as quick as my writing. I always write in pubs and always longhand. So I'll have all these notes, and then I will start the actual process of writing it out, and I'll be crossing out, and question-marking – is this the actual word I want, and so on – and then I turn that into these nice clean white pages of typed-up script, and that's when the real process of editing happens. Then after that I may do a bit more, but in fact it's really gone from me by then, and I can't be objective about it any more, though I might be able to be in six months or something. And also I think, well, that bit could go but I really want to say that, and a director might too, so wait and let him see it.

But presumably you may find that people say, this is too long and this needs clarifying, and so on – you're not opposed to that.

Elevenses with Twiggy needed five thousand words cutting out.

Five thousand words! That's a lot!

Yes, but it was far too long, and too repetitive. It was a bit painful at the time, like cutting the legs off my baby, but now I think, yes, it really needed it, it's stronger now. You have to remember that anything that is going to help your play is a good idea. If it's going to change it, that's different.

And you're writing a novel as well?

I started it in January.

Because it's unusual, certainly among the people I've talked to, to have a playwright who happily turns to writing novels. I mean some do – David

Storey's written novels as well as plays, and Sebastian Barry – but a lot of playwrights don't want to write novels.

Yes – I wonder how they make their money!

But is that the reason?

No, it's not the reason at all. It's simply a case of – I didn't realise till I started it how much fun it was. I've always written short stories, I write short stories a lot, but with the novel, I hadn't realised just how enjoyable it is. Because you're writing different things other than just character and dialogue. I don't know how true this is, but I think theatre is, or should be, quite questioning. And sometimes you don't really want to question, you just want to reflect a little.

The answer some playwrights give is, well, I'm good at writing dialogue and I'm lousy at writing consecutive prose. But you obviously don't feel like that, if you've written short stories.

No. I like the way you can go off in so many directions with a novel. It's such a different thing. I'm still learning what I'm good at and what I'm not so good at.

One big difference when you write a novel is that you just give it to a publisher and it comes out and people read it, whereas with a play you're handing it over to a huge bunch of people who take it over.

I like the idea with a play that you can actually see people reacting to it too, but I also like the idea that with a novel you've got something which is preserved.

I came here the other night to an award being given to Elyse Dodgson, and the title they gave to the presentation, was, 'Can Theatre Change the World?' In fact they never got to that in the debate, but I wonder whether playwrights think, 'Ah, someone will see this and something will happen to them when they see it.' Do you ever think like that?

Well yes, because I think when you write something and someone sees it, even if it's only one person, that it does change the world. Whatever the play's like, you don't come out of the theatre exactly the same. It's given you something to think about. But for me personally, if I wanted to change the world, I wouldn't write plays. I'd probably be a politician or some-thing. I think my agenda when I'm writing a play is that there's something I want to share, or I want to tell a story, or create an atmosphere, or impart something, or say, this is how a life goes wrong – I want people to think about that. And that's enough. I don't know how seriously drama is taken, even by people who go to the theatre all the time. I take it very seriously, and it does influence my life. I do think about things, and when I'm in a certain situation I might think, it's like that bit in so-and-so. Your conscience changes, or your attitude, because of a piece of drama starting you thinking, and that's good. But I don't think it's necessarily the purpose of it. I'd find it dangerously pompous, for me, to say anything more than that. I suppose in a way writing's an egotistical thing, because you think people are going to be interested in what you're saying. For me, what prevents it from being that is it's not so much that you want people to know what you're thinking, or what you've been through, it's just that you want to throw up a talking point. I don't, or only rarely, write about things verbatim that have happened to me. There's a mistaken belief that just because something's happened in real life it warrants being written about, it's inherently dramatic, which it isn't. I find personally with writing, it's not to put a point across, it's actually a journey, to find out what you the writer think about something. But plays do change the world. They certainly changed my world. Strangely enough, issue-plays don't do that much for me. I think they're like preaching to the converted, like going to a church and hearing a sermon about when they became Christian, and they're all Christians sitting there – I think it's weird. It's like going to a play telling you about how much misery racism causes, and even racists know that.

Quite.

But thinking of the things that have changed my life . . .

What has? Can you think of any examples?

Well, Mark Ravenhill again, not that he's a terribly important playwright to me or anything, but I do remember going to see *Shopping and Fucking*, and I remember that line at the end where the boy says, 'I want a dad.' I will never forget it. I will never be in a situation again where I walk down a street in King's Cross, and see a rent boy, and don't think of that scene and automatically wonder what his background is, what his story might be. Not that I go wandering about King's Cross looking at rent boys by the way. And things like that speech in Trevor Griffiths' *Comedians* about the Holocaust – of all the things I've heard about the Holocaust, I've never had anything affect me like that speech. And in Scotland, Peter McDougall's plays made me aware of the Catholic–Protestant thing, that went on every day, the bigotry towards Catholics. No one in England has much idea about that. Another play that made a huge impression on me more recently was Patrick Marber's *Closer* – I thought that was incredible. It's just such a good play, so well written and so sharp. You think, that's articulated something and that's absolutely right.

What seems to interest you – it certainly comes across in Rainbow Kiss – *is human relationships, and sexual relationships.*

Yes. I am really interested in that because although it's the staple of drama – adultery and all that, it's the staple of everything – still there are so many areas that don't really get talked about. But I'm also fascinated by class, which I suppose is not something people write about much these days. Maybe it's not such a pressing issue in today's society. But I am fascinated because I'm in an unusual position, with a working-class background but brought up in a middle-class environment, something like that.

Why did your parents send you off to public school?

I think they were typical working-class parents, who thought, because they'd never had any money, that money solves everything. I don't mean that as a slight against them, but I think they just thought, your education will be better if we send you there. But it was all so strange to me – I felt like I came from somewhere really different – being at public school in the south of England in the 1980s, and in the summer going back to this village in Scotland.

It must have been extraordinary.

It was, but it was really interesting. It gave a good sort of contrast. Some of the experiences I've had in my life I could have done without, though. I'm chucking them into things now like lead that I hope will turn to gold, so maybe it was all worth it.

Peter Gill

Peter Gill is one of my oldest friends. I first met him when I was about sixteen, and really got to know him when we both worked at the Lyric Hammersmith, where John Dexter was directing a double bill of plays by Willis Hall. Peter was the assistant stage manager and I was a sort of assistant assistant stage manager, runner or dogsbody. We became instant friends and were soon inseparable. We went everywhere together – parties, films, exhibitions, plays – and he spent much of his time at my house, where my mother seemed immediately to accept him as part of the family. He moved in as a lodger fairly soon, and has only recently moved out. He was still living there when I interviewed him, in December 2004, in the flat at the top of the house in which Tony Richardson once lived.

Peter has had a distinguished career, as director, writer, and as Artistic Director of Riverside Studios (1976–80) and Director of the National Theatre Studio (1989–90). His once-black hair is now white, and he is less skinny than he was forty years ago, but his eyes still sparkle as they always did and his conversation remains as challengingly digressive and wide-rangingly intellectual as ever.

So – you started in the theatre as an actor and only later became a writer. What made you go into the theatre in the first place, and what was it that attracted you? Can you remember the first time you went to the theatre?

Well, I must have gone to pantomimes when I was a child, and I can remember the parish pantomime, the youth pantomime, that my brothers were in. But the first play I saw was at school. There was a big assembly hall, with a stage, and a couple of friends of mine found out that if you put the chairs out for the caretaker, for the amateurs who used it for their shows, then you could see the play. So we put the chairs out, and the caretaker taught us how to stagger them. I remember the first play I saw was Molière's *Tartuffe*. I thought it was the funniest thing I'd ever seen.

And how old were you?

About eleven. I think it must have been the Miles Malleson version, which he'd made for the Bristol Old Vic. And after that we always put the chairs out for the amateurs, so we saw *Much Ado About Nothing*, and various strange kinds of plays that had been done in London and then used to be done by the amateurs. And that's how I got interested. It was a curious school, because there wasn't much going on, but I realise now that they always responded, funnily enough, to things that we wanted to do, though they never started anything themselves. So we tried to have a magazine at one point, that had just two editions, and then we asked them if we could do a play. So they put a play on for us, *The Wind in the Willows – Toad of Toad Hall*. I played the lead, and my friends were all in it. And we did the scenery, and that was the best bit – the excitement of being in school in the evening, painting screens with paper on them. So I got more and more interested by those means, and then I went to a local drama school.

So this was in Cardiff – Cardiff Castle?

Yes – it's now the Welsh College, but this was when it was just a local drama school. It was very much still in the tradition of the Welsh amateur theatre, with teachers who weren't professionals, except for an interesting man who didn't come back after the first term, who was called Rudolf Shelley – a movement teacher. He was one of those people who'd fled from Hitler, and he became a big influence at the Bristol Old Vic. And he was nice to me. Anthony Hopkins was in the year above me, and he was a friend of mine. But at the end of the first year I wanted to leave. By this time I'd been to see plays in school, and at other schools, little touring things done by the Arts Council – so I knew the name Arts Council. And I found out they were sending a tour from London round South Wales and the north-east, so I wrote a letter to them asking for a job. And I remember my mother waking me one morning – because we didn't have a lot of post – to say I'd got a letter! They were asking me to come and audition. So she lent me the money, and I went to London, to St James's Square, where the Arts Council was, and met the director, Frank Dunlop. He gave me a job as an ASM on this tour, and I then rang Tony Hopkins, and he came up and was one of the other ASMs. It was a tour of *She Stoops to Conquer* and *Look Back in Anger*, the first production of *Look Back in Anger* not at the Royal Court. I was about nineteen.

And then after that you came to live in London?

No, then I went to the Nottingham Playhouse as an ASM, and there we were so overworked that all the boy ASMs were taken to hospital at one time or another. And then I came to London. But I'd already auditioned for the Royal Court somewhere in between. I did an audition for Ann Jellicoe's *The Sport of My Mad Mother*, and that was where I met Miriam Brickman, the casting director, who was a much loved person, a very kind woman, a very good woman, who was a very good casting director. So I'd auditioned for John Dexter and Miriam and Ann Jellicoe, and then I auditioned for Anthony Page and Lindsay Anderson. And finally they asked me to be an understudy in Willis Hall's *The Long and the Short and the Tall*, and that's how I first worked at the Court. I used to go on quite a lot – I understudied three parts – Alfie Lynch, David Andrews and the Japanese soldier. And I played one of the parts for a long time in the West End, and then Lindsay decided I looked too young next to Peter O'Toole! The Royal Court was often a very bruising kind of place – because there I was playing that part and then I went back to being an understudy. Michael Caine was the other understudy in the West End. And in those days the successful West End plays used to go on a tour, and I remember Wolf Mankowitz, who was one of the managers, said, 'Oh, you can go on the tour, don't worry,' so I waited. Michael Caine was doing it, and various other people, and I was waiting for the rehearsal call, and nothing happened. So I rang up Anthony Page, who was the assistant director, in a rather tetchy way – and I found out that this very good-looking boy had just left the Webber Douglas, and they'd given him the part. This was Terry Stamp. That was typical of the Royal Court in those days. But I was in some Sunday shows, Arnold Wesker's *The Kitchen*, and something by Christopher Logue.

By this time were you thinking about writing, or directing?

Well, I'd already written on the quiet – plays – that's all I ever did, ever could. But I went and did lots of telly, and films, and I went to the Aldwych in the first season that they came in from Stratford – the first year of the RSC – and I was in Bill Gaskill's production of Brecht's *The Caucasian Chalk Circle*, during which I kept a diary, which I found only the other day, and some of it's fine, but most of it's not very good. But interesting.

When you were writing it, were you thinking of it as 'writing'? Or were you just scribbling down?

Mostly scribbling down, but then I got interested in writing. But I was really not good at formulating that kind of writing. I was better at accruing dialogue.

That's fascinating to me – because I've never had the first desire to write a play. I don't naturally think about writing dialogue. But obviously for people who write plays, that must be the primary thing that they are good at. And I wonder how you get good at it. Is it just instinctive?

I think a lot of people are not good at the other kind of writing, and believe dialogue is something they can tell the truth with, or can feel satisfied with, because the more abstract conceptual writing is difficult for them. It's a different type of temperament.

So can you remember the first play you ever wrote? Did you write plays that got put away and never done?

Bits and pieces of things. It was always difficult to formulate them. A group of my friends and I wrote a play when we were young, and we all wrote different parts.

Oh – like Snoo Wilson and David Hare!

Well, yes – but we were only kids. I remember my friend Stephen, who's now a painter, wrote the avenging brothers in rhyming couplets, and I wrote the girls in free verse. John James, who has become a poet, wrote the hero and the philosopher in graphic poetry that descended to points. It was terrible – absolutely shocking!

So it was a collage.

Yes. But later, when I was at the RSC, when I was about twenty-one, I wrote a play, or some scenes that amounted to a play. I knew one of the sub-editors of a little magazine called the *Transatlantic Review*, and I'd met the editor through him. And this bloke had said they wanted to do a playwriting competition, because plays were the thing then, very much. So he asked me if I would read the plays, but I said no, I will enter it, and I put a play in under a pseudonym. I suggested Keith Johnstone or Bill Gaskill to be the person who read the plays. Then one day when I was leaving this house with Bill to go to Kew Gardens, he said, 'Would you read a play for me, because it's set in Wales?' . . . and it turned out to be by me. Now when it came to judging them, typical of Bill – he could have said, 'Well, I know this person, but I came by the play by honest means,' but instead he said, 'They're all dreadful plays except for this one which shows a little bit of something or other.' They published a couple of scenes, but he put in a kind of disclaimer saying they were all bad but this was the least worse one. And at twenty-one that's exactly what you don't need.

But that was not the play that got done as a Sunday night?

No. At that time I decided to stop acting, because I'd been in a film, and I didn't feel that I was a good enough actor, or that I was a natural enough actor in my head. I'd become interested in the theatre as a whole process by that time, and I'd become very involved with the work at the Court. Stephen Frears and I were taken on as assistants in Anthony Page's season, which was the season of John Osborne's *Inadmissible Evidence*. So I worked as Anthony's assistant on *Inadmissible* and Lindsay's assistant on *Julius Caesar*. By this time I'd written another play, and Desmond O'Donovan did a beautiful production of it on a Sunday night.

This was The Sleepers' Den?

That's right. With Eileen Atkins. Well, we enjoyed doing it, and I think the Court liked it; I know your father enjoyed it very much, because Desmond had done it very very simply. There was no attempt to put in bits of scenery, which people sometimes did. It was just marked out with tape. And that was how George had imagined the Sunday nights, that people really wouldn't enter into the area of design, but would present, as it were, the last run-through. But I was terribly self-critical, and I thought, if I'm any good they'll put this on, which didn't happen of course.

Then you started directing D. H. Lawrence?

That's right. When it came time for me to do a Sunday-night production without décor as a director, I'd not done anything; I'd not been to university, so I'd got no experience. I'd never done a production, and having been an actor I was hypercritical of directors and so I found it very daunting. But it became inevitable that if I wanted to direct I had to overcome any worries and just do it. So I'd heard that D. H. Lawrence had written a play, and I rang the British Drama League and they sent me a little tiny green book, the first edition of *A Collier's Friday Night*, which had never been done. And I read it, and I was fascinated. But I thought, Well, it's not a new play – who, except me, will want to see this? But people were enthusiastic by this time, so I showed it to George, and he read it. And he had a very good quality, George, of making you feel that he'd be interested, and that counted to somebody like me, because you had a kind of safety net, somebody who was on your side. So I cast it, and we did it, and people liked it.

But when I looked up the dates of all this, it seemed to me that he can't have seen it.

He didn't. Because he had his heart attack on the day it was going to open. I saw him putting Helene Weigel into a taxi – I'm pretty certain I saw it – and when I came home, Sophie said, 'Georgie's had a heart attack.'

So he never saw that production.

No. And it's a sadness for me, as you can imagine.

Yes, but still nice to know that he wanted you to do it. So you were thinking of yourself more as a director, but still thinking about writing?

Yes, well, I was directing, which is a time-consuming thing. I was writing, but it was a kind of private thing to me, writing, a secret activity. Because I've never been very good at getting up and doing a fixed number of words.

So when you write, what's it like? Is it hard or easy?

Not easy. Well, it's easy after a point. Once you've got to a draft.

But when you start, you have in your mind a concept, something that you want to say? No?

No. It's altered slightly, but then it really was a sort of accruing of notes, or forays into an area that somehow seemed to keep recurring.

So in the end you sort of stand back and say, 'Where's this going?'

Yes. And you don't quite know why – afterwards you can rationalise it, but at the time you don't seem to know why – it has a kind of life of its own. There are obvious rules you know about that you then apply.

But what comes first? The characters?

No – for me originally it's a sort of language notion. I don't know really – it's difficult to analyse. I think at the beginning it was just a kind of language game.

And is there any way, beyond the plot and so on, that you can say, 'This is what my plays are actually about. This is what I'm interested in saying'?

No.

132

Your plays are essentially realist, aren't they?

No – well, it depends what you mean by realist. I think nowadays people think it means that they are about characters who aren't rich. But in fact I've recently been called a modernist.

Could you say a bit more about what you think that means?

Well, I think it's because I sometimes deal with time, jumping about in time. There's a play called *In the Blue*, which started as a short piece and then was developed into a longer play, which was sort of fragmented, so I suppose people might say it was a slightly expressionistic sort of play. Also *Certain Young Men* is a play made up of a lot of different separate scenes. But *The York Realist* was an attempt to write a particular kind of play which you could say was social realism, a play set in the period we've just been talking about.

So do you know they are going to be experimental before you start? Are you setting yourself a task?

No. *The York Realist* kept recurring as an idea, and that was a kind of image of the characters, and a kind of play, and it wouldn't go away. It was in the system, as it were, for ages before I wrote it.

In fact your output of plays is not enormous, by any means.

Well, there was a whole period early on when I was directing all the time, and running things.

But if somebody said to you, you have to choose between being a director and a writer, or we'll shoot you, what would you do?

Well, it alters. I thought last year it would be a writer, but I haven't written anything for a few months so I don't think that at the moment.

I know you've often directed your own plays. But do you think you've been well served by other directors?

Yes – because when I directed my own work after Desmond had done that production, what I had to remind myself was that he'd done a beautiful production of that play without me. He was a friend of mine so we got on fine. I think there's a problem if you direct your own plays – not that you necessarily don't direct them well, but people start thinking you're one thing rather than another, people want to compartmentalise. After a bit it's very enjoyable directing your own play, funnily enough. The few times somebody else has directed them, I've never really had much to complain about, but they haven't been the first productions. When they did the Sheffield season of my plays, I was available – there was a very low budget, and there were three directors, and there had to be a permanent set, and I helped at that stage, and then after that I was just at the end of a phone. I never went to rehearsals, or to a run-though, I just went to see them. I think the thing is, in the period when I started writing, I'd have been luckier in the directors than I would now. Because the whole dramaturgical side of the theatre has grown, the whole notion that plays are there to be workshopped. But I think a lot of the success of the new writing at the Court at the beginning was due to the peculiar talent of the directors – a kind of collaborative nature, in a sort of unaffected way. I remember all the early good productions, like Bill doing Henry Livings' play, or John Dexter doing Wesker, or Lindsay and David Storey – the collaborative nature of author, director, designer (in that case always Jocelyn Herbert) and the casting director was what made them work, and gave the plays an incredible sense of importance. Now I don't remember witnessing any abstract discussions, or things of a self-consciously collaborative nature. No dramaturgy, no rewriting. I've just read some new young plays for an award scheme, and they're all talented, but I don't think the writers are aware how difficult they are to direct. I think people are too concerned at the moment with how they can improve the play by rewriting, rather than how can they make it look all right by directing it well.

I wonder if you can teach people to write better?

I think you can if someone's got a good idea, a lively idea that could be developed. But different writers are different, and some writers are good rewriters. Joe Orton was a good rewriter, John Osborne and John Antrobus weren't. It wasn't their bag.

Christopher Hampton

When Did You Last See *The Philanthropist* 1970
  My Mother? 1966 *Savages* 1973
Total Eclipse 1968 *Treats* 1976

Christopher Hampton hasn't had a play done at the Royal Court since 1976, by his own choice. He has become famous and distinguished since then, and his association with the Court has continued, as he is one of the trustees of the George Devine Award. I never got to know him in the early days, though I did meet him once, at the end of the 1960s, in the pub next door to the Royal Court. He doesn't remember, luckily, that I twittered away foolishly about being high on a macrobiotic diet. This must have been when he was still at Oxford and about to take over my job as the Court's literary manager. I went to talk to him in February 2005, in his working environment, a top-floor flat in Notting Hill.

So what's your first memory of going to the theatre?

Well, the first play I ever saw was Ibsen's *An Enemy of the People*. That was a school play at a boys' school in Alexandria. I was absolutely riveted.

How old do you think you were?

Eight.

Quite an ambitious project all round, really.

Well, it was a boys' school that went from five to seventeen – this was the big boys. I can still remember it quite vividly, including the fact that in Act Four, when Stockmann makes the big speech and the townspeople all shout at him, they planted all the boy actors in the audience, so suddenly somebody two seats away was shouting at the stage. It was incredibly exciting. And funnily enough when I translated it for the National Theatre a few years ago I got a letter and a clipping from the actor, now settled in England, who'd played Stockmann in that production.

He knew that you'd been at the school?

Well, I wrote this autobiographical play called *White Chameleon* and I'd talked about it in that, the fact that I'd seen this play at school and that it made me become interested in theatre. But I hardly ever went to the theatre. My parents weren't theatregoers, not in England. But I went on school outings, and those school outings did include Olivier's *Uncle Vanya* at Chichester and – the real sort of road to Damascus for me – Peter Brook's production of *Lear,* which was my A-level text. We all came up to London to see it.

By this time you were at school in England.

Yes, by this time I'd been sent back to school in England, to Lancing. I was not very much looking forward to seeing *King Lear,* but I was so wiped out by this experience that I remember thinking all the way back, I really want to work in the theatre.

And when you thought that, were you thinking of yourself as a writer?

No, I think I was thinking of myself as an actor. I was already writing. I started writing while I was still at school, I wrote a novel and I guess I'd already started that. And when I finished the novel I couldn't get it published, and that's when I wrote *When Did You Last See My Mother?,* which I wrote in what they might call the gap year now, between leaving school and going to Oxford. I mean I had a series of dreary jobs, to stay alive, and I used to write in the evenings, and wrote this play rather quickly.

So this was the outcome of that moment of thinking, oh my God, the theatre is where I want to be?

I guess. I have a feeling that at the time, the day that I saw the play, I suppose I was thinking in terms of being an actor. So I suppose I wrote the play thinking I'd like to play the part, which I did. Which somehow both cured me of wanting to be an actor any more, and confirmed me in wanting to be a writer.

So having written a novel and now writing a play, did you find you preferred the experience of writing a play?

Well, certainly the dialogue was what had come alive to me in the novel, and I had realised that when I re-read the novel, when I was thinking about whether I should revise it. I remember thinking perhaps this is what I should be doing, writing plays, because the novel seemed to come alive when the characters were talking to each other. So I felt I had a sort of ear for dialogue. But you know the play was written in complete ignorance. I had never seen a play at the Royal Court, until I saw *When Did You . . .* But I knew all about it. We were very interested in the theatre at Lancing, and we did readings of John Osborne's plays, and Pinter's plays – we did a sort of rehearsed reading of *The Caretaker*, in which I played Aston. We kept an eye open. For some reason we were never allowed to do those as the school play, we always had to do Christopher Fry or Robert Bolt. But my French teacher, Harry Guest, who was very influential in my life, was a most enormous fan of Beckett, and I remember going to listen to *Endgame* on the radio in his room – he would invite pupils he knew were interested. We did a reading of *Godot*, as well. At that time we were for some reason obsessed with theatre, and we built an open-air theatre, which is still there now. It was something you were allowed to do – an afternoon's labouring – and eventually Dame Agatha Christie came, who was married to someone who'd been at Lancing, and opened the theatre, which was rather beautiful, like a Greek amphitheatre. I was in a play by Goethe, in German, called *Iphigenie auf Tauris*, which the *Times Literary Supplement* came down to review. They said as far as they knew this was the first production of the play this century, and now they'd seen it they could understand why. But it was an enormous role, bigger than Hamlet and all in German, and I was about fourteen or fifteen. So I had this enormous enthusiasm for theatre, as many of us did. David Hare, whom I was at school with, once gave me for a first night present a photo of us both in a school production, in baggy tights.

So this play, once you'd written it, you thought, 'Now I'll send it to the Royal Court'?

I did not. I didn't do anything with it. Which is why it came to be two years before it went on. I didn't know what to do with it – I had no idea. And what I did eventually was I entered it in a play competition run by the Oxford University Dramatic Society, and it didn't win. But a few weeks after the beginning of term, the secretary of OUDS came to see me and said that one of the plays they had was too expensive and mine was very cheap so they'd like to put it on. I think they had about three and a half weeks. So we got it on in February 1966 and it was reviewed in the *Oxford Mail*, and got a very good review in the *Guardian*, and I started to get letters from agents.

That must have been very exciting.

It was exciting – it was also slightly bewildering. So I talked to my tutor, Merlin Thomas, who was very interested in theatre. He was on the board of the OUDS and he knew the woman who ran the Oxford Playhouse who was called Liz Sweeting. He said I should go and ask her advice. So I went to see her and she said – this must have all happened very quickly, a week or two after the play was on – she said, 'Send the play to Peggy Ramsay – she's the only agent who's any good.' So I sent the play to Peggy Ramsay and she contacted me right away, and took me on, and phoned Bill Gaskill while I was in her office. And I think six weeks later we were in rehearsal. Amazing. Robert Kidd had never directed a play before – he was an ASM – he was given it to direct, and Victor Henry played the part I'd written for myself, a good deal better than I did. It was a Sunday-night production, very successful, and they repeated it on a second Sunday night, and then Michael Codron decided he was going to move it into the West End, which he did – this was the summer of 1966 – just for a month. It was a production without décor – and it was moved into the West End as a production without décor.

Michael Codron's name pops up a lot at that period, as somebody was who very interested in new theatre although he was a West End manager.

Well yes, he was. And when I wrote the next two plays, *Total Eclipse* and *The Philanthropist*, both those plays were optioned by Michael Codron, and he also put money into the production of *Total Eclipse*. And he produced these famous souvenir programmes, with watercolours by Patrick Proctor, which sold for a shilling, till some bastard came in during the second week of the run and bought all the programmes. I remember not having one at the end of all this, and Donald Howarth organised a raid into a sort of recess off the artistic director's office, a sort of hole in the wall full of old programmes. Donald took me in there one day, and I remember crawling in and pinching a couple.

So one minute you're having a Sunday-night production done of your first play and the next minute you're invited in as literary manager. What was the leap between those two things?

You'd have to ask Bill – it was his idea. I came down to see either *Time Present* or *Hotel in Amsterdam*, I can't remember which now, in 1968, and Bill was there, and I had a drink with him afterwards. I was coming up to my finals, in June, and he said, 'What are you going to do afterwards?' I said I'd no idea. He said, 'Have you got a job or anything?' I said, 'No, I just want to write.' He said, 'Well, leave it with me, I'll see what I can do.' In the meantime I had a very tempting offer from Peter Wood, the director, who was embarked on what I think was his one and only feature film. He rang me up and said, 'Come and live in the South of France and write this feature film.' And I said, 'I can't, I've got my finals.' He said, 'A clever boy like you, what do you need with a degree?' So I was terribly tempted, but I turned him down. I stayed and did my finals. And sometime when I was gearing up to do my finals Bill came to Oxford with Bob Kidd and made me read to them. I read them *Total Eclipse*, because Bill was undecided whether he would do it or not. And at the end Bill said he would do it. And so they were going to do that in September of 1968. And he said, 'I've been on to the Arts Council, and they're going to stump up a bit of money for you to be resident dramatist.' I said, well, that's fantastic. It was £1,000 a year, £20 a week, very good. And he said, 'But you needn't think just because you're called resident dramatist you're going to sit around doing nothing. You're going to have to do lots of other things too.' So I said fine, whatever. But the principal thing I had to do was run the literary department. And I also had to go – you can't imagine it these days, because such a thing doesn't exist – I had to go all round the country to reps that were doing new plays. And then there would always be the Monday meeting where you had to report on all the plays – and writing reports – and I didn't see how I was ever going to get to write. So that was when they let me hire David Hare.

And you stayed as resident dramatist for how long?

Two years – they gave me an extra year. I wrote *The Philanthropist* while I was there and it was done at the very end of the period. That was a play that was hanging around in the system for about a year, because first Bill was going to do it and then he decided not to – he suddenly rang up one evening to say he didn't want to. Then Anthony Page was going to do it – they couldn't get a director. Robert had been fired – Bill gets angry when I say this, but I contend that he was fired for getting very good notices. He had been fired and he had gone to work in television, in Manchester. So we went through Bill, Anthony, who wanted to do it with Alan Bates who didn't want to do it, and he couldn't persuade anyone else, Ron Eyre, Michael Blakemore – and finally I think Bill got impatient and reached for the phone and called up Bob.

So was that a rather painful time, when everybody was saying no? Did it feel as if they didn't like the play?

Everybody liked the play – that was clear – with the possible exception of Lindsay, who said he thought it was a bit frivolous and couldn't I be a bit more serious. But he quite liked it – given that he detested everything, he was quite positive. So I didn't feel that nobody liked it, nor did I have any very exalted idea of how good it was or how successful it was going to be. I mean, people were pretty gloomy about it right up until the time the first audience came in. I remember a long, long meeting after the dress rehearsal in Bill's office when he was trying to analyse what was wrong with it, or what was wrong with the production. Bob was there as well. And I remember one of those long Bill silences, after which he sighed and said, 'Oh well, I suppose it's the play.' So we were pretty gloomy by the time it was ready to open. And then as soon as the first audience came in it was obviously . . .

Suddenly everything changed.

Yes – and I was a bit sheepish about it, given all that.

So we've gone from you as a schoolboy writing plays to you as the resident dramatist – thinking, okay, now I'm a playwright. But I'd love to know – what's the process like for you? You've done a lot of adaptations, or things based on other things – Les Liaisons Dangereuses, Carrington . . .

Well, *Carrington* I think of as an original.

Yes – but it was based on letters.

Yes.

Looking at Total Eclipse, Carrington, *even* Liaisons Dangereuses – *each one of them is a group of people, whether it's the aristocrats of the* ancien régime, *Bloomsbury, those peculiar French people, it's all about . . .*

They're all about sex.

Peculiar relationships, really, within famous communities of people.

Yes – but they're all about sex, really. So there's a strand in my work which deals with sex and sexual problems – because that's something that's always interested me. And that goes right up to the last play, which was about Jung and Freud, *The Talking Cure*.

But you don't sit down and think, okay, now I'm going to think of another subject that will enable me to write about sex and sexual problems, do you?

No. Not at all. It's very mysterious, how these things come about. I mean, *Total Eclipse* for example, that was the play I really wanted to write. I wrote *When Did You Last See My Mother?* as a sort of practice.

So the idea for Total Eclipse *was sort lurking about in the back of your mind?*

I knew I wanted to write a play about Rimbaud and Verlaine, from when I first found out about them, when I was about seventeen. I thought this was a great subject for a play. And somehow *When Did You Last See My Mother?* was an easy way in. What was very confusing was that it got such great reviews, and *Total Eclipse*, which I thought was a better play, got terrible reviews. And of course that was just the mechanism of being the second play, or a more difficult piece in some way. But I'm about to do *Total Eclipse* in Paris this autumn, not for the first time. It's done quite well in France. It gets revived a lot. It's probably the most performed of all my plays. And it was such a catastrophe at the Court. The reviews were ghastly. It ran for three weeks only, in a sort of three-play season of new plays, but it was only fifty or sixty per cent full.

But that's a sort of honourable state of affairs at the Court.

Yes. But the strange thing is that so many people that I've subsequently met seem to have seen that production and been sort of marked by it. People remember it very vividly. And it did look great, because Patrick Proctor, who'd never designed a play before, designed it, and he painted the whole proscenium arch and the whole back wall pink, and he had a sort of Moroccan lamp hanging down in the middle of the auditorium over the stalls, which spun during one or two of the scenes and threw these patterns all over the theatre, while the play was going on. And it was very much of the moment in some curious way, and people reacted to it very strongly. But going back to your question as to what the process is – the process is very mysterious. You get an idea which just sort of nags, and won't go away. *The Philanthropist* is a completely different sort of play – but, on the other hand, I'd had this idea of doing a sort of mirror-image kind of play of *Le Misanthrope*, which kept coming back into my head . . .

And do you know, when you sit down at your desk and think, now I'm going to start writing my new play – do you have a sort of shape? Do you know where it's going to go, who the people are?

Yes – I spend a lot of time preparing. And then I write very fast.

And often you have to research a lot?

Not always – but some plays can take a long time. I mean, *Savages* took two years to research and a trip to Brazil – and I guess, though it was very on and off because I was doing other work, that the Jung play took about five years.

So when all that's done and you sit down, the writing is fairly straight-forward? And you enjoy it?

No – no, it's always very stressful.

Getting it right, you mean? Making it work?

Yes. I mean, I love being a writer but I can't say I've ever enjoyed actually writing.

And do you revise a lot?

No. But more as time goes on. And this is something I kind of attribute to the Court, that they really understood from the word go that what was interesting about the play was the individual voice – and that if you sort of mucked about with it, or editorialised, or told the writers what to do, to rewrite, then you started to lose the individuality of it. I've often quoted this in interviews, what Bill Gaskill said about *Total Eclipse* – there was a run-through he came to, and he was very happy with the play and how it was done – and he took Bob Kidd and myself out to lunch. And Bob and I had been talking about the play – what wasn't working and so on – and he said, 'Don't change anything. It's very valuable to see the play as you wrote it. And if there are things wrong with it, you'll only really see that with an audience.' And so we didn't change anything. We just did the play as it was written.

And did you think that was true?

Well, twelve or thirteen years later, when David Hare directed the play, I rewrote it quite a bit. But I was able to rewrite because I'd seen it several times with an audience. I could see what wasn't working. And so that's how I do it now. With *The Talking Cure,* which was done at the National Theatre a few years ago, what didn't work as I'd hoped became clear during the first run, so I rewrote it for the American production.

What the play is on paper is one thing, but what goes on in the theatre is another.

But now I think writers – I think people fall on them like a crowd of locusts and say, change that . . .

Well, they do. Talking to the young dramatists at the Court, it's very clear that a lot of stuff goes on now. A play turns up in the literary office and hours may be spent on that play – what are you trying to do in this scene, and that scene doesn't quite work, and maybe we should change the ending . . .

I remember Howard Brenton had a very good play called *Magnificence* at the Court – he was probably the resident dramatist then, because he took over from David – and I remember having read the play when it first came in and somehow being aware of the various stages it had gone through, and somehow feeling that by the time it got on stage it had not been improved. It had been diluted in some way.

I guess that was in the period David Hare talks about a lot – the unhappy 1970s, when there was a lot of dissent at the Court. He has talked about how Lindsay hated the new writers.

He certainly did hate the new writers, but then his stance was always oppositional. I mean, I remember when there was a reading of *Lay By* – and this was again after I'd left the Court – and he turned to me and said, 'I suppose you're responsible for this.' I liked Lindsay – I mean, I admired him enormously. And I remember one of the big bonuses of being resident dramatist was that I was able to go and sit in on the rehearsals of David Storey's *Home,* which was just great. He was a marvellous director, but for some reason he, and some of the other directors of that generation, derived their energy from sort of detesting things. It was the sort of ethos of the Royal Court in those days. We used to go out in sort of marauding gangs – we used to go to the RSC, and at a certain point we'd all walk out.

It was the same with my father – I don't think I ever saw the end of any play I went to with him, because he always used to leave after the first act. So after you stopped being the resident dramatist, you stopped being so connected with the Court?

No. *Total Eclipse* started rehearsal the week after I arrived, and *The Philanthropist* opened a week or so after I left, so that spanned my time at the Court. But then there was *Savages*, which was 1973, because that took me two years to write, and then *Treats* in 1976, which was my last play at the Court. And that was absolutely a conscious decision. Because there'd always been these conversations at the Court about who the Court was for, and the thought was always that it was for new writers and new writing. You had a sort of sense, for example, with John Osborne's plays, which were all done at the Court, that there was a faction that went, 'Oh, can't he get his plays on somewhere else?'

I see – so it was a conscious decision that it was time to move on?

Yes. I'd been there ten years. And I remember when Max kindly called me in and said would I write a play for the Court, I said no, I don't think I will. Because – thank you very much – because I'm sort of established now. I've done ten years at the Court, five plays and a couple of translations, and I can get my plays on anywhere – I shouldn't really.

That's interesting. Because I've talked to lots of writers who have been at one time associated with the Court and for whatever reason are not any more, and I don't think I've heard anybody put it quite like that. I think some of them feel rather peeved they're not being done there any more.

I might be hypersensitive or sort of paranoid, but when I did *Treats* I didn't feel that the mood in the theatre was in favour of the play. I was quite sensitive to that sort of thing. I slightly felt that they would do it because it was me. Then the play was a box-office success and transferred to the West End – and I felt I'd better move on. Anyway writing *Treats* was such a kind of bruising experience because it got such terrible notices – I didn't write another play for five years.

Because of the reviews, even though it had been so successful?

Yes. But then I got interested in working in the cinema. So the two things I wrote after that were first a TV play and then *Carrington*.

You wrote that because you had read the Holroyd biography, and you were fascinated by that whole story? So you say it was an original work, but based on things that really happened?

Well, I'm very interested in history plays, or biography plays, as it turns out. I mean *Tales from Hollywood* was as well – a play based on research.

I guess in a way that's something I keep on coming back to, because I think if you sort of brood on people's lives, and keep on coming back to those people, for a long enough period of time, it clarifies your own thinking on these matters. The great thing about *Carrington*, for which I just took a year off and wrote, was that although she and Strachey lived together for sixteen years they wrote to each other every day, and we have all those letters. So for nearly twenty years you have almost daily accounts of their lives, and these were people who told each other everything.

When I was reading it, I was thinking of their voices and wondering whether some of the things they say in your film, they actually did say to each other in the letters?

Yes.

So sometimes you are doing your own version and sometimes it really is their voices?

Certainly with Lytton, a lot of the things he says, he said.

It's a wonderful story. I can see why you were fascinated by it.

Yes, and I couldn't see how to do it on stage, either – and in any case I was interested in having a serious go at writing a film.

And then later you wrote Dangerous Liaisons – *but that started as a play, an adaptation,* Les Liaisons Dangereuses.

The thing about *Liaisons* was that I offered it to the National Theatre, who then didn't want to do it, so the RSC did it. I think I was slightly goaded into doing it by Peggy Ramsay, because I'd talked to her about it. I said I thought it would make a very good play, and she was really hot on the idea. She kept on and on at me. It took about seven or eight years for me to get around to doing it, and then I gave it to the RSC, and they hummed and hawed, and then put it on in The Other Place. It was written for the Barbican but they put it on in The Other Place because they were uncertain about it.

It would never occur to you now to do a play at the Court?

No – I was there not so long ago and Ian said, we'd like to do a play sometime, and I thought how nice it would be to come back. But I don't really write them very often these days, although I am writing one at the moment which doesn't have a particular home.

So why don't you write them so much any more?

Well, here's the answer. I always have a play on the go, but I've discovered that they sort of marinate – they take their own time. So it suits me to do other things while that's happening. I keep a notebook, and keep going back to it and thinking about it, and sitting up in the middle of the night and so on – and eventually I'm ready to do the play. But it might not be more than once every few years. I mean, I think I've averaged a play every three years or so, but I can't imagine upping the rate, really. So in a sense it suits me to do other things, because the rhythm of writing a play seems to be something I got into around the time that I left being resident dramatist, and I remember with *Savages* thinking I needed something else to do, because there were long periods when I wouldn't be writing. And somehow when you're doing something else you may get an idea that may progress the play.

One more question – is there any one thing that your plays are about? You said sex and sexuality.

Well, some of them are.

How do you react to something my father said in an interview in 1960: 'Plays should be disturbing'?

Peggy Ramsay once said, 'There's always something ugly about new work,' which was a very interesting remark. Because there's a truth that has to do with exactly that – that somehow something being expressed in a way it hasn't been expressed before is troubling. And it does sometimes jar and it is ugly. I think that's true. No, I don't know what my plays are about really. But I think in all these interviews I did for a book with Alistair Owen [*Hampton on Hampton*], we came out thinking that they were about the debate between liberals and radicals – because he seemed to find that in a lot of them. But since my aim is to be as sort of multifarious as possible, what I suppose I've tried to do is the opposite of what a lot of writers do, which is to create a sort of unmistakeable style. I've always tried to be as various as possible.

That's why Dominic Dromgoole calls you the invisible man.

Is that what he calls me?

He says with a lot of writers you can sort of see who's there behind the play, but with Christopher Hampton you can't. Even when you write about yourself, as in White Chameleon, *he says you don't know.*

I just love doing new things. The last thing I did was an opera libretto, for Philip Glass, and that was great. And I really said yes to it because I'd never done it before. And a lot of the stuff I do because I've never done it before. Because one of the things that was borne in on me when I was at the Court was how dangerous it is to repeat yourself, because you tend to repeat yourself with less energy than you put into it the first time. And it's very hard not to repeat yourself if you're writing over a longish span of time. You know, I was twenty when I started, so I thought, I've got to find out some way of keeping going and not driving myself demented.

David Hare

I had never met David Hare before I went to visit him in his place of work, a very impressive studio in Hampstead, in January 2005. He had started working as literary manager at the Court shortly after I left at the end of the 1960s, and all I knew of him then was that he was one of the two people who were doing the job I used to do. No one nowadays with half an interest in theatre could avoid knowing about David Hare, of course.

So can you remember the first play you ever went to?

I'm just trying to think. Not really. My mother was an amateur actor, and because she was Scottish – the amateurs used to act with the professionals. I remember her telling me that Duncan McRae had acted with her amateur dramatic society. And she had a book of cuttings and reviews – I remember that very clearly.

But was she still doing that when you were growing up?

Yes. I was brought up in Bexhill, and I certainly went to see my mother in plays. The thing I always remember, because Julie Christie was in it, was Molière's *Malade Imaginaire*. And my mother was a flunkey – I remember her well, in plus-fours, those sort of servants' costumes, and Julie, who was eleven or twelve, a very striking girl – everybody in Bexhill knew Julie. But the first real theatre I remember going to was a festival which was held at Glyndebourne – in fact the only time to this day that I've ever been to Glyndebourne. I went to Glyndebourne with my mother, and there was an incredibly silly play about Shakespeare hiding in a trunk. I don't know what this play was, but I have a very strong memory of a farce about Shakespeare hiding in a trunk. I guess I was about five or six.

You didn't immediately say, 'Oh my God this is what I want to do,' then?

No. But I was very drawn by it. Also I had Pelham puppets . . . I loved acting out little scenes with my puppets. And three of us, schoolboys, we all started doing little dramatisations with our puppets. And this blew up and blew up until we finally did *Busman's Honeymoon* by Dorothy Sayers, with puppets.

What an interesting choice!

Lord Peter Wimsey, and – well, I loved thrillers, I loved detective stories, and I loved Agatha Christie. And then I think in an insanely ambitious moment when I was about twelve we tried to do *The Importance of Being Earnest* with puppets. I think by then I'd begun to see the limitations of the medium. But there was a little amateur drama school in Bexhill that Julie went to – she was the star pupil – and my mother went to teach Scottish accents there. I didn't go to it formally, though. I didn't have an ambition to act.

But were you writing? Did you like writing?

Well, you know there's this extraordinary coincidence of my being at school with Christopher Hampton and Tim Rice – so when I went to school I started writing ridiculous plays. And I can remember writing a play and certainly sending it in to the Royal Court when I was about fifteen or sixteen. And they were terrible, N. F. Simpson-influenced, absurdist sort of pieces.

Because you knew about the Court – you'd been to see things there?

When was Barry Reckord's *Skyvers*? 1963? That's when I started going to the Royal Court. Because I remember David Hemmings being in *Skyvers*, and that I think was the first play I saw at the Royal Court. But the most extraordinary thing that happened to me was that I was walking past the Royal Court when I was about sixteen or seventeen, and I didn't know what was on, and I saw that it said *Inadmissible Evidence* by John Osborne. I went in and said, 'Do you have a ticket?' And they said, 'Don't you know it's the first night tonight?' And I said, 'No, I don't know it's the first night, but have you got a ticket?' And they said, 'Yes, we've got one ticket,' so I said, 'Well, I'll have that.' And there was this, to me, incredibly glamorous crowd of people – I remember Vanessa Redgrave being in the circle bar – and I remember also being absolutely knocked out, and thinking it the most incredible play. And that's the first time the Court took root in me, seeing *Inadmissible Evidence*, and seeing Nicol Williamson's performance.

And then you went to Cambridge – and after Cambridge came Portable Theatre?

What happened was that I was very anti-established theatre, so to speak. Tony Bicât and I started Portable Theatre in order to set up a political theatre as a complete alternative to the regular theatre, but we weren't making any money. So Christopher Hampton, who of course I had known at school, rang me and said, 'I am literary manager at the Royal Court but I'm not getting any writing done.' And he asked me to go to the Royal Court to read the plays. And so I went to the Royal Court in 1968 or 1969, grandly titled Literary Manager. I was in the position of being all of twenty-two and being the person who advised the Royal Court on its repertory.

Yes – just like me, really.

It was three days a week, and I got £7–10–0 for reading about twenty plays a week – it was heavy work. I was using the £7 a week to subsist. But I wasn't a writer, I was a director.

But you'd written something when you were with Portable Theatre, hadn't you?

Only because another writer – in fact Snoo Wilson, who was still an undergraduate, at UEA – was meant to be writing a play for us, and he didn't deliver the play. And so on a Wednesday I had to sit down to write a play so that we could start rehearsing on the following Monday. And the play was absolutely terrible. It was ghastly. But Michael Codron read it and then commissioned me to write something. The Royal Court never thought of me as a writer. They thought of me as someone who read plays, and directed.

Did you ever direct plays at the Court?

Yes, I directed plays in the Theatre Upstairs. I directed Howard Brenton's *Christie in Love*, which was a Portable Theatre production that came in, and I directed another play of Howard's, *Fruit*. I directed Snoo's plays, and finally, *Teeth 'n' Smiles*, but that was some years later. But, in other words, when you talk about the Royal Court, and the extraordinary aura that it then had, and what was a Royal Court writer – I was certainly not considered a Royal Court writer, and would not have dared to put my own plays forward. Did you ever try to write a play when you were there?

No! I certainly wouldn't have dared.

When I finally did write a play, which was *Slag*, I never even considered showing it to the Royal Court, I would have been terrified. So Michael Codron said, 'Do you want to show it to the Court?' and I said, 'No, I wouldn't dare.' Because – by the time I got there, it was savage, absolutely savage. Not so much Bill Gaskill. Though I was very frightened of him – he was a frightening man to me – I understood him in the sense that I understood his taste. When I put plays forward, Bill would very much engage. You could have a very serious discussion with Bill. But then after about a year the triumvirate took over and I had Lindsay Anderson to deal with, and I found him incredibly trying, because he wouldn't engage. He would just roll his eyes and say, 'This is rubbish.' And if you were a literary manager who was seriously trying to get work that you liked on, well, there were three of them already, with Anthony Page, Lindsay Anderson and Bill Gaskill running it together, so as literary manager you were effectively powerless. And Lindsay Anderson was so – I felt – childish and capricious. He was a very difficult man. So, frankly, he put an awful lot of writers off because nobody wanted to be put through the indignity of being told your shortcomings by Lindsay Anderson.

So you didn't send the play to the Court, but it ended up at the Court.

Yes. I did *Slag* at Hampstead and it was a great success, but not enough of a success for Michael Codron to put it on in the West End. So a year later, while I was working at the Court, Bill finally summoned me into his office and said in a tone of total despair, 'Well, I suppose we're going to have to put your play on.' As if that were the most terrible defeat! But he said, 'We're not having it in that awful production, we'll have a new production.' And I said yes, okay, fine. And that was his way of salvaging his self-respect, to get it redone completely. Because it did look a bit silly, that the literary manager had a play that had been so successful, and I was winning a lot of awards as most promising playwright, but the play hadn't gone on at the Court. Bill said okay, I'll put it on, and it went very well at the Court.

And Teeth 'n' Smiles – *did that come quite shortly after?*

No – what happened was I'd had a very difficult time at the Court. That early period was not happy. And once Anthony, Lindsay and Bill took over, I found it impossible. And there were a whole lot of writers who . . . I mean crudely, it was a generational problem, which was that the people running the Court didn't like the new writers. They didn't like me, they didn't like Howard Brenton, they didn't like Snoo and they didn't like Howard Barker, they didn't like Trevor Griffiths, they didn't like David Edgar.

And why didn't they like that generation?

I think there were different reasons for disliking us. Oscar Lewenstein, for instance, was very candid about it. He disliked British political work. He once said to me, 'With my personal history as a Jew who came to Britain in the 1930s, I'm not going to put on work which is so savagely critical. You must understand that for me this country is a haven, and to have it talked about in this way – I just don't accept the version of England that you have.' So there was a feeling that we were a lot of arrogant young guns, who were intellectuals, which was held against us. We hadn't been to Oxford, which I think was also held against us, and we were political in a way that Lindsay certainly found very uncomfortable. Lindsay was an anti-political man. He was a conservative anarchist. And my position as literary manager was basically saying, look, you may not like this bunch of writers, but they're where the energy is now coming from in theatre. And whereas all the energy in the fifties and sixties came from Royal Court writers – John Osborne, Arnold Wesker, Edward Bond – this is where the energy now was. And I would say to them, look, those writers are now known – if you want the next generation, you have to put on the plays of Trevor Griffiths. You just have to. You can't ignore them, if you want to keep up to date. And Anthony Page was the only one who said, 'We are looking silly by not putting on the work that is attracting the most interest and excitement.' But Lindsay Anderson was absolutely dead set against it, and just said, 'If it's living in the past I want to go on living in the past. I don't like these writers and I don't want their work to go on.' So there was a real split. And anyway, more theatres were beginning to put on new work, so it mattered less if your work was not put on at the Court.

And in fact you quite quickly moved to the National . . .

I moved to the National. And there was a moment in the early 1980s when the National Theatre had on a play by Christopher Hampton, a play by Athol Fugard, and a play by David Mamet, and as it happened, all these plays were playing on the same night in each of the three theatres. So you thought, oh I see! These were the authors who ten years ago would have been at the Court – Christopher Hampton and Athol Fugard were central Royal Court writers, Mamet was exactly the sort of young American writer who would once have been done at the Court – and the Court, for one reason or another, was not presenting the writers that people were most interested in. Once it had had a monopoly of them, and it had lost it in the 1970s.

So in your own history, though you've been almost entirely associated with the National Theatre, you have twice returned to the Court with Via Dolorosa *and* My Zinc Bed. *Now why did you do that?*

Because they kept asking me. All through the years that I was at the National, certainly when Max was running the Court, he kept asking me, and I would say, but I have no reason to betray the National. I went to the National because I was not wanted at the Court, and then there was no reason to go back. Stephen Daldry was always asking me – Max was always asking me – and in fact it was Elyse Dodgson of the Royal Court who said to me, 'Would you write about Israel?' In fact she paid for me to go to Israel and the Palestinian territory – it was her idea. The intention was that I was to write a play, but instead of writing a play I wrote a monologue. Stephen Daldry was running the Court at the time, and so he offered to direct me – it was always a Royal Court project. And then with *My Zinc Bed*, it simply was that I'd had such a wonderful time working with Stephen that he said, could you give your next play to the Court, and I said okay. It's usually to do with being asked, and made to feel welcome. When Nick Wright was running the Court we did *Teeth 'n' Smiles* there, again because he made me feel welcome. One of the things Nick Wright did when he became artistic director was to say, I feel terrible about this division that's grown up – there's a whole lot of writers who feel that the Court doesn't want their work. And Nicky, you know, whose years as artistic director with Bob Kidd were not very happy ones, for all sorts of reasons – one of the things he tried to do was heal the wounds. I admired him for that.

I suppose one of the things the Royal Court always has to do is to find an identity.

Well, I think that its identity – because it isn't run by writers, it's run by directors – its identity comes from the alliance of a director with a major writer. In other words, in your father's day plainly it was John Osborne, and so John gave that theatre its existence – everything comes from your father and John. And that's why I've written a lot in defence of John, because I regard him as someone who made it all possible. In other words it's because of John that that theatre has existed and flourished. And similarly when Bill was artistic director it was Edward Bond, and Edward Bond was his cause. And Edward Bond was a great, major European playwright, who the Royal Court propagated. Also you have Lindsay Anderson and David Storey, Oscar Lewenstein and Athol Fugard. In Max's years you would say it was Caryl Churchill. And now – which is what I've argued to Ian Rickson – you have to say, who is the writer that you believe in? Who do you exist to propagate? I think that the artistic director has to give the theatre an identity by saying, 'This is the writer we truly believe in, that's what gives the Court its identity.'

So – tell me about Lay By.

What happened was, there was a theatre conference going on at the Court and I found it unbearable. So, as a counter-measure, I said, 'Oh, for God's sake, instead of talking about writing plays, let's go and write one.' And I said, 'Anyone who's interested in writing a play, come into the back bar, that stalls bar, and we'll write a play in there.' So eight people came in and we started on an idea – and then we said, 'Let's meet again on Wednesday.' And the astonishing thing was that seven of us did turn up on the following Wednesday. And we started saying, 'How, physically, are we going to write a play together?' So we decided the only way was to do it on wallpaper. So we pinned up a lot of wallpaper, and we all got crayons, and we had several sessions. And at the conference I'd said to Bill, 'Look, I've got all these writers, and they're pretty good writers, will you guarantee us a slot?' And he said, 'Yes of course, whatever you write can go on.' So we delivered the play and the artistic directors were absolutely horrified by it, because it was obscene, or pornographic. I mean we said it was a serious investigation of pornography, but it was a pretty hairline business. And Lindsay was absolutely determined it should not be allowed to go on. He said we could have a reading, and we did, and he was sitting next to Christopher Hampton, and he said this famous thing, where he rolled his eyes and said, 'I suppose this is all your fault.' He was just incredibly hostile. So they went back on their promise. Although they did finally let us do it on a Sunday night, one performance. So we went and did it at the Traverse in Edinburgh. But it was everything that they hated. Group authorship was very much against the principles of the Royal Court. And I do remember John Antrobus, who was an old Royal Court writer, saying, 'Why on earth do you want to write together? In television I have to write in groups – I love the theatre because it's the individual voice.' And we said that was exactly what we meant – we were socialists, we wanted to write as a collective. And this was what they found very hard to understand.

It must have been very different from how you normally write?

Completely. But you see I didn't feel like a writer. It's very hard to explain – I usually wrote satire, and I was deeply influenced by directing plays by Howard Brenton and Trevor Griffiths. And if you met Howard and Trevor in those days – they felt a calling. They were *vocationally* writers. Howard had got himself terribly into debt, he lived like a pauper for years and years, to become a writer. Trevor was older, and he'd spent ten years thinking before becoming a writer. So they were driven. I didn't feel driven. I felt like a satirist. I also had an agent, who said to me, 'You're not a play-wright, you're a satirist, and you make jokes.' So when I started to think that I'd like to write a serious play, which was *Knuckle*, my agent said to me, 'This is a terrible mistake. You're not a serious writer and you shouldn't try to be serious.' And so I actually left that agent and went to Peggy Ramsay, because my agent told me that I couldn't write serious plays.

So when you wrote Knuckle *did you then feel, okay . . .*

Well, *Knuckle* was a tremendous campaign, in the sense that it was commercially mounted, and there was only a very small group of us who believed in it. It went on during the three-day week, and it was a flop, essentially, though Michael Codron tried to cover that up by running for four months, very loyally, for which I will always be grateful to him. Essentially those people who believed in *Knuckle* believed in it passion-ately, but we were a very small group. So once you become involved in a campaign like that – I'm not putting myself on the same level, but when I arrived I could see that Bill had had to fight for Edward Bond, and similarly those of us who fought for *Knuckle* – that tempers you, that marks you for life. And I can't say that I understood Edward until I had a much smaller fight. Edward had a major fight to establish his reputation, and he put up with an incredible amount of abuse. Now on a much lesser level, I began to understand – oh I see, when you really have to fight for some-thing, as we had to fight for *Knuckle*, then it changes you, it toughens you, it hardens you. I mean, Edward has plainly reached a point where he just doesn't accept the view of the world about his work at all. He accepts only his own view. At some level you have to do that in order to survive as a playwright. It's a very hurtful profession.

Is it? You still say that having been so stupendously successful?

You say that – but last night I was at a performance of my work where, if I had allowed what was going on to reach me, in terms of watching a play not well performed – I just ran from the theatre, I certainly didn't stay to hear anybody's comments afterwards. The experience of putting your work under the scrutiny of four or five hundred people is intensely . . . Nicky Wright asks in his book why so many playwrights' lives end so badly. It's very rare to end like Noël Coward, with a huge revival in your reputation. I mean John Osborne – okay, he self-dramatised to a degree – but I knew John Osborne very well at the end of his life, and he said, 'You know, it made absolutely no difference – I don't think it would have made any difference if I hadn't lived.' I remember we were in a taxi together, and he said, 'I knew it would end badly, but not this badly.' Tennessee Williams I knew very well, and really he had a recurring theme in his conversation: 'Why does everybody hate me, why is it so impossible to get my plays done?' How do you come to terms with the first half of your life being celebrated and proclaimed, and that slump in reputation in later life? It is common to playwrights. If you are lucky, as Noël Coward was, then you get an upward curve at the end of your life. Peter Nichols has endured years of not getting his work done – now it's coming back – at least, the early plays are getting revived, he still can't get his recent work done. But at least his classic plays are being revived. There's this terrible thing about theatre and fashion, it's very tough, and the scrutiny is unpleasant.

Tell me about the actual process of writing. How do you find that?

Oh, fun. Yes, it's a struggle, too, but it's a good struggle. That's a private struggle – but the scrutiny is the tough thing.

But you never have a time when you think, 'Oh God, I'll never be able to write another play'?

Yes I do. There have been two. But this is me, and I'm completely un-typical. I have to know – I have to have some sense of what I believe and what I'm trying to say before I say it. Most writers say that they blunder about in the dark, and they don't know what they're saying.

David Storey is an extreme example of that kind of writer, but others have to do lots of research and know what they're doing before they start.

But there are three conspicuous examples, in the first category – and they are the most celebrated writers of the age – Harold Pinter, who finds his way without knowing what he's doing, Samuel Beckett who found his way . . . and David Storey. So they're quite a strong group. Then on the other side there's us lot – like Brecht, who's much more in my category, which is somebody who has to know what they believe before they can work. And I have a gap in my writing life, which basically happened at the end of the 1970s, which is when, having been a socialist throughout the seventies, and fundamentally a socialist writer, history turned to the right, and I had no response. I didn't know how to write. So then, for four years, I think, I didn't write a play – and it was because I didn't know how to respond. And in fact since I've written *Stuff Happens*, which is about the diplomatic process leading up to the Iraq war, and since Bush has been re-elected, I've been very confused about my own writing. Because again history has taken a turn that I don't really understand. And until I understand it, I can't write.

So your politics drives your writing.

Yes, though I wouldn't define politics narrowly. I mean I had an email just now from another playwright, an American playwright, saying, 'What the hell do we do? How do you respond to what's happening?'

Obviously there's a political agenda in all your plays, but that's not all they are, surely? Amy's View, *for instance, did not seem to me to be political.*

It's not received as political. However, I intend it as such. And I can't write unless I know what the politics are – in other words, there are politics behind that play.

You also seem to write a lot about women – you seem to have a fascination with women, and how women behave in, and deal with, the world.

Absolutely.

But maybe that is secondary to what you think you're doing in your work?

No, in fact nothing annoys me more than when people can only see the politics in my work and can't see anything else. For me it's like a skeleton of scaffolding – it won't be seen by everyone, but it's there. Just to give an example from when I was writing *Racing Demon*: to write seriously about the church, which I wanted to do, is to say, these are very well-meaning people, but the institution is decaying, and it's tragic. And I wrote the first act from that point of view. Then I suddenly thought, hang on, I'm writing as if I were a Christian. But I'm not a Christian. I don't believe in this God that they follow – and actually if the Christian church died, and people stopped believing in Christ, I might quite like that. I think the world might be a better place. And as soon as I saw that, I had a much richer play. I went back, and rewrote the whole first act, because I realised I'd been writing the first act from a lazy point of view, which was, oh it's all so tragic that this is dying. As soon as I rewrote it from the point of view that perhaps it's a good thing that this is dying, the play became more interesting, and as you would say, the people became more interesting. That's what I mean about working out what you believe. Now you may do that through writing and you may discover it as you go along, which is why I always say the most difficult character to get right in the play is yourself. Because you're the person who's providing the viewpoint, so unless you can write your own character, and unless you're sure who your character is . . . I was reading Chekhov's letters over Christmas, and I thought, oh, I see why you're the greatest playwright of the last hundred years. Because he has this utter, almost preternatural conviction, from the age of about eighteen, of who he is. He has no doubt about his own identity. This is one of the things that makes him so incredibly attractive to women. Women are falling in love with him all the time, because he's completely sure about who he is – his own limitations, his own strengths. He's a brilliant self-analyst – he's not completely at peace with who he is, but he accepts who he is. And of course it gives those plays this incredible authority. Sam Beckett was the same – I've never met anyone who was more wholly themselves. He knew exactly who he was, he knew exactly how he wanted to live, he knew how he wanted to conduct himself, and it's a big plus, isn't it?

Looking back over the many plays you have written, could you say any play is the one you feel particularly pleased with?

I think *Plenty*'s the play. Because my voice is there. It took me ten years to become a writer, and *Plenty* is the play in which I can hear my own voice. It's a finely balanced play, in the sense that the audience has to make up its own mind how it feels. It's a disturbing play, and it's a play that is morally quite unsettling. There's something magnificent about the character of Susan Traherne, but there's also something very destructive about her. So it helps people, I think, who are disturbed by elements in themselves to come to terms with that. And it still has that power – when it was revived in the West End with Cate Blanchett, it still drives people crazy, it hasn't lost its power to annoy. So I'm very fond of that play.

And how did it arrive with you?

Really it's to do with the Second World War – I only see this with age, with perspective – that I was born having just missed the most important event in my life, which happened just before I was born. And I can now see that my parents' behaviour, which I didn't understand at that time, was related to that event I had missed. I remember throughout the seventies, when I started writing, saying I wanted to write about the Second World War. Because most work was Kenneth More-ish, and Richard Todd-ish – there was that sketch in *Beyond the Fringe* – but no one had looked to see if people really behaved in that heroic fashion. So then I had a wonderful period when I wrote *Licking Hitler*, about black propaganda. At that time the people who'd done black propaganda were still alive, and I managed to travel all over the country meeting the people who'd been in this absolutely disgraceful unit doing black propaganda. Then I began to meet people who'd been in Special Operations (SOE), and I began to understand that the war wasn't that fight that had been presented to us as completely heroic. So I had what I imagine feminist writers have, a sense of discovery, of finding women who have been hidden from history – and a whole lot of writers immediately began to get interested in the same thing. But it was very exciting, showing that the war had been quite different from how it was represented. And people who'd lived through it, like John Mortimer, were kind enough to say to me, you're the only one who's presenting it like it really was.

Donald Howarth

Lady on the Barometer 1958
Sugar in the Morning 1959
Ogodiveleftthegason 1967
Three Months Gone 1970

I first met Donald when I was a teenager, though there have been long periods when we haven't seen each other. He moved into the upstairs flat in my mother's house in Hammersmith in 1961, and he has lived in the house on and off ever since – he and George Goetschius bought it from me in 1971. I have seen a great deal of him in the past few years, and have talked to him endlessly about all kinds of things, including this book. He was one of the first people I recorded, in November 2004, but I asked him some more questions in June 2005.

I always ask people about their first experience of theatre, and it's struck me it's a generational thing. With the older generation it's usually pantomime, but for the young ones it's often Theatre in Education.

A lot of worthies – *Ragged Trousered Philanthropist* sort of Joint Stocky kind of thing.

So what about you? Can you remember?

It was always the Alhambra in Bradford, and it was always variety. Mrs Greenwood, who was our surrogate mother, took us – there was a rep, but she would never have gone to see a play, or taken us to see a play. It was always Ethel Revnell and Gracie West, Wee Georgie Wood, Arthur Askey, Hutch singing 'Begin the Beguine', Avril Angers – they were all variety acts. The pantomime was the only thing that wasn't variety – Norman Evans, 'Over the Garden Wall', as Dame Widow Twanky in *Aladdin*. My first play was when I was in the fourth form at secondary modern school – it was the school play, *The Ascent of F6*, by Auden and Isherwood. This geometry master, William Ormes, put it on – Ginger Ormes, we called him. His claim to fame was that he'd invented a theorem called the Ormes Theorem. It's in all the obscure geometry books. He was homosexual, as I found out later – a big red-faced, ginger-haired man. The play hadn't gone down at all well, and he'd been told to do Shakespeare or something next time. So the following year he said, 'Anybody who wants to be in the school play stay after school.' So I stayed behind with my schoolmate Leslie and we said, 'We'll do it – we want to be in the school play, sir.' And the school play was *Twelfth Night*. Shakespeare! And I was cast as Olivia, and Leslie was cast as Maria, because we were chums in the class, and Maria was the handmaid of Olivia. We both thought it was very strange that we were cast as women – it was a boys' school. But then of course I had to learn the lines, and that was it, really – I mean learning Olivia (and I still remember the lines, you always do) and this teacher, this horrible geometry master, suddenly became this person who loved Shakespeare, and obviously was in a rotten job teaching maths and wanted to be in the theatre. He was absolutely besotted, and so was I. I just fell in love with Olivia, and not just with Olivia but with Shakespeare, and the lines. And I could understand it, you know. 'Go to, you're a dry fool, I'll no more of you' – and it was just ordinary! 'Oh, I know what that means!' Because before then you don't understand a word of it, but when you have to learn it, and speak it, it suddenly comes to life. So Ginger Ormes was a member of the Bradford Civic Playhouse, which was an amateur dramatic society, and he said, as I was so good as Olivia, why didn't I come and join the Bradford Civic Playhouse, which I did. They had evening classes, once a week, and Tony Richardson was in the third year and I was in the first year. Anybody who was in the Civic could read a poem on a Sunday-night coffee evening. I got a book off the library shelf, knowing nothing about anything, and it was Faber and Faber, *Another Time* by W. H. Auden, whom I knew about because I'd seen the play. There was a poem in it in doggerel – 'Let me tell you a story about Miss Edith Gee. / She lived in Cleveland Terrace at Number 83.' And I thought, that's me – so I read this poem. Tony was in the café having coffee, and he came up to me afterwards – he also knew about Auden – and he said, 'I thought that was a wonderful poem.' He then started Shipley Young Theatre, and because I'd read that poem by Auden, and he was doing *Comus* by Milton, he cast me as the Attendant Spirit, and I had to learn all this poetry suddenly! So it was Auden, really, who brought me and Tony together. Then he did *Romeo and Juliet*, and I played Paris, and then he went to Oxford. By then of course I was hooked on the theatre, although I was a commercial artist – well, writing signs for the cinema.

But you were already thinking about acting, although not about writing, at that stage?

Oh yes, acting, not writing at all. But yes, I met someone called Margaret Dick, who was a student at Esme Church's drama school in Bradford. She saw me going to work one day, at lunchtime, and said I should go and audition for the drama school. But I said, 'I've no money, miss' – I was only about sixteen. But Tony rehearsed me in my audition speech, which was Hamlet – 'Speak the speech, I pray you . . . ' Tony rehearsed it, and told me how to do it, which was brilliantly Tony. He said, 'Come on, turn your back on the audience, and speak it all upstage, because the players are all upstage, and you're directing them. Don't look at the audience at all.' So I did the whole thing with my back to Esme Church and the rest of them – it was brilliant – and I got in – they remembered that! Someone who did their audition with their back to them. That was Tony – brilliant. So then he went off to Oxford and I went to drama school. And after a couple of years at drama school Esme told me I wasn't any good as an actor, and I started to direct plays – still not writing. I went into rep and I was a stage director, a play a week, playing parts as well – that's where I got my apprenticeship really. Because if you do a play a week you do bad plays, good plays, farces, Somerset Maugham, R. C. Sherriff, *See How They Run*, *The Sacred Flame*, *Journey's End*.

So how did it happen that you started writing?

Well, being in rep – learning lines – taught me without realising it. Because when I sat down years later to write a play, I realised I couldn't have had a better apprenticeship. Because I'd learned dialogue, all sorts of writers – and the lines you couldn't learn were the ones that were badly written. If you couldn't speak it, it was stilted. So I knew as a bad actor – don't give them sentences to learn, give them the literature of talking. Don't give them literature to speak. Also I learned construction, exits and entrances – why do people come and go? Length of scenes, small parts – so you knew what the part had to do with it all. It was all much more practical. So I was very glad for rep, though I didn't know till years later.

Tell me what you meant by the literature of talking.

Well, in rep we did all these wonderful writers – Restoration comedies, a fantastic *She Stoops to Conquer* – such wonderfully rich stuff. But I thought, that's not really what theatre's about, plays now. Dialogue is not literature, or shouldn't be, though it was when those plays were written. So I invented something for myself and called it 'literature of talking'. It's written, so it's got to be literature of a sort, but it's not wonderful sentences, like wonderful Shaw or wonderful Oscar Wilde: 'It seems to me, Mr Worthing . . .' So I just thought the literature of dialogue is the literature of *talking*, where you still have to choose the words actors memorise and say. That's what I did, a bit later. First, I started to listen. I was on a ship, as a merchant seaman. There were eight of us in a cabin, and every night these morons in the cabin, who had the same four-hundred-word vocabulary, said the same things. I used to write down everything they said, not joining in any of their conversations. After a week or so of this, I suddenly realised something different was happening every night – they shuffled these four hundred words, and it was the moods that were different. One night somebody didn't say anything, and another night somebody else said things – somehow the conversation ebbed and flowed between them, and that's when I sort of realised that my snobby attitude about vocabulary, words, text . . . that what people say is not what it's about, not what the scene's about, or the mood of the play.

But you didn't make that into a play, did you?

No – that was just getting through the day, really.

So that was learning to write dialogue?

Yes, though I didn't think of it like that at the time. I wasn't in the theatre at that point, I'd signed up as a merchant seaman. I went to New York, and Esme Church, who'd taught me at drama school, was playing in Tyrone Guthrie's production of *The Merchant of Yonkers* on Broadway. We docked in Hoboken and I went to see her in the play, went backstage afterwards, and she said, 'Oh, hello Donald, what are you doing here?' I told her I was on this ship, and she said, 'Oh, you should write your experiences.' So I went back on the boat, and we sailed to the Caribbean, and every two weeks we were back in New York. She had said, bring me what you've written, so I did. And that was the basis really, later, when I came to write dialogue, because I'd actually been forced to listen to these seven people with that minimum vocabulary. So that's just academically how I came to be thinking about playwriting and dialogue.

How long after that did you decide to write a play?

Quite a while, about two years or more. I wrote my first play in Manchester. I'd decided I didn't have enough education, so I went to an adult college in Manchester – evening classes. I worked from eight till one o'clock in John Lewis, cooking chips. I had a bed-sitting-room in an attic and I thought, I'll be a writer. I can write in the afternoons when I get back from John Lewis, and I wrote a little one-act play.

So you knew there was a theatre in London which put on new plays, and you thought you'd have a go?

Yes I did, but I didn't think I'd write it for the Court. No, I thought I'd send it to television because there was a television company in Manchester. I just wrote it and sent it in and got it back, of course. And that was that. Then I went to see *Look Back in Anger*, at the Palace Theatre in Manchester. This must have been 1957, when it had gone on tour. I hadn't seen it and I wanted to know what they were all talking about in the papers, this play at the Royal Court – revolution – John Osborne – kitchen sink drama. I went to see it and I thought, oh, so that's *Look Back in Anger*, and carried on with my work, my job. But then Esme Church had come back and she asked me to go back to the theatre, taking a children's play around the schools, playing Henry VII in a play about Sebastian Cabot. We had two weeks off when we weren't touring, and I went down to my mother's bungalow in Haslemere – she wasn't there – and I had two weeks doing nothing. That was when I wrote *Sugar in the Morning*. I didn't write it for the Court. I wrote it in two weeks, and it was set in the lodging house I lived in, in the centre of Manchester. It was virtually word for word what had happened in that house, practically verbatim – very little was changed, it was just that experience. And I stuck in a chorus, because at that time I was very interested in Greek drama and the fact that they had choruses, and I thought – how could you have a chorus in a modern play? So I had the main character talking to the audience, which comes out of my interest in *Oedipus at Colonus*.

And was it easy to write?

No. I sat there for two days thinking, what am I doing? I'm all right here for two weeks, no rent. I had this paper, and I scribbled a bit, and I started with this chorus, this man setting the scene.

So you'd been sort of brewing up to this, had you?

No, no. I just thought, oh, I'll write a play. What shall I write about? Oh, that woman in Manchester. And I started to write. After about two days I thought, oh, get on with it, write a scene. So I wrote the first scene. And then I just wrote the next one based on the last one, and then it built from there. That's really how I started to write.

When you'd finished, did you go back and think, 'Oh, it needs revising'?

I didn't, no. I finished it and sent it as it was, to the Court. Keith Johnstone read it, and didn't know who I was. Bill Gaskill and Tony Richardson, whom I knew, were there but I didn't send it to them. Keith wrote on the card 'very talented' and 'to be seen', or something like that. And I was asked to go and see Keith Johnstone. That was when Bill made that famous remark, 'Oh, I know him, it can't be any good.' I saw Keith and he said, 'Is that the end of the play?' Well, of course, I didn't know if it was the end of the play or not. I'd just stopped because the two weeks ran out, and I'd had to go back on tour. So I said, 'Oh, well, isn't it long enough?' and he said no. 'Oh, well,' I said, 'I could write some more.' I went back on tour, and as we were playing in the day for the schools, in the evenings I read what I'd written and then I wrote the end, another twenty-four pages, in four nights, really just to complete the play. I sent it in, and they did it. But, in fact, I wasn't writing a play to be performed. I wanted to be a director, like Bill Gaskill and Tony Richardson. I'd done rep, and I knew I wasn't an actor, but I thought I would like to be like Tyrone Guthrie. So I thought the only way I'm going to get to do a production is if I write a play with lots of stage directions, showing how I would direct a play. So I didn't really know I was writing a play – I was writing stage directions, there were loads of stage directions in it. Well, they agreed to do it on a Sunday night, and I was rather upset because they said, oh, this is a good play, we'll do it, and then they gave it to someone else to direct, the casting director, Miriam Brickman! As it turned out, she cast it brilliantly, but she'd never done any productions, so as I'd been in rep, where you had to bang out a play in a week, I really took over rehearsing after two or three days. We only had ten days to get it together. And that's how it was done.

And then it went into the main bill?

Yes. And then Georgie commissioned me to write another one, which was *All Good Children*.

And then they didn't accept it when you'd done it!

They said they'd do it on a Sunday night, but I thought, well, I'd had a play done in the main bill, and it was not what'd been done with other playwrights, with John Arden and John Osborne. They'd had their try-outs and then they'd been done in the main bill, so I thought I'd try to get it done for a run somewhere else. And George was quite agreeable, you know. He said, 'Well yes, go.' Because I could always have gone back and done it as a Sunday night if I couldn't get it done anywhere else. But I did get it done, at Bromley.

But by that time you were thinking of yourself as a writer?

I had to, really – I'd been commissioned to write another play.

Was it hard to write the second one?

The first one took only two and a half weeks and the second one took eleven months! The first one was just experience, and I was writing it as a production. But the second one – I thought, 'God, George Devine's asked me to write *a play* – I don't know what to write about!' Then I went to see Ibsen's *Rosmersholm* at the Court, with Peggy Ashcroft, and I thought, 'How can I write *Rosmersholm* today?' and that's how it started. So *All Good Children* was originally called *Donnisthorpe* – Rosmersholm was the place, and Donnisthorpe was the manse, the vicarage. It was changed to *All Good Children* later. But it was about a minister who was retiring, and it was based on the parable of the talents: I have three talents, I have three children. One doubles his capacity, another makes half, and the third buries his talent and doesn't do anything with it. And that was the daughter. There's a scene in the play where the father, the vicar, says 'I have three children: Clifford's made a lot of himself, Maurice left home to be a merchant seaman' – that was my experience on the boat – 'and the other one, my daughter, has stayed and looked after her mother and has not multiplied her talent.' She buries her talent in Donnisthorpe.

So it was agonising working on it?

Yes – it was sort of mind over matter. I wanted to make a well-made play, because that's what Ibsen had done with *Rosmersholm,* but I wanted to make it contemporary. It's about incest, the play – well, the incest hides the homosexual content of the play. You couldn't then be homosexual in plays, so it's incestuous because that's kind of understandable. But then the other two plays followed from that, because I used the same characters in them, you know. So that's how I kind of drifted into writing, really.

What about rewriting – has anyone made you rewrite your plays?

After *Sugar in the Morning* was staged at the Court, it was done on television. The Sunday night was absolutely as I had written it. But when it was done in the main bill, Bill Gaskill directed it, and he wanted the time sequence to be linear, where in the original the time sequence jumped about – now; a year before; ten months later; six months before that. Bill changed it because after the Sunday night it was going to be done on TV, and it was the agent Elspeth Cochrane and the TV director who wanted it to be in sequence.

And were you happy about that?

No, miserable. They changed the end of Act One, which was the death of the grandmother – she dies ten months after they've been in that house. After they changed it, she dies two-thirds of the way through the play, near the end, which is completely the wrong place for it, because you're leading up to the end of the play and then this intrusion comes. But it wasn't actually Bill's fault. Bill just followed what they had suggested.

So did you feel like a Royal Court writer?

Well, with Tony and Bill being at the Court, and me suddenly being a writer, and not having been to Oxford, like they had – I don't know if this is the reason, but I did feel a bit . . . as Bill said, 'He can't possibly have written a good play.' So I think there was a bit of that. I wasn't considered intellectual or something. I do often think about the Court, as David Cregan said to you, that if your plays were at all lightweight, or weren't Ibsen's *Enemy of the People*, you weren't somehow regarded. Though it's not true of N. F. Simpson.

Yes – he had his moment, but he didn't last all that long. Very few playwrights lasted all that long, apart from Caryl Churchill, who's lasted from the early 1970s right up to the present. Most writers have their little moment – even David Storey, or Bond, just had a run of a few good years.

You know what it is – you have to have a director. Arnold Wesker had Dexter, Storey had Lindsay, Bond had Bill Gaskill.

Yes, John Arden said this. He only had a handful of plays done there, and he said, 'I never got my director, that person who saw me through.' There's a myth that prior to Max Stafford-Clark the play was a sacred object and no one would ever work on it. But David Cregan said, 'Donald was great because he worked with me on the play, edited with me.' I'm sure you can't have been the only person to work on someone else's play?

Well, George did it with Arthur Miller! He cut a character out and had to put him back. So if Arthur Miller wasn't sacrosanct . . . In fact I remember

George coming to *Sugar in the Morning* when it was in rehearsal and saying, I think you should cut that bit with the gas meters. We talked about it and Miriam Brickman said, no, she thought it was necessary musically, so we didn't cut it.

But the suggestion was made. So it's a myth. David Edgar said somebody should have told John Osborne to change the last act of The Entertainer.

John was difficult – he probably wouldn't have agreed to any changes. In fact perhaps the whole myth has come from that. But think of Keith Johnstone and all his improvisation – and Ann Jellicoe's *The Knack,* made up partly from improvised scenes.

Ann Jellicoe

The Sport of My Mad Mother
   1958
The Knack 1962
Shelley 1965

The Rising Generation 1967
Two Jelliplays 1974

Ann Jellicoe was the first woman to have a play produced in the main bill at the Royal Court after 1956, the first woman to direct a play at the Court, and the first woman literary manager of the English Stage Company. She has spoken of how hard it was to be a woman in that male-dominated environment. She was a member of Bill Gaskill's Writers' Group, and it was there that Bill and I improvised the scene that she put, more or less verbatim, into *The Knack* ('It isn't a bed, it's a piano' – 'It's a bed' . . .) A few years later she gave me a part in the Sunday-night production of Barry Reckord's play *Skyvers*, my only appearance on the stage of the Royal Court. I have seen Ann from time to time since then – she always comes to the presentation of the George Devine Award. But for many years she has lived in Dorset where she has become a world expert on community theatre. I went down to Lyme Regis in December 2004 and spent an enjoyable day in the delightful house where she lives with her husband Roger Mayne. We talked all day, on and off the tape, with breaks for coffee, home-made soup, tea and chocolate cake made by the Women's Institute.

Can you remember your first experience of going to the theatre?

No – but I think I know what it would be. I was born in Middlesbrough and lived not far away. There was an Empire Theatre there in those days, so I suspect it would have been a pantomime. But I also remember my grandmother lived in London, and there used to be a sort of family get-together – by that time my parents were separated – and I remember a series of wonderful London pantomimes. There was also a wonderful *Sleeping Beauty* at that theatre that was turned into a dance hall.

The Lyceum?

The Lyceum, yes! The pantomime actually had a harlequinade in it. Those pantos were usually fantastic. And I think I went to the occasional variety show at the Empire in Middlesbrough with my father, who probably wondered what the hell to do with this child he had to entertain.

And were you taken with theatre?

Oh, absolutely, absolutely. When I was four years old I went to a kindergarten, as they were called in those days and, I suppose at Christmas, when we were there we put on *Sleeping Beauty.*

And were you in it?

I was Sleeping Beauty! So my first words on any stage were, 'May I try?' and the finger gets pricked, you know – and I remember that vividly, oh so vividly. I never looked back, I knew that was what I wanted to do from then onwards.

And that's what you did, you acted to begin with? Did you go to drama school?

Yes I did. I went to the Central School. And I did well there. I went back to teach later.

But what about the writing? When did that happen?

Oh – well that happened way back, at school. I went to boarding school and one was always encouraged to do little shows. Charades was the great format, but what that really meant was three or four scenes. I had an amazing way of writing, which I wish I could do now. I would lie in bed – for an hour or so – visualising the scenes, writing the dialogue in my head. I would compose the whole thing like that, and I would just be able to tell people what to say and do. I don't think I ever wrote it down – I didn't need to, I could remember everything. And then, as a child can, I would fall asleep afterwards, and have a full night's sleep. I certainly couldn't do that now! It was great – it was wonderful.

So the ideas would just pop in?

I never had any difficulty in finding them. I never thought it was anything very special. And then at Central, you often only did scenes from plays. I was teaching and directing by then, and I remember if I had to do scenes from *School for Scandal*, for example, in order to give the girls more parts I would write an epilogue in verse saying, 'You don't know what happens next. Maybe . . .' It was around that time that I got the idea of writing plays, but I never had the drive to finish one. Then the *Observer* Play

Competition was announced and I thought, well, if I don't do it now I never will.

So you wrote The Sport of My Mad Mother *for the competition rather than using something that already existed?*

I wrote it for the competition.

So how on earth did it happen that you came to write such a play? Because it was very experimental, wasn't it?

Very experimental, very ahead of its time, but it's never quite died. Recently one or two people have picked it up and had another look at it – a revaluation. Where did the influences come from? First of all there was a terrific air of excitement around, there were a lot of teenage gangs, of a rather innocent nature.

Yes – mods and rockers.

I had all sorts of newspaper cuttings about all these things pinned about my room. I was intrigued by Noël Coward's dialogue: clipped and superficial, but very spare and tight, masking what the characters are really thinking. There was T. S. Eliot's 'I knew a man once did a girl in' – *Sweeney Agonistes*. Casual violence and threat and tremendous internal rhythm. I think I first read that when I was about thirteen. There was a lot of Central School influence, from improvisations, for example, which were sometimes incredibly interesting. I remember one in which a boy was blowing a trumpet and it became a bird and flew away. And of course by this time I did know a lot about theatre. I'd done all that work at school, always knowing that I wanted to go into the theatre. I'd set up my own theatre club, an open-stage theatre club – oh, I wrote something for that, that was my first play. A little one-acter – a sort of translation of Aristophanes' *The Frogs*. I think I wrote two plays for them. And I'd directed a lot of plays there, experimenting with the theatre. So by the time I came to write *Sport* I did know something about theatre. I had a real feeling for it.

And so it went into the Observer *– but you didn't send it to the Court?*

No, what happened was – it was great fun, that *Observer* thing, because Tynan began to write about the competition in his column. He'd say, 'We've had two thousand scripts' – obviously many more than they'd expected – and then he'd say, 'Those we don't want we're sending back.' But mine didn't come back . . . and didn't come back. Then one day the phone rang, and someone with a very Foreign and Commonwealth Office accent said, 'Oh, didn't you write a play for the *Observer* competition? Well, it's won a prize.' And being me, I said, 'Which prize?' and it was a joint third with N. F. Simpson's *A Resounding Tinkle*. Obviously they couldn't agree. The committee could agree on the first two, which were rather boring and conventional plays, but us two, they thought, we'll put them in as third, because we don't understand them but they look interesting. The prize was going to be a production at the Arts Theatre. Someone, I don't know who – by this time I must have got Peggy Ramsay as my reluctant agent – or somebody from the *Observer* rang up and said, 'Would you like us to show it to the Royal Court? Because they're interested.' So of course I said yes. Much more fun to go to the Royal Court than the Arts Theatre. It was the first of the new plays – produced in 1958. I lived in a flat with my first husband; I had a little workroom, and I had sat in there writing this play, and within hours I was having lunch with George Devine and Tony Richardson at the French pub, and Jocelyn Herbert was bringing round designs to my workroom – it was wonderful!

And the actual process of writing that play – can you remember, was it easy, was it difficult?

Oh, I loved it, I really enjoyed doing it. I worked very hard at it, but I didn't know what I was writing – I created it as a blind man creates sculpture. What I mean is that I was sensing all the time that I was getting true to what I wanted to say, but I was never quite sure until I finished. And then I revised the whole thing and I finally knew what it was about! I didn't have a pre-laid plan, not at all. Another thing I remember – there was a little restaurant, which you either loved or hated, at the back of the Court, and it was very, very intimate, half the size of this room. And in there one day I heard somebody talking about this extraordinary Australian girl with a mane of red hair – and I almost said, stop talking, I don't want to hear any more. I felt it was very significant.

When you heard that, you thought of putting that person in the play?

Yes, it began to grow in my mind – a woman like that.

Many writers have an idea where it's going before they start – but David Storey told me that he never knows. He just sits down and starts. With Home, *he didn't know it was taking place in an asylum till he got to the end of Act One.*

Well, I can absolutely understand that – because I used to write a bit, and then say, oh well, this is where it must be happening.

But what drives it? Is it the language? I always want to ask where the ideas come from, but nobody can say, because I don't suppose anybody ever knows.

Ideas create ideas.

You must have been interested in language.

Oh, yes. I've spoken poetry as long as I can remember. It was great thing at school – it was called Diction. It meant – not exactly acting lessons, but poetry was the great engine, you know. I learned reams. In a sense it's been a great comfort to me all my life. It's lovely being able to remember it, when you're somewhere . . .

Sad that doesn't happen any more. It seems to me in your early plays that you're experimenting with language.

Well, it interests me very much. Speech rhythms fascinate me.

So you just sat down and started and saw where it would take you? Are there occasions when you've tried to work from a different perspective?

Well, in the later plays, which aren't published, all the community plays, you do start with a great mass of material. But I remember, with the Danish community play, sitting for months in front of a blank pad of paper, trying to find a way in, knowing that at the end of it you had to produce something that could be done.

But you said you wrote Sport *and then you revised it?*

Howard Barker said the other day that he never rewrites. I always rewrite. I won't say I rewrite every word, but the first draft is a process of discovery, and discovery also includes discovering the language, discovering all sorts of things. Then you go back and make it into a coherent – whatever. If I were to define artistic truth, I would say it was trying to get nearer and nearer to some central integral idea, and that everything must support that. And I think that the process of revision was getting into that. You've got your rough material and now you make it go into one idea.

So perhaps you don't know that idea until you've finished writing the play?

Well, until you've finished the first draft, anyway. What would happen was, I would get halfway through and then realise that in order to discover what the end was I would have to go back and rework the first half so that its direction was more clear.

Is there some overall idea you're trying to convey in these plays – some continuity? What do you think Sport, *for example, is about?*

It's so long since I thought about it – I don't know what it's about. It's something to do with women, it's something to do with inarticulate people, it's something to do with people who need myth and ritual and all that sort of thing.

That's good enough!

'Birth, birth, that's the thing!' to quote the play.

The title – did it come after the play?

Oh, the title came after. It was actually rather a cheat because it was a quote from *The Outsider*, the book by Colin Wilson that was popular in the fifties – 'All creation is the sport of my mad mother Kali.' I picked it up – it must have been while I was writing the play, certainly not before.

It suggests the world is a chaotic place.

Yes – I think probably, that is what the play is about. I mean, 'Rules, regulations, into the pot with the whole bloody lot. Birth, birth, that's the thing.' That's practically the last line of the play.

If it is about that, it's interesting that it's couched in quite rigidly ritualistic language.

Well, in fact it's not. In a sense the language and the speech rhythms often drive the people. If you take scenes out of *Sport* – the trio, they get absolutely as if they're on drugs – the words drive them. I think that's what it's actually about – this chaotic thing.

I saw that play in 1958. I was very young, but I have such a vivid memory of Sport *– I can see it in my eye now. And* The Knack *– you used rhythmic language in that too.*

Yes – the bed scene.

I improvised that scene originally, you know, with Bill Gaskill, at the Writers' Group. When I started thinking about how plays get written, you have the David Storey model, but then you have someone going to the Writers' Group, and you have, as it happens, me and Bill Gaskill doing an improvisation about whether something's a bed or a piano, and then that comes into the play. But the play was already under way by then?

It was. I'd reached somewhere like that in the writing, but I was blocked so I set up the improvisation. I set it up simply with a bed in a scrapyard or some place with a beggar, or maybe a scrap-iron merchant. But it began to change: Bill began to insist it was a piano, not a bed, and demonstrate: pling plong, etc.

And elements of your own life at that time went into that play.

Oh yes – I have no hesitation in saying that. Almost all the characters were based on real people. The only non-ready-made one was Patti, the girl. Practically autobiography.

So really what we're talking about is two different processes. Sport *kind of came out of God knows where, but . . .*

Oh well, but *The Knack* came out of nowhere in the sense that I did not know what I was going to write about when I started.

It sounds as if writing was an easy process. You weren't struggling?

I don't think it's ever easy. Easy writing's damned hard reading, as I think Chesterton once said. No, it wasn't easy, but I won't say it wasn't enjoyable.

But with that play as well you went back to it, and refined it . . .

Oh yes.

And who directed The Knack? *You didn't direct it yourself?*

It opened at Cambridge, directed by Keith Johnstone. It was his first production and I wasn't completely happy with it. But people don't always want the writer to direct. Your father was wonderful with *Sport* because I wanted to direct and – it's incredible – it was a thousand per cent more difficult then for a woman to direct, almost unheard of. And your father sort of respected this – he said, 'We'll do it together. I'll protect you.' And then he came to the first few rehearsals, and obviously decided I could direct, and after that he would only come to about one in five. But he did protect me, you see. But when *The Knack* came along, Bill was the artistic director and you had this old bloody nonsense about how the writer shouldn't direct.

And did it go down well in Cambridge?

Yes. The undergraduate audiences were wonderful – they were so quick. They would laugh twice at the same joke – they would see the joke coming, and they would laugh when it came.

Did you know it was so funny?

It was meant to be funny. But we didn't know what a success it would be. We were just blessed with that undergraduate audience. There were queues round the theatre.

It must have been so exciting.

It was wonderful. And then they decided to bring it into the Court, and I refused to ditch Keith, though I hadn't liked his production. So I said right, Keith and I will do it, and that they bought. So after that I think I'd more or less established that I could direct my own plays, until there was a play that Oscar Lewenstein put on which was a ghastly failure, though it was a huge success in Edinburgh!

What was that?

The Giveaway. It came into the West End, to the Garrick. It was never a Court play.

Did you write it thinking it was not a Court play?

I don't know. I had ideas above my station and thought I'd like a West End play, something like that. But I was about eight months pregnant with my second child, so Richard Eyre directed it.

But you did have another play at the Court – Shelley.

Oh yes – I directed that.

Was that play a happy experience?

Well, I enjoyed it enormously. What happened was, I was on holiday in Italy and we found Shelley's house in Lerici, and there was actually a plaque on it saying 'I still inhabit this divine bay, sailing and listening to the most enchanting music.' And I was intrigued by this. Later I found the true quotation in his letters: 'I still inhabit this divine bay, reading Spanish dramas, sailing and listening to the most enchanting music.' I was amused that the Italians dropped the Spanish reference. I think it all started from that. But I began to have such a reverence for the man, and reverence for his work – a feeling you couldn't muck about with it, and I think the play suffered from that, my leaving nothing out. I had a terribly vivid dream while I was writing it, of trying to pack everything into a suitcase and not being able to get the lid shut.

So you must have had to do research?

Oh, an awful lot. I remember going to the Bodleian Library, because they have all his letters and things – that book that he had with him when he was drowned, Keats's poems, thrust into his pocket – it's all stained with water. And a lovely sort of constant doodle he did of a big tree, and two slightly less big ones, which were clearly him, Mary and Claire. And you know how when you're away on holiday you add up how much money you've got left? There were lots of little scribbles like that.

Of all your plays, could you say one or other of them is your favourite?

The Knack, without question. I'm not talking about community plays now.

Did you write the screenplay for The Knack?

No – Charles Wood wrote it.

And how did that feel, just having to hand it over?

Oh, I disliked it intensely.

You didn't have the option to do it?

I don't think I did. I do remember I had nothing to do with it, and being so irritated when they mistimed the jokes. It was agony to me.

You really didn't like the film?

I won't say I didn't like it. Some things I liked more and some things less.

It must be strange seeing what someone else has made of your work.

Yes. But I've directed that play quite a lot in various countries and seen various productions – it still goes on, that little play, after all these years. It's amazing, I still earn trickles of money from it. I've had a lot of fun out of it. There was a time when I seemed to be going abroad a lot, and I would go backstage for some reason, and I could say, 'I wrote The Knack,' and people would fling their arms round me and say, oh, I played such and such a part.

You said that when you were at the Court it was difficult for a woman to be a director – do you think it was as difficult for a woman to be a writer?

No, although it was quite difficult. But the play stands away independent of you – you write the play and it doesn't matter if it's written by a man or a woman as long as it's well written. Sex doesn't come into it. Of course forty years ago it jolly well mattered if you were a man or a woman when it came to getting a job, as it were – if one wanted to direct, for example, because there was money and power involved. But writing, you produce the goods, and it doesn't matter if it's by Bill Smith or Sally Jones – it doesn't make any difference at all.

Although some women writers in the eighties made conscious feminist statements.

Oh yes – but that's a different thing. Anyway, the time was right for that. It created interest.

About being the literary manager – was there any one criterion you used to apply? Did you open up a play and say, I can tell within a page whether this thing's any good? Or, like Donald Howarth, did you say, no, I've got to read it from cover to cover before I can tell?

Well, I could open a play and within three pages I would know, but I always read the whole text to be sure. But I did second readings – we had readers, so they came through to me already sieved. But I always did read them and I always could tell very quickly if something was any good or not.

Keith says in his book Impro, *'I would first read plays as quickly as possible, and categorise them as pseudo-Pinter, fake-Osborne, phoney-Beckett, and so on.' But that can't be the whole story, can it?*

No, because it could easily be one of those things and still be a very good play. But I did keep my eyes open for women writers, and I think I found three – among them Mary O'Malley, who wrote *Once a Catholic . . .*

What made you move into community theatre?

Well, coming down here, really. I'd had a very pleasant year, eighteen months, as literary manager, which I'd really enjoyed. I'd written children's plays that had been done at the Theatre Upstairs, enormous fun. But we very much wanted to be in the country, and I could see no reason why I couldn't go on writing down here. I think that was a part of it. Roger, being a freelance photographer, could operate from here, so in theory I decided I could operate from here too. I had two children of school age, and I'd cottoned on to the idea of writing for schools, and I think I'd even approached a big London school. But I'm extremely glad nothing ever came of that, because I think I'd have been crucified in a London school – they're very tough, and they were just as tough thirty years ago. But when we got down here, there was this local comprehensive where my daughter was about to start her first year – and the place was just lying like a virgin bride waiting to be taken advantage of, really.

The writing must be a very different kind of experience? Or is it the same – you just have more people to work with?

I've written a book which has got everything I know about community theatre. There are about six basic rules that I tell any other writer. It has to be about the history of the community. It has to have many more women's than men's parts, because always many more women want to be in it. It should have an 'up' ending, if not a happy one – you want the community to feel good about itself. You have to have about a hundred and twenty people, and it's not enough to say, we'll have thirty washerwomen and a hundred horsemen or something. Every one of them must be a character. And there are certain techniques, like you can divide them into families; and then suppose you've got, say, ten families, you can put all the teenage boys together in certain scenes, or all the women together. There are sub-groups, which feed into other groups – this gives them varied relationships and quite a rich life. I don't like too huge stars. What I aim for is about eight important parts, and so you go on till maybe you have somebody who is just holding a horse and saying, 'Yes, your worship.' But even that person has a family and peer groups and other relationships and is part of the action the whole time, since they are promenade performances.

A very different sort of writing – it sounds as if it could be formulaic?

No, its not formulaic, but it must conform to certain rules. You can't write a four-person play when you've got a hundred and twenty people.

But is it just as satisfying?

Oh, just! And what's wonderful is having a hundred and twenty people – it's marvellous. But you have to do an awful lot of work in the community to rouse interest. David Edgar was very good at that.

Well, it's all very interesting – because writing a play is not just sitting in a room somewhere waiting for inspiration to strike. It's got to have this kind of pragmatic side to it. If you've got any sense at all you're going to be thinking, well of course I want somebody to do this play, so I have to write within certain sensible constraints, otherwise they're not going to do it.

Yes, but you see, theatre is a collaborative art. You can't do it without other people. I won't say theatre is about compromises, but in a sense . . .

Well, it's about co-operation.

It is, isn't it?

Terry Johnson

When I reconnected with the Royal Court in early 2004 I read a lot of plays very quickly to get myself up to speed. One of those I enjoyed the most was Terry Johnson's *Hysteria*. I wished I'd seen it on stage because, as well as being intelligent and funny, it had dramatic and farcical elements which obviously were at their best in performance. I met Terry Johnson in the Royal Court bar in February 2005. He was ill with flu and had almost decided to cancel the interview.

Do you remember the first time you went to the theatre?

I think it was a pantomime. I remember walking past the Watford Palace Theatre and saying to my mother that I wanted to go. I don't think she'd ever been to the theatre – she walked into the box office as if it was a cinema. I think we got the last two seats at the back of the upper circle. It took me twenty-two years to get back to the Watford Palace, but I did sit in the same seat to watch *Elton John's Glasses* by David Farr.

And how old were you?

Tiny.

What did you think of it?

I was delighted by the transformations – carriages and mice and the actress . . . I immediately knew how the actress had transformed. And in my teens I did props for a couple of amateur shows.

You were interested in being involved with theatre?

I love pass doors – I love the weight of the pass door, and I still find it a fairly magical transition to walk through a pass door. I still to this day get a sense of moving onto a magic space. And it's something to do with the forbiddenness of the space, the heaviness of the door.

So when you were making props, you were still at school? Did you do any drama there?

No, I was too shy to do anything like that. I finally took the plunge when there was a sixth-form revue. I was in the Lower Sixth, and the Upper Sixth decided they were going to do a play. And I nicked the scenery from the Rickmansworth Players' old-time melodrama – a very ingenious piece of scenery which was on wheels, so it went round and round. I nicked the entire contraption for this very funny twenty-minute melodrama which we put on. It was a great hit, and the next year I did the whole revue myself. So I was an actor in disguise. I was too shy to go to drama school, though I finally did a degree in drama, which meant I could keep up the pretence.

So when did you think, 'Oh, I'll write a play'?

I tried to write a play quite early, but that was silly. I remember recording a Whitehall farce off the telly and having my mother type it out for me – and halfway through she said, 'You haven't written this, you know.' And I went, 'I know that.' I'd attempted things, but mainly it was about stealing comedy, and reinventing comedy. Then at university I tried acting and was never happy at it, never happy in an actor's skin. My body never aligned with the fantasy, with the imagination. The energies would never align with the imagination. So I could be sitting there in character, and I'm saying this, and I have to move to that chair. And I could understand it cerebrally, but my body would sort of groan. So there was a physical lack of attunement, I couldn't become an actor. But I started directing there, and I started writing. David Edgar was teaching undergraduates there at that time, so he kicked me off. And by the time I finished I had a couple of one-acters, one of which went to the Bush, and they commissioned a full-length from it. That was the beginning. So about a year and a half after leaving university I had a play at the Bush.

Do you think of yourself as more a writer or a director?

It took me a long time to happily acknowledge the playwright label, because I'm not really a writer. I don't take to writing naturally, I don't enjoy writing. I don't write anything except plays (apart from letters to Wandsworth Council). I don't write to order. I was always a play-maker. I think if I'd met the right mentor at secondary school, if I'd been sent to Oxford or Cambridge, I probably would never have written a play. I'd have directed. So I've always thought of myself as someone who's creating a theatre event. The fact that I'm best known as a playwright is actually a sociological phenomenon – because it was the only way I could get in. Working-class, non-Oxford, no money, no resources. The only way to get the resources was to prove myself on one hundred pages of paper. So then it's a natural development to become a playwright. And it turned out that I could do it. It was an insane way of becoming a playwright, though quite an intelligent way, as it happened. So I'm over that particular chip on the shoulder, but it was there for a long time.

You say you don't enjoy writing. You never get any pleasure out of it?

Maybe when a play is scheduled to happen.

But this is after you've finished it?

Not really, because I go through three or four drafts between the acceptance of a play and the performance. Maybe a couple of those drafts are quite fun, because you know where you're going, and obviously it's in good nick already. Maybe the final draft is fulfilling – but the actual process is not enjoyable.

Tell me what the actual process is like – from start to finish.

That's very hard to answer, because for me no play is the same. I have no writerly discipline. If I was the sort of person who sat at a desk from nine till four, maybe a pattern would be describable, but for me it's very hard to describe.

Could you say what starts it off?

Well, you can start with an idea, but you usually waste huge amounts of time starting with an idea. I usually don't get started until something has occurred that I call the car crash. And the car crash is two ideas hitting each other head-on, and throwing you into a world in which you know immediately there's a dynamic. In my own work, the car crash would be, a fascination with Monroe, and a fascination with Einstein. Either of which I could have written a play about. The fact that I found out that they met, that was the car crash. Wanting to write an anorak play – *Star Trek*, it was for some time – knowing about comedians, a dead comedian – a student workshop in Birmingham – one scene about sex therapy going extremely well – Benny Hill dying, Frankie Howerd dying, in the same week. Car crashes. Car crashes of two completely different things, and an instinct that one will fire the other. Dalì met Freud – you're kind of waiting for a car crash. But there are no rules. People talk about a block, but that's a misnomer, it assumes that there is something to be blocked, and there isn't. There's nothing, and then there's you, and then there's a play.

So the car crash happens – and then what do you do?

Well, you start, really. I try to remember that rule – look after your characters and they will look after the plot. Different things. For a Freud play, you read Freud, and then you put it away because you don't understand it. And then you read it again. Seven years it took me to write about Freud, because I didn't understand the books. The fourth time you read the same chapter – oh, I know this, maybe I can have a bash at Freud. But it's very hard to write in a linear fashion. I tend to write very patchily, and discard more than half of what I write. If I really started to describe the process of writing, I'd get instantly scatological. I don't know how fit your colon is, but I've had quite a bit of colon trouble in my life, and if you imagine not being able to regulate what you produce, no matter what you eat – you can eat curry, or you can fast, you can enjoy your food or you can hate your food – if you've got a badly regulating colon, you don't know what's going to come out. You may not shit for a week, then suddenly there's a four o'clock outpouring. It's an appalling metaphor, but sadly it's the most accurate one I can think of. It's not controllable.

But at some point you've put your pieces together and they more or less fit, and that's what you call a first draft?

Yes.

And then you show it somebody? Or you wait?

Lately I get people round, and read it. I tend to know when it's ready to go out.

In the process of revising, is it helpful to have feedback from people – your agent, or a theatre?

Yes. Well, the whole process of putting a show together is keeping your ears open, working with your ears rather than your mouth. And, especially if I'm directing something of my own, you have to listen. I mean obviously you pick and choose according to how alert you think people are to the material. You can send the same play out to two producers, and one of them will sit opposite you and say some really unimpressive things, like, 'Why is it set in Greece?' But somebody else will say, 'Why don't they drive a bus?' – and that's fantastic. So you do pick and choose your feedback.

I try to do a draft for whatever actors have been cast. So the last draft tends to be for the actors playing it at that moment. And there are drafts in between. The drafts can be numbered anything from thirteen to twenty-two. A little of that's down to word-processing efficiency, but it'll give you some idea that it never stops.

If a play gets revived after twenty years, do you revise?

Yes – I rewrite sometimes quite substantially. For *Insignificance*, I put in a lot of physics in 1996.

So, what about your association with the Royal Court?

One was always aware of the Royal Court. I think it was my third play that came here, *Insignificance*. I did a reading of it in a pub in Hampstead, and Rob Ritchie turned up, and made me an offer in the urinal.

But you've never been somebody who's given your heart and soul to the Royal Court and never done anything anywhere else?

Really, it's only been the Bush, because that's where I started, and Hampstead, and here. And the National, of course.

If the Royal Court and the National both commissioned a play, would you consciously produce a different play for each of them?

I think I would. I don't take commissions, for that very reason. But one of the staging posts on the journey would be some kind of unity in your head – where it's set and what it would look like. You see it in a particular theatre. So at that stage if you looked me in the eye and said 'What theatre are you writing that play for?' I'd probably be able to say.

But that's to do with the space, rather than the ethos or the content.

Yes.

Why do you have this recurring thing about writing plays about real people, yet not write biographical plays about them?

I don't know – I find it interesting. It just gets me going. It takes me a long time to invent a real person. Maybe I'm an iconoclast rather than a humanist. I know what it gives me aesthetically – it gives me a head start on the audience, and the audience have a head start on me. It's like we've done Act One – well, in Aristotelian terms we have done Act One – which gives people a good feeling. And you have preconceptions you can play with, you can reverse. You just have more ammunition, and you hit the line running. On the whole my work is at its best in that way. I have written some good characters, but I'm not an Arthur Miller, I haven't written a Willy Loman. I don't think I'm an inventor of enduring, statuesque characters, but most of the theatre I write involves kind of statuesque people. That's not a good word, is it? But I can't invent 'em, so I nick 'em.

But you need to know about those people.

Well – how much does Rory Bremner know about George Bush?

Okay. But did Marilyn Monroe really know Einstein?

She had a signed photograph of him among her things when she died. And she had put him on the top of a list of people she would like to fuck.

Had she really? Good for her.

Well, good for him.

Yes – but good for her too. Okay, you've written a play about X and Y and Z, but could you say that there is one thing or collection of things your plays are about, something you want to say?

It's an interesting question at this point, because I've run out of plots. I'm not entirely sure it would be wise for me to try and formulate that, really. When you are in the middle of a thought about infidelity, you remember all the different plots in which you've included infidelity and you get the heebies. So I don't really want to go there. I'm sure there's quite enough petticoat showing.

Would you say your plays have any kind of political agenda?

Most plays do have a political agenda. Do you remember there was some-body who said he'd give money to anyone who came up with a good right-wing play, and nobody did? So I understand where he's coming from – it's a perfectly valid utterance. There's a degree of social analysis, if only in the process of getting the plays on. It remains almost always a kind of radical gesture.

In a theatre like the Royal Court there must be an agenda to make people think, in one way or another.

Yes, but the boulevard remains the boulevard, and I've been down it quite a bit myself – it's a very enjoyable place. And much of my stuff kind of borders – tips over, some people might say – into the populist. Deliberately so. I'm still actually writing from my background, I think.

And do you consider yourself somebody who writes comedies?

Apparently we're not allowed to any more. There are going to be no more awards for comedies, we just have to muck in with the best plays. Which is very flattering, and means that we'll get fuck-all from now on.

I heard Pinter being interviewed the other night, and he said, 'I make myself laugh a lot.' Do you?

I consciously make things funny, yes. I like the reflex, I like the hysteria of laughter. I like that we do it, but it's very odd that we do it – it's a completely overt hysterical act. Imagine coming from a different planetary species, you'd think, what the fuck are they doing? It's an amazingly odd thing, and it's an opening thing – it leaves people vulnerable and open to your storytelling in a way that non-funny stuff doesn't. I don't enjoy non-funny stuff half as much as I enjoy funny stuff, as a writer or as a member of the audience. Yes, I write comedies. But it does make my hackles rise a little that it's still regarded as the 'lower form', because it's more popular than the 'higher form'. That's aligned to the same class bullshit that took me ten years to get a theatre to let me direct. The idea that comedy is a lower form is all-pervading. And it's not a lower form at all, but it's always been the way, that – I don't know. People thought my plays were delightfully funny at the Royal Court, and when I did exactly the same thing at the National, it was kind of deemed that I oughtn't to be there. There was this kind of undercurrent of, should the National really be doing stuff that is quite so popular, so potentially populist? I'm not talking about the management or the audience. Absolutely not. Trevor Nunn was very supportive, it was his idea. I'm talking about the criticism.

Well, it's encouraging that they aren't saying that here, that the plays are welcomed here.

Yes – there's a kind of irony, isn't there? Especially as the pieces were obviously calculated as investigations into populism, rather than being populist themselves. But no, it was not embraced. It was slightly sniffily regarded.

And now you're attached here as what?

Literary Associate.

That's like being a resident dramatist without being resident?

I suspect it came out of my having been around for quite a time. I like to think that somebody might have perceived that I needed a home, actually.

But it's also associated with the process of selecting work, isn't it?

Yes, and also having a hands-on role. Being another voice, capable of pushing a writer in the right direction, through drafts, together with Graham Whybrow and Ian Rickson. We all have a go at the writer.

There's a lot of having a go at the writer here these days, I understand.

Oh – it's absolutely necessary. That concentration on script development I think is absolutely crucial.

Does it happen with established writers as well?

It shouldn't have to happen with established writers. I mean, I'm a very simple man. If somebody offers me a play to direct that's not finished, I'll go once round the houses. I'll do a very detailed study of the play, I'll meet the writer over a couple of sessions. Then they'll take the play away. If the play comes back – and I'm not saying the play has to come back and conform to my thoughts, but if the play comes back and it's better than it was, and I like it, I'll do it. If it comes back and it isn't better than it was, then I pass on it straight away. Because it's such a chemical thing. You don't know who's going to help a writer to that final thing. Finding that chemistry of who to put with who is the trickiest job. When it goes right it goes very, very right, and when it goes wrong it goes pear-shaped.

But is it actually a case of saying, 'Do this, do that,' or is it more saying, 'What are you trying to do here?'

It depends again what the relationship is. But the thing about the Court, for all the pressure it puts on writers, is that there's no other space where the writer is the primary artist, and they feel it, and know that it's genuinely felt by every department. Especially now, at the Court here now, it's particularly true. I find it extraordinary – there isn't a department that isn't dedicated to that play, to creating it the best way it can. And that, I think, is what really should be written above the door here. There is no other place that's quite done it. I mean, the boats that were launched to get *Hitchcock Blonde* on were phenomenal, and yes, okay, the National can launch the same boats, even bigger boats probably, but the integrity with which the building conspired to make that show what it was still gets me quite emotional. And one knows that would be the case whatever one brought here.

That's very good.

And another thing: I was here when Max was here, and then Stephen and now Ian, and there's always a buzz of respect conduiting round the corridors. You've probably felt it. It's an incredibly positive feeling, very valuable. I've never quite experienced it anywhere else.

Ayub Khan Din

East is East 1996
Last Dance at Dum Dum 1999
Notes on Falling Leaves 2004

Ayub Khan Din became instantly famous when his first play *East is East* was made into what turned out to be a very successful British film. I saw it when it came out, without initially realising that it had started life as a Royal Court play. When that fact dawned on me, it seemed particularly interesting and relevant to my thoughts about how 'serious' drama related to commercial success. So Ayub was someone I was looking forward to talking to, and we met in the Royal Court bar on 24 May 2005.

You shot to fame because of East is East, *which was a huge success and got made into a film – but where did it all begin?*

Well, it began with acting – because up until *East is East* I was an actor, and writing was something I did when I wasn't working as an actor. It was a hobby. It was not something I ever thought people might take seriously. So it started with me going to Salford Tech, doing a two-year foundation course in drama, then coming down to London to go to Mountview Theatre School. Then leaving drama school and discovering I was never going to be seen as a white actor. It was 1984 when I came out, and in those days reps very rarely took black actors or Asian actors – there was nothing for them. So my idea of ever doing Shakespeare or Chekhov went right out of the window. You came out of drama school with this invisible stamp on your head: Black Actor. In those days whether we were Afro-Caribbean or Asian, we used to call ourselves black actors. Now it's become very divisive, so there's Afro-Caribbean and Asian. So it was then that I was made to do something with the writing. I got together with some friends of mine, and we had the idea that we would do something to get our Equity cards, because in those days it was a closed shop. We decided we'd put our own shows on to try to get contracts – you had to have so many contracts to get a card. So we put our own show together, called *Slightly Schizophrenic* – it was like a sketch show. And that was the first time I actually wrote something that an audience saw. And we ended up just doing that one show. Before that I'd done little bits of writing at Salford Tech and at drama school, mainly monologues, for exercises. But I never really thought of it seriously.

So you're from Salford.

Yes. Down by the docks.

Can you remember the first time you ever saw theatre?

Yes – it was a school show, in the form of six actors coming along and singing about the spinning jenny – they wore clogs and black caps. It was Theatre in Education, and we all hated it. Every year you were dragged down to see these actors, singing about the spinning jenny, and Lancashire, and Arkwright. It was coals to Newcastle for us. Do a different kind of show and we'll watch it! That was the first theatre I saw. My dad ran a fish and chip shop, my mum worked in there, and that was our life. I suppose the first show I found entertaining was at the Contact Theatre in Manchester. There was one boy in my year at school who was really into youth theatre, and he dragged me and another boy along. It was the Contact Theatre Club, and again it was a Theatre-in-Education show. It was based on Shakespeare's *Henry V*, but in a précised version, and it made Shakespeare look really exciting. I stole the prologue for my audition speech for drama school later, and did it in exactly the same way. So that was when I discovered theatre could be really exciting, as well as the boring sort we got at school. But it wasn't till much later that I started writing bits and pieces, monologues.

Did you like writing at school? Were you good at English?

It was the one subject I was good at. I came out of school with three CSEs. English was one of them, Art was next, and Human Social Biology – I don't know why I did that one. I was in the main stream for English, but I never thought about writing – you don't, do you? It was a very working-class secondary modern school, with very few people who went on to university. My brother was the only one from his year who went on to further education, and to university. I was always under his shadow, because he was a really good artist at school. Most of my other brothers and sisters ended up as hairdressers – when I left school I had to go and work as a hairdresser because my mum said I wasn't allowed to go on the dole straight from school. And from there I suddenly decided I wanted to try being an actor, and acting opened up this whole other world of writing, and writing became a hobby when I wasn't acting. I started *East is East* when I was at drama school, the first draft in about 1982. But for me it was just something that a few friends read.

And you wrote it to entertain people? 'This was my life' kind of thing?

Well, not working as an actor, rather than just sit at home I thought I'd get all of these things down on paper. And then, much later on, I was working at the Albany Empire, as an actor – they'd had a play-reading festival, a competition, and I was one of the actors in the two winning plays. And I was talking to one of the directors who'd organised it, and I mentioned that I had this play I'd written. I showed it to him and he said, 'It's really good, we'll do a reading.' So that's when it had its first reading. That was 1986. And this guy who ran the Albany Empire said perhaps we could take it further. He wanted to drop all the seriousness of *East is East* and keep it as a comedy. But then I got a part in my first film, which was *Sammy and Rosie Get Laid*, Hanif Kureishi's second film. So I just forgot about writing and got enamoured of doing TV and film. But one of the girls who was in the reading of *East is East* was a friend of mine from acting days, when we both used to work at Tara Arts. She and another girl set up their own company, Tamasha, and then in 1995 or 1996 they said, 'Look, we're doing these workshops with the Royal Court – have you still got that play we read? We're looking for new Asian writers, because eventually we want to do a production, and the Royal Court are helping to fund these two weeks of workshops, to look at and encourage new Asian writers.' So I brought *East is East* along. I was quite wary about going to the Royal Court – it always seemed a bit highbrow for me, as a writer. I thought all writers had degrees, English degrees, and they'd all done this and that. But I came to the workshops, and worked with the people here, and just kind of thrived. I hadn't felt like that since first leaving drama school – the excitement I used to have as an actor when I first went to Salford Tech and then on to drama school, I had it again. I thrived in those two weeks here.

So the play you brought here in 1996 was essentially the same as the one you'd written in 1982?

It had gone from a very rough stage play to a more polished stage play, and I think I rewrote it as a TV script for fun, and then changed it back from a TV script to a stage play. So it went through all these different phases, and each phase helped it.

And what happened in the workshop?

We were all given writers to work with, and I worked with David Lan. He was great. He just pointed me in the right directions. He said, you know which way to go with this, but you just won't do it. Because so many things in it were so personal, it was hard to get a distance from it. He was really able to give me that.

Did the play change very much?

Not drastically. But I think the whole two-week process – just being focused on it, instead of doing a little bit here and there and then saying, oh, I'm going off to film in the morning, being able to focus purely as a writer – changed things completely, changed my way of thinking.

And then the Court picked it up from there.

Yes. Tamasha said they were going to do it, and then Birmingham Rep were on board, and then the Royal Court said they'd be involved as well. So it was a three-way co-production. It started at Birmingham Rep, and instantly did really well there. The Court was closed down for refurbishment, so we were in the Ambassadors, and it did incredibly well there, and the Court said they wanted to bring it back in the New Year, at the Duke of York's. But in between Stratford East took it as well.

What a year you had!

It was really hard, as well, because I was holding down two TV jobs. For the last three years I'd been doing this soap in London, called *London Bridge,* and another programme called *Staying Alive,* where I played a surgeon. I had these two hats on, and that's when I thought, I'm going to stick with the writing. The impetus was that those two programmes just stopped that year, so that helped. I've never said, never again – as actors, both my wife and I did really well, luckily, so we were living in Chelsea, with a big mortgage. That was the only problem, because I had to do more and more film work and not enough theatre work to keep up with it. And now we have children, it's happening again – I have to chase film and TV work when what I really want to do is theatre.

So how quickly after this theatre success was East is East *picked up for the film?*

Within a year. I remember people telling me this was the quickest turn-around ever—to go within a year from theatre success to writing the screenplay to going into production. People said it will never happen again – you will be really lucky if it happens again. And now, five years later, I've adapted two books, and written three of my own screenplays, and I'm still kind of struggling along trying to get these done. It's certainly a different world.

But you've had other plays done here.

Yes. Straight after *East is East* there was *Last Dance at Dum Dum,* and then a year ago there was *Notes on Falling Leaves,* which was done on the main stage. *Last Dance at Dum Dum* had a kind of mixed reception – some people liked it, some people hated it, the reviews were mixed. *Notes on Falling Leaves,* which was only on for a week, was really well received, just like *East is East.* It's just been done in Athens, and it's gone really well there, apparently. So it's been great that it's had a second life.

Everybody says that the hardest thing is to write the second play – it seems to be such a hurdle to get over, especially if the first one has been hugely successful.

Yes. *East is East* was such a particular piece, as well. I think everyone expected I was going to write something similar, but I wanted to do something completely different. I wanted to show that I could write a West End play, which is what *Dum Dum* was, really. I mean, it did all right – it did very well on tour – but a lot of people thought I fell at the second hurdle. But that's other people, putting those kind of pressures on you – it's like in film. I've written five screenplays since *East is East,* and it doesn't matter that those films haven't been made. Because the standard is just as good as *East is East,* that's how I get my next project, because people read those scripts. My wife and I have formed our own production company. She's always script-edited for me ever since the early drafts of *East is East* – she's very good. So if anything goes into production, we'll produce it. We work quite well – she's very clever, she knows when something's not working and puts her finger on how to make it work. And she's not nice just because we're married. We have massive arguments.

And do you find it easy to write, hard to write?

I find it hard. I do enjoy it, but I find it hard. I have the characters, and the dialogue, and the idea – it's hard finding the form that I want to do it in. With *Notes on Falling Leaves,* I started to write an ordinary play, a two-act play, with a beginning, a middle and an end. I'd written something like twenty-five pages, and it didn't ring true to me. So I blanked it out on the computer, and I was just left with one speech – half of a speech. It looked good on its own, so it just turned into two monologues. It was about Alzheimer's, but I didn't just want to write a play about someone with Alzheimer's, I wanted to find a voice for that woman, so that an audience could see what she was going through as well as what she was putting a member of her family through. I wanted to find a voice for her as well. And it was by blanking those twenty-five pages that I suddenly realised that was what I wanted to do, that was the area to go for.

And did the writing go well after that?

Yes, but it took a year to write. It was a really personal piece, because my mother had Alzheimer's. So it was very hard to write. And no matter how hard I tried, it was never going to get any bigger than what it was. I think it played for just under an hour. And also it was really exciting because, having to find this voice, I had to find a way of writing this voice. I don't know if you've read the play, but it's very kind of particular – the words, and the sounds the character makes. At moments it's like a poem. And I thought while I was writing it, this is mad, I don't know if it's going to work, if people are going to take me writing in this way. But they did.

It just felt right to you to do it that way. So that's all you can do – and hope that other people will cotton on.

That was what was exciting about writing it. Suddenly I found myself in a whole different area. I think that's what you do when you write. If you keep on pushing to make your writing different, not just for the sake of it, but to try and broaden your writing, that's what keeps the excitement going – and writing for the theatre, you can do that. As an actor I used to hate rehearsing, but as a writer I love to watch actors rehearse, watching them put the puzzle together, putting in those little moments of their own.

So Notes on Falling Leaves *went well.*

Yes. I didn't think it would be as powerful as it was in performance. I was really interested to see it on a big stage. It never felt like a studio piece, even though it was just two actors and two monologues, because the subject was so big. And I didn't want any set at all, apart from the stage, full of dead leaves, and a bench, and the bare wall at the back – just that Court stage. We came on a tour here, a lot of the writers, when it was still in refurbishment, and the stage was completely bare except for that brick wall, and I thought, 'God this is fantastic, it's such a great space.' I kind of kept that in the back of my head. And it just fitted perfectly for the play.

I wish I'd seen it. Why was it only on for ten days?

I don't know. It had taken me a year or more to get it done, and then I'd sent it in, and it got lost in the post. I was thinking, oh, the Court don't like it, then one day I met Graham Whybrow at a party and asked, 'What do you think of the script, then?' And he said, 'We never got it.' So I sent another copy, they asked a couple of actors to do a reading, I did some more work on it, and they said, 'Look, we want to do this. We've got this break at the beginning of February, let's do it.' And it did really well. It's supposed to be done in Ireland soon – it took a year for the production in Athens to happen. They've just taken an option in Turkey, and there's one amateur production happening here. They're doing it in schools, so they asked if they could take the bad language out, and I said okay, because it's for schools I can understand why, and that's fine. And I think Rose Bruford are going to do a production.

But Last Dance at Dum Dum *was less successful. Was that from your own point of view as well as its reception?*

No – I was very pleased with it. But people thought it was old-fashioned. I mean, the subject I was dealing with wasn't old-fashioned, it was about racism in India today. There was a production in New Zealand, which won lots of awards in amateur festivals, so somebody must have liked it. It was in form they thought it was old-fashioned.

Would you say that issues to do with race and racism are of interest to you because of your particular background?

Not really. I've always fought against being typecast as an Asian writer, or a black writer. I see myself as a writer first and foremost, and my colour or my ethnicity doesn't enter into it. If I write something that's got an Asian theme to it, fine, but I'm not going to be restricted to doing only that, and I don't want to be seen that way either. That's one of the reasons why in *Notes on Falling Leaves* the characters didn't even have names, they were just called Man and Woman. Because I wanted people to look at the work without going, oh, Ayub Khan Din, he's a Pakistani writer. Just being a writer, that's what's more important to me. But I will write more pieces about Asians, if the idea comes into my mind.

Do you know where your ideas come from? The first and third plays sound like they came from your own experience?

Yes, and the fourth one, which I've started, is also from experience. But someone said to me that a running theme through my three plays is communication, or lack of communication. It's not that I've actually gone out there and said, oh, I'm going to write a play about lack of communication, but other people have seen it as a theme that runs all through. In fact a drama teacher said that. And looking at the idea for the next play, it's also about that. But if you came to me and said, 'I'm going to commission you to write a play about communication,' I wouldn't have the slightest idea how to do that. I think, though, that the idea comes through unconsciously in the work.

So you're writing something now.

Yes – again, it's taken me a year to get started. I knew what I wanted to write about. It's a play set in Salford – the old Salford, that's gone, been killed off. Even the Salford I grew up in has been demolished, physically demolished – all the terraced houses, near where the Copthorne Hotel is. I mean, Salford Quays to me will always be Number Seven Docks, no matter how they tart it up. My eldest brother died a year ago, and I didn't realise until I started to think about this play that it was going to be about the death not only of someone in the area, but of someone in a family, a big old family. And then I started kind of going through that process, the things that happened during my brother's illness and his death. All this year I was thinking, do I dare do it? What are my family going to say? But in the end, I'm just going to do it anyway, because these are things that affected me. It doesn't necessarily have to be directly about him, but just about the process of illness and dying. I'm just going to write about the process and see what happens.

It's interesting to be writing all the time so near the knuckle. It must be painful, I would have thought, at times – writing about your mother and Alzheimer's, and now your brother.

Yes. But it kind of clears something.

Almost like writing as therapy?

Yes.

And what do your family think of the plays? Did they like East is East?

They all liked the play – some of them didn't like the film so much, they preferred the play. They said there was more of an argument in the play.

Was it imposed on you to change it when you wrote the screenplay?

I think somehow in films they underestimate their audience, thinking they can only understand just one argument. They tend to break it down to just a couple of protagonists. So rather than all the brothers taking part in the arguments as their own characters, they made it focused on one brother and everyone else went along with that. There was nothing I could do.

But how did you feel?

I felt that there was no reason why I couldn't have the same arguments in the film as in the play. You could have the same arguments and everyone could take part in them. I don't think it affected the piece that there was only one main argument in the film – but anyway that's just the way it is. I got ninety-five per cent of what I wanted in that screenplay, which is more than most writers get, even if they end up still writing their own screenplay. I think that was partly because I had a very protective director, who believed in the piece. I got a special-endeavours clause put in the contract to have Linda Bassett, because no one else could play the mother – and at that point all the usual suspects were being pushed forward for that part. So I had a protective team behind me, helping me. Because it's not just me as a writer when I'm writing the screenplay, there's a whole team: producer, executive producer, director. The director didn't want to direct a film version of a play, he wanted to find his own way through it. I was very pleased with the film. I'd like it to have been a little darker, perhaps, but it was extremely successful. It was the first Asian breakthrough film, the first to break into commercial cinemas. It took something like seventy-six million pounds worldwide. I think everyone was really pleased with it. I can't complain – it gave me a different kind of career. I love the process of writing screenplays, and working with a team of producers who know what they're talking about, that's really important. But I've been working with people who are 'in development' – that's what they do, they do development – and half the time they don't know what they're talking about. You just know what book they've read, by the way they talk – character arc, all this kind of thing. I find it incredibly frustrating.

And the play you're writing now – is that a commission?

Yes – for the Court.

Hanif Kureishi

Soaking the Heat 1976
Borderline 1981

I first met Hanif Kureishi at a party in the summer of 2004. I'd been looking forward to meeting him for many reasons. He was such a star. I'd read his books and seen his films, but also heard him spoken of by friends who knew him and by writers who'd been taught by him. Unfortunately the only thing I could think of to say when we finally met was, 'Oh, I've heard of you,' to which he replied, 'Well, I've heard of you too.' Not a terribly good start, really. But things went rather better when he came to Lower Mall in March 2005, and we sat in the downstairs front room (which was once my bedroom) and talked about his writing. I was also interested to hear about his experience of working with young writers.

Can you remember the first time you ever went to the theatre?

We were brought up in the suburbs, in Bromley, and there was a little theatre, so we used to go there. But then we used to come up to London to see the ballet, because my mother and my sister were mad about the ballet. So at least once a year we would come up and see girls in tutus doing *Swan Lake* and the *Nutcracker* and things like that. So going to see live performance was kind of built in.

And were you struck by it?

I always loved it, yes. I fell in love with the darkness, something about being in the dark. And when I first came to work at the Royal Court I was an usher, and I used to see the shows every night. I'd stand at the back, because I loved being in the theatre. That was the time when Nicky Wright was running it with Bob Kidd, and I must have been eighteen. I was at university at King's College, and in the evenings I'd go to work at the Court, where I'd been hauled in by Donald Howarth.

Let's backtrack a bit.

Well, I was very excited by television drama. If you're in the suburbs you don't get to see a lot of live theatre, but what you do – or at least did – see were David Mercer plays, Alan Plater plays, you saw Ken Loach, you saw Dennis Potter and Alan Bennett and all that sort of stuff. And so I began to be interested in contemporary writing.

Did you like writing yourself? Did you write at school?

Well, I decided when I was fourteen that I wanted to be a writer.

And what did you write then?

I wrote several novels. And then I wrote a play called *Soaking the Heat*, which was about students, and my dad found it in my room and sent it to Donald Howarth, who was the literary manager at the Court. And Donald wrote a letter saying, 'Come in and see me,' which I didn't. And my dad then found this letter, and said 'Oh, you should go in, you must go in and see them.'

Why didn't you go?

I was shy. You know, we were from the suburbs and it was a sort of class thing – the Court was a very upper-class place, compared to us.

You felt like that? It shouldn't have felt like that!

Absolutely! There were all these men from army families, who were upper-class, and they were terrifying. But anyway, I go in and talk to Donald and he gives me a job. So that night I become an usher. He also gives me a pile of scripts and tells me to write notices on each one of them. I was eighteen. Then Donald took me into the auditorium – I remember this vividly – and said, 'Sit down.' Beckett was rehearsing *Footfalls*, with Billie Whitelaw. And at that moment my life completely changed, because of my dear friend Donald, who was very generous and kind to me. And every afternoon I'd go in and sit at the back, and I became involved in this wonderful place. Lindsay was doing a David Storey play, Bill Gaskill was around, Max Stafford-Clark was there, and so I fell in love with the whole thing.

So when you'd been writing novels and you suddenly decided to write a play, was it because you'd enjoyed plays on the telly and thought you'd have a go?

I'd started to go and see plays, because I was in London during the day, at King's studying philosophy. I started to go to lunchtime theatres, at the

Open Space and the Almost Free and Soho Poly. London was pretty derelict in those days, it wasn't as wealthy as it is now, so you could make theatres in old buildings. I became very excited, because this was contemporary. And I'd go to the ICA and see Gay Sweatshop and stuff, and I thought, well, this is a theatre that's concerned with contemporary life, what I'm living in, in a way that the novel wasn't. Because you could throw on a play in three weeks. You could do a play about trades unions, you could do a play about class, about gays, about Asians, about whatever. They were like sort of newspapers. I was really turned on by this, it was very exciting.

So it was the immediacy of it . . .

Right. So then I wrote other plays.

And that was when Soaking the Heat *was put on Upstairs?*

Yes. It was given a Sunday-night production, directed by David Halliwell. And I remember Nicky Wright came, Gerald Chapman came, and David Lan – I remember them all being there that night. I've described it in my last book, which is about my father. Then I left university, and went to work for Steven Berkoff, and then I went to Riverside as David Gothard's secretary.

But he wanted you to go because you were a writer?

No – he wanted a secretary, he wanted a typist. So I went there and started typing, and then David tried to sack me because he said I wasn't a quick enough typist. But Peter Gill rescued me and gave me a job in the bookshop, which was great for me because I just sat there all day reading the books.

You must have been writing during all this?

I wrote a play that was done at the Soho Poly, which was then run by Verity Bargate and Barrie Keeffe. Then, in 1981, I retired from work and decided to become a full-time writer. Then I had a play done at Riverside.

But did you not send any of these plays to the Court? It seems as if you landed on the Court briefly and then flew off in other directions.

Yes – because I was working at Riverside, I guess. But then Max Stafford-Clark came to see a play called *Mother Country*, which was done at Riverside, and he gave me a job at the Court, as Writer in Residence. And while I was there I wrote *Borderline*. I was Writer in Residence for ages, and I had a workshop at the Court for years, and I still do sometimes – even two years ago I had a workshop there. And that was my thing, really, working with the young writers. That's what I wanted to do. I had a group every week, and I enjoyed teaching, and encouraging people to write. I liked being with the kids – that was my place. I did that for years.

So the Young Writers' Programme, was that up and running when you started doing it?

It was originally called the Activists. There was an acting bit and a writing bit, and I ran the writing bit, and I had a workshop at the Court, and also used a building in the Portobello Road.

Were these people who'd sent stuff in?

I think so, I guess so.

You didn't have anything to do with recruiting?

No, I just turned up. They were a mixture, as you can imagine from what the Royal Court was like – some very well-educated upper-class people, and some working-class people, and black kids, and people from the States.

But they had to be young?

Well, some of them weren't as young as they said they were. Some of them were pretty old, really – I mean in their late twenties rather than seventeen. But I didn't care, I taught whoever turned up. And these workshops went on for years.

And what on earth did you do with them every week?

Well, first of all we'd play games, which is a sort of Royal Court thing. Theatre games, just to get people kind of wound up.

Give me one example.

Well, you'd stand in a circle and do all kinds of things – shout things out, and touch each other, and so on. Then there would be a writing exercise, and then people would read their work. Normally I would encourage them to be working on a play or a film, and each week they would bring it in, and we would read bits out. And someone like, say, Sophie Okonedo, who's just been nominated for an Oscar for *Hotel Rwanda*, that's how she began to act. She was in the writing workshop, but she found she really liked playing the parts. Because someone would bring a play, and you'd say, you read that part, and you read that part, and then we would discuss the work.

And good things came out of it? People went away and wrote producible plays at the end of all that?

Some of them did, some of them didn't. In fact more people did, but that wasn't the point of it. I mean, my intention was not to produce writers, my intention was to have a workshop, to provide a structure, so that they could write. So during the week they would write and they would bring it in, or they would give it to me to read, and I would read it privately if they didn't want it read out. So it was just a place where they came, and they knew that there would be other writers there. That's all it was. And you could come as long as you liked.

But it cost people money to come, presumably?

I didn't get paid, and I don't know if they paid either. Because they were all skint. The only structure I had was that I'd be there every week and they'd turn up at seven o'clock on a Monday. And some people came for years. I loved doing it. I liked the company of the other people, and the idea that you were making a space where people could talk about writing.

Did you bring your own writing at all? Did you join in?

I did at first, yes. Between *My Beautiful Laundrette* and *Sammy and Rosie Get Laid,* both of which Stephen Frears directed, I remember bringing in some of my own writing. But that wasn't the point – it wasn't really a place where I could show off, it was a place where people with less confidence could show their work, and spend time with each other. And also they could be at the Court, be in the building, and go and see plays. Then actors would come in, and I'd bring in my writer mates to come and talk to them, or we'd show a movie he or she had written and we'd talk about it. It was terrific.

So Borderline – *that was something to do with Joint Stock?*

It was a co-production between Joint Stock and the Royal Court.

And you hadn't worked with Max before that?

No. Max was smart enough to realise that there was this new subject, which was race, which was immigration, these new communities – and he had always understood that part of the Court's brief was to put on plays about people who weren't represented. So whoever it was, whether it was Arden or Osborne, or whoever, they'd brought a new community onto the stage. Max understood that the Court's purpose was to do that. So suddenly he saw that immigrants, and black people, and Asians were fascinating subjects that hadn't been done, so he brought me in. And we all went out to Southall – the actors, and Max, and everybody. Wherever the Court was, they did workshops.

So you went to Southall, but how did you find people to talk to? Did you just find people in the street and buttonhole them?

We'd go to community centres, mostly, day centres, we'd go to restaurants, we'd go to shops. We'd have someone doing research first. The person who was in charge of doing the research was Danny Boyle, who'd worked for Joint Stock, for Bill, on *The Ragged Trousered Philanthropists*. So Danny's job was to go round Southall and get hold of these poor people, and then we'd go and interview them. And he of course toured with *Borderline* as well, and then Max gave him a job later. I remember him saying, I've no idea whether Danny Boyle can direct. So that's what it was like.

That was a completely different way of writing for you, presumably?

Yes. It was like being a journalist. I loved doing that – I loved every minute of it.

But you were still in control of the material – it came in large lumps and you had to go away and do something with it.

I had to make a play out of it, yes. Very difficult.

More difficult than normal writing?

Well, you couldn't just put anything in. You had to work around what you had. And you had to write parts for the actors you had, because by then it was cast. It was cast in advance.

So you have to say, 'I want a young girl and a young lad, and the parents, and these other people,' and then write a play for those characters?

Exactly. And then they go – I haven't got enough lines! My part's not big enough, I've been doing this for weeks! So you go, oh, okay, I'll write a bit more for you. It was wonderful, I really enjoyed it.

The process of writing – what is that usually like for you? Do you write like Pinter or Storey, not knowing what is going to come out?

I would say that I have a vague idea of some of the characters, and some of the situations, and the world in which it is going to be set. I would know unconsciously – and I'm sure Harold or David would know – that they were going to write a play about rugby. But the idea of not knowing what you're doing is really the idea of being surprised by what you write. Because the surprise that happens to you as you write it – when something occurs to you and you think, oh God, that person has got to do that, but that's terrible! – you know that your shock will be the audience's shock. So the writer is standing in, as it were, for the audience. The unconscious, you might say, knows what it's doing, and you are watching this and being shocked and involved in it. So that's how it works. It's a wonderful way to work, but it's very difficult because it doesn't always work out. I mean, it's easy to make it sound as if you just sat down and wrote it, but in fact it's not always as simple as that, it has to be difficult at times.

But is there a sort of agenda when you start? I mean, with Borderline *there was an agenda, and it was set by someone else, presumably – someone said we want to talk about what happens with second-generation immigrant families.*

You would be thinking about lots of things, all the time, in terms of your life – being a teenager, or being married, or being divorced, or having children, or being a child, or your father, or your family, or your class. And all this would go into the work, which would eventually produce some sort of dramatic idea.

If you looked at the whole body of your work, could you say there is one or more things to which you constantly return?

I would say that all writers have a certain field, an area of interest. I mean if you look at Harold Pinter's plays you could say all his plays are about power.

Well, he says all his plays are about politics, even the ones that he wrote when he wasn't thinking about politics.

But that's just another way of saying they're about power. I would say that I'm interested in dramatic moments in people's lives, moments when people change, and moments when they have to think hard about who they are, and what they want to do and be. And as a writer I would look for a dramatic moment – say, for instance, in my film *The Mother*, the moment when this woman falls in love with this young man, and wants him, and she has to make a decision whether she wants to be with him for a time or not. At that moment you have something exciting, and as a writer I'd look for that.

Can you talk a bit about the Court?

I'd like to say what it was like for me to go there, as a young man from the suburbs – to go to a place where the people were intelligent, and were profoundly absorbed in plays, in culture. Because people in the suburbs mostly have a very sneery attitude towards culture, they think it's posh, it's not for us, these people are showing off, this is all silly. So to go to a place where people would really seriously argue – you know, many people at the Royal Court hated each other, and they argued like cats in a bag, but they were arguing about plays – you thought, my God, this is really serious. They're taking this stuff, this culture, really seriously. They live in it all the time, and they would fight to the death over something that to people in the suburbs is of no interest and no importance. That was very moving and important to me, so that I felt it was a place where I really belonged, with these people who were arguing about this stuff, and about acting, about what an actor would do, how much this mattered, and why it seemed important. Or they would argue about the set, the writing, every-thing. I loved that. Also, to me it was like being at university, in the sense that I felt I was surrounded by people who were very intelligent, much more intelligent than me, who could teach me a lot, and did. So I'd turn up at the Court really early every night – when I was working in the box office or as an usher – and I'd go to the bar. And Beckett would be there – he was often in the pub next door – and there were the younger writers, Christopher Hampton, David Hare, and of course Peter Gill. So I would just go up to these people, and sit next to them, and talk to them. So that's where I had my education. Because they would talk about actors, they'd talk about writers, they'd talk about music, and cinema – and I'd never heard of Bergman, I didn't know who Fellini was – so then I would go to the cinema, and gradually become educated. They didn't teach you about Fellini at school, or at university, so where the hell could you learn? The atmosphere of seriousness, and intellectuality, was very impressive to me.

So do you think you would have been a different sort of writer if you hadn't found that?

You need to find other people who are doing something similar to you, and are serious about it. You can't be a writer in isolation. You need other writers, you need publishers, you need bookshops, you need magazines; you need a world of culture, which I joined when I went to the Court.

And you've continued to write in lots of different forms – novels, films and plays. Is there a hierarchy in your mind?

I'm just involved in whatever I'm doing at the time. I think, I really want to do this. But I've never felt I only wanted to be a playwright, or that I only wanted to be a screenwriter, or that I only wanted to be a novelist. I mean David Storey is a wonderful novelist too – so I don't think I ever felt I had to choose.

Is it a different kind of experience, though?

What I love about the theatre – you think it's just you, and the director, and a couple of actors, and you're in a room together. With movies there's a hundred people on the set. And I love the intensity of the rehearsal process, of seeing the actors gradually build into playing a part. But each form has its virtues. I mean, if you're writing a novel you're completely free – you don't have to go, oh, I can't have too many actors, or, can I cut from here to there? I'm writing a novel now that starts in the 1970s and ends yesterday, so I can put in what I want, I'm completely free. So each form has its virtues. But the Court was a very important place for me. And we still talk about it – if I see Nicky Wright, or Stephen Frears, or Roger Michell, or Danny, or Max – we still talk about how important the Court was to all of us.

So you couldn't possibly say, I suppose, of all the things you've written, which is your favourite, your pride and joy above all the others?

It's always the thing I'm working on at the moment, that I'm really involved in, that's a nuisance and I can't get right, that nobody else understands – that's what I'm interested in. And then it's gone. I mean, which day was the best day of your life?

So writing's a struggle, but it's an enjoyable struggle – would you say that?

You've got to have the right amount of difficulty. You want it to be difficult. You know, if you're playing table tennis there's no point in playing against a three-year-old – you want some kind of challenge. You want it to be hard. You want there to be real problems that you're struggling with.

So yes, it has to be difficult. You have to feel you've taken on something that's just beyond your reach.

And do you revise a lot?

There's only revision. I've been working on this novel and I've revised it over and over again, but I've only written a third of it. I'm revising it but I can't get to the end. I'll go back . . . it's like having a run-up. I mean, writers do numerous things to try and trick themselves into getting to the end of some piece and just finishing it.

It's good, though – it sounds good.

It is – it's a very pleasurable life. It's a good way to spend your life. Hanging around the theatre, and writing. That's all I've ever done, really.

So, here's something I've been trying out on various writers. My father said in 1960 that he wanted Royal Court plays to be 'disturbing'. Do you think that's what theatre, or any other writing, is for?

I think your father was right. We have to live in a culture that's alive. We have to have a culture in which people are asking important and difficult questions. Otherwise there's nothing, there's just vulgarity and stupidity. You've got to have some kind of penetration, some kind of interest, some kind of challenge to the status quo, otherwise we live in some kind of state that's authoritarian, or totalitarian, or fascist. So I would say that the purpose of culture is to cause disturbance, to ask questions, to be a nuisance – otherwise why are we alive? Why do we have parents, why do we get married, why do we have wars, why do we have class? To ask the most challenging, the most important, the biggest questions. Absolutely. Yes – yes. That's what culture is for. And I learned that at the Court.

Conor McPherson

The Weir 1997
Dublin Carol 2000
Shining City 2004

I was longing to meet Conor McPherson. I'd loved all his plays, and also he was clearly the playwrights' playwright, overwhelmingly the one that was named when I asked other writers whom they admired. But all our attempts to meet were doomed to failure – on one occasion I actually saw him from a distance at Luton Airport, getting off the Dublin flight that I was waiting to get on to. So in the end we had to settle for a telephone interview in May 2005.

Can you remember the first time you ever went to the theatre?

It was probably to see my cousin – I have a cousin who's an actor. I've actually just directed him again in a play, but he used to be in the theatre in Dublin and I suppose I was brought along to see him in things. I remember seeing him in Woody Allen's *Play it Again, Sam.*

So theatre was kind of built into your life as you were growing up?

Yes, I suppose it was. He would bring us backstage and so on, so there was an early introduction to it like that, perhaps.

And were you thinking to yourself, oh, this is great, I want to be involved with all this? Or did that come later?

No, that came much, much later, when I was grown up. Music really had been the huge thing that I wanted to do, and then I got kind of sidelined. What happened was, I grew up just wanting to play music, and my parents were a little bit worried about that, they wanted me to get an education. I wasn't doing very well in school, but I knew I didn't want to go back and repeat my exams or anything, so I managed to study for about six weeks and pass my leaving certificate, which is the exam you need in Ireland. It wasn't that I was stupid or anything – I wasn't – but I just couldn't get on in school, I just couldn't do it. But I did end up going to University

College Dublin, to study English and Philosophy, which I thought were the subjects I wouldn't have to work at very much.

A common mistake!

Yes, it was. But then a great thing happened when I went along – I suddenly found that I was really interested in everything. I'd grown up that little bit, and it was the first time I'd come across plays, texts – and that really blew my mind. And philosophy too – it all kind of came together. So I wrote this little one-act play. There was a drama society in the college, and I thought I would just come back in three weeks and watch the play. But they said, 'Who's going to direct it?' And I didn't know anyone, so I thought I'd just have to do it. That was it – and that's exactly what I'm still doing. I was about eighteen at the time.

You were lucky, then! So what were these plays that you were reading?

The first one that really blew my mind altogether was David Mamet's *Glengarry Glen Ross*. I just loved the freedom of it, the freedom of expression – it was just so not like anything else. The language was atrocious, and I thought that was brilliant. So the first thing I wrote was just an imitative form of that – that's how I started.

Then what? You thought, okay, I'm going to do this professionally?

Then you begin to meet all these other people, and they're going to be actors, and you're going to do it all, and . . . somehow it all came together for me at that time. I was a very diligent student at university, and I was writing these plays – it was just sort of nuts really, because for a long time in my life I'd been failing completely, so that was great. And we kept putting these plays on, and at the same time I was winning these scholarships, and I won a scholarship to do a postgraduate degree in philosophy. So I was writing a thesis in philosophy and I was writing these plays, and then suddenly it was all coming to an end. So then I had to make a decision whether I was going to keep going, try and do a PhD and stay in college or whether I was going to face the world. We left college, a lot of us at the same time, and continued to try and put on plays in Dublin, in small venues like pubs. I was working at the time in a shoe shop. And that was our lives. It was amazing, really. Then that began to become very difficult for all of us, because no one was making any money, and I suppose there was pressure coming. So people drifted off, or went abroad – at that time there weren't many jobs in Ireland, the Celtic Tiger hadn't exploded, and a lot of people were going away. I don't know why I didn't do that. But I just kept going, and kept on writing these plays.

And by this time were you sending them to larger professional theatres?

That was the next thing, really. I thought, all right, what am I doing here? I mean I was still living with my parents – I was about twenty-three or twenty-four – and I thought, well, I'd better do something serious now. And so I wrote a play called *This Lime Tree Bower* and I sent it to the Abbey, and the Gate, and RTE.

And they all turned it down?

Yes – I got a meeting, I remember, at the Abbey to talk about it, but nothing happened. So I just decided I would put it on myself. I put it on in this place called the Crypt Arts Centre, which is in the middle of a church, at Dublin Castle. It was part of the first fringe festival, during the Dublin Theatre Festival in 1995.

And was it successful there? It must have been.

It was really successful, in terms of what it was. It was only on for two weeks, but it was one of those experiences where everything went according to plan. The cast were great. It really worked. And at that time I had been approached to write a screenplay, and when I was writing that the producers said I should try and get an agent. So I approached an agent, whose name was Nick Marston, and he came to see that play, scouting around, looking for things, and he said to me, 'Well, you know, I think we could get this on in London.' So this was just brilliant, because my parents had said, 'Look, what are you going to do with yourself? Because this is mad.' So I was able to say, 'Well, I've got this agent now.' He got the play and sent it around, and the Royal Court wanted to do it, and the Bush wanted to do it. The Royal Court wanted to do their own production of it, but I didn't want that, I wanted to do the production that I had already done. The Bush were happy for me to do that, so I brought that production from Dublin.

That was incredible – you had them fighting over you!

Yes, it was amazing, really. But I think Nick Marston is a really good agent, and he was able to make it work for me.

And you directed it yourself?

Yes, that was the thing – I had directed it in Dublin, so I directed it again at the Bush, with the same cast. Because that's what I'd been doing, writing these plays and then directing them, ever since I started.

So you'd always directed your own plays?

I'd always directed them. The first time that I didn't direct was *The Weir*.

That's really unusual. A lot of writers have had an association with a director from early on, and very often that's been important in pushing them along. But then The Weir *– that was commissioned?*

Yes – what happened then was that the Bush offered me a commission, so I wrote a play for them called *St Nicholas*, which was sort of a one-man play that I did with Brian Cox. We did that at the Bush, and then in New York, which was sort of mad for me – all this was happening really quickly. And then the Royal Court had asked me for a play, and I'd had that idea for *The Weir,* and I wrote the play and met with Ian Rickson, who was going to direct it. And I expected to have to go through lots of drafts, but they told me they were just going to do it as it was, and they did.

And it was a huge success.

Yes. I felt extremely lucky. It's a lovely experience when you're working with a director and it's all going very well. It's probably something I should not be afraid of, really.

From then on your plays in England have always been done at the Court?

The next one was *Dublin Carol,* which Ian directed again. That was the one they reopened the theatre with. Then the next was a play called *Port Authority.* I don't know why, but I ended up directing that myself, and it played at the Ambassadors Theatre in the West End, and then it came to the Gate. I can't remember why I didn't do it at the Royal Court.

And then Shining City.

Shining City, yes. I hadn't written a play in about four years, and I sent it to Ian as someone that I knew, working in the theatre, and he said, 'Yes, we can do this play.' So he wanted to know would he direct it or would I? And I just kind of knew instinctively that I should direct it, and I did.

It was terrific. But can I ask you what it's like, writing a play? How does it come about? I know this is a difficult question, but is it possible for you to say where the ideas come from?

For me, it's not like you have a choice. It's not like, oh, I'd like to write a play about, say, corruption in the NHS – it doesn't happen for me like that. It just comes, and that's it. Suddenly it's in your brain. All these people sort of standing in your mind trying to tell you something, or trying to talk to each other, or something, and you're thinking, 'Who the fuck are these people?' And it's just there, and it just keeps growing, and it becomes clearer and clearer until you get to a point where you're scribbling notes, scribbling in your mind all the time, and then you just have to do it. And if you don't do it it'll be gone. For me, it just comes – it's like I can't control it, really.

So there's never a sense of struggle, or agonising over it?

If it feels like that to me, I don't do it. If it feels like, 'Oh, what's next?' – if it's not happening, I just leave it. And then when I'm doing something else, not writing at all, it'll come to me and get very clear. But it's never what you think it's going to be, anyway. You have this vague, ghostly idea of what it is and then it comes in its own way. It's fascinating, really, because that's the magic part, that it's very unclear. And the more you actually manage to do it, the worse it gets, because then it becomes real. Reality has a very deadening effect on what was this beautiful dream that you had. So it's like when Woody Allen talks about his films, I can really identify with that. Because he says he can never watch any of his films, because he had this great idea, and then as it went along, because of his own failings . . . and that's how I feel, because of my own lack of talent, I damage the idea at some point in the writing, and then in the casting, and then in the directing – so it gets to the point where I don't really go and see my plays. Because I only see what it isn't.

Shelley wrote something about that – the purity a poem has when you first conceive of it. When it comes out it's never going to be that thing you had inside the brain.

I know. But there must be a trace of something left, because when the audience relate to it, that's what they're relating to.

I must say the first night of Shining City *was so exciting. The buzz, you know, in the theatre, and in the bar afterwards – there was such an incredible sense that everybody was just wild about it.*

I know. It was overwhelming.

So it's not a very long-drawn-out process when you write.

No, it's quick, it happens very quickly. But the thing is the thinking about it, when it's in your mind, that can be hanging around like a bad smell for a long time. And then suddenly it has to get down there, on paper. And if for some reason you don't do it or you do something else, then that's the shocking thing. You have to be very careful – and as a writer and a director, I have been in the middle of that kind of feeling when I've had to go off and direct something. And then when I come back, it's gone. Your energy went somewhere else.

So you do many drafts, a lot of revision?

It's usually there the first time, pretty much. I just write with a pen, and the next draft for me is when you go through that, you have to type it into the computer, and as you're doing that you're sort of changing it as it goes, just neatening if you can.

You've worked with Ian, but do you still feel you'd rather direct your own plays?

I don't know. For me it's still part of that same feeling – it's part of the completion of the writing of it, of the getting it out and putting it on. As you learn to become more visually literate, and better at putting plays on, over time, and you learn how to use light, and sound, and all of that – then the whole thing for me should be like a musical concert, it shouldn't really be like a literary experience.

Most writers are happy to have that aspect taken care of by somebody else, who can perhaps add their own vision to your vision, as it were. But it sounds as if in your case your own vision is so complete that you want to follow that through to the end.

Well, that's it. It's like if you are listening to some music that you just can't get out of your mind, there's no point in trying to work with somebody else to get it out, you've got to play it. But I suppose it depends where you are with the play. If it was a play that you had written and for some reason it didn't get produced till later, maybe you would. To me it's so exciting putting the play on, working with actors, watching it come alive. And honing it, and realising it could work, is a wonderful feeling – it's fascinating, a privilege, really.

Supposing in years to come people are sitting in a university somewhere and their topic is the plays of Conor McPherson. The question is, 'What are these plays actually about? What is he really trying to say?'

I can't really say anything, because I don't know anything. All I do is make a picture of the confusion. This is basically like a cave drawing, on a cave wall, of the world, by a very ignorant person. It's a picture of the sort of unknowability of the human condition, and simply being trapped in that, being animals that are conscious. And the curse of that, and the uncertainty of it, and the tragedy of it, and the amazingness of it, and all of that, but no answers. It's just a picture of it, I suppose, almost as if you took a picture with a camera. That's what it is. It's probably in some way a picture of myself. Probably any writer who's relying on their unconscious is writing about themselves – it's a picture of the different motivating factors that are in your own life. But having said that, I don't know. I can see it somehow as a snapshot.

Is there any sense for you when you are writing that you are hoping people will come out of there looking at the world in a different way?

It's a much more inarticulate feeling, probably – a sort of pleasurable feeling, I hope.

You're not out to change the world?

Only by trying to spread . . . I don't know, human warmth. If you can. I think as human beings we have lovely facets about us, but ultimately we're just animals, and we're very flawed. And a Utopian vision of society is something I can't envisage, so I write about what I see. Again, it should be like music. To me the sort of theatre that I would try to create doesn't really need to have a point, it just needs to be like music. It seems to me to be then unconditionally good. You know what I mean? It's art, you know.

But theatre is the place where you want that to be expressed? Rather than a novel, or . . .

Well, that's beyond my control, because the rhythm that seems to suit me, the way that I write, seems to be this way. I find – this is my own failing – I can't really express myself properly with words on a page. I need someone else's voice, the voice of actors, and their appearance, and I need to be able to move them around in a space to express what I'm trying to do. I become very self-conscious when I'm trying to write prose. I hate it. I just hate that voice – perhaps that's what it is, I hate my own voice. It's like when you hear your own voice on a tape recorder! That's what I see when I hear my own voice in prose. It seems so definite – that's another reason why I don't go and see my own plays. They're too definite.

Do you have any sense of loyalty to the Royal Court?

For me, having been someone who was reading these plays, and being very impressed with these plays, that had been done at the Royal Court back before I was born, working there is an amazing feeling. But it's also a depressing feeling, like you don't want to meet your heroes. It's like Groucho Marx said – who wants to belong to a club that would have them as a member? I feel I've ruined it for myself. But it's great, because a place like that, it's very inspiring, a sort of beacon for people to look at, to aspire to go there to work. And for me it was like that too.

What are you doing now?

Well, I'm trying to write a play at the moment, waiting until each moment in the play feels alive and real before committing to those moments. Writing a first draft can be a very alienating experience. You can become very self-conscious. Sometimes you crave a mindless activity instead. I've also been adapting a book by David Guterson, *Our Lady of the Forest*, turning it into a screenplay for FilmFour.

What's that like, adapting somebody else's work? It must be strange.

You just have to be ruthless, and think, well, if this is not exciting me, what I'm doing now, it has to change. That's your job. And *Shining City* is scheduled for a production in New York, so there's been all the head-wrecking of that. Trying to deal with producers, trying to make decisions that protect the work, but really wishing I didn't have to think about it any more!

Mustapha Matura

As Time Goes By 1971
Play Mas 1974
Black Slaves, White Chains 1975
Rum an' Coca Cola 1976
More More 1978

I visited Mustapha Matura in his enviably beautiful large Victorian house in Queen's Park, London, on a hot day at the end of April 2005. We sat in the big bright living room, surrounded by colour – paintings, textiles, and artefacts from India and the West Indies. The evening before, Donald Howarth had given me an ancient, yellowing script to return to Mustapha – a play called *Black Slaves, White Chains*, which had been done in the Theatre Upstairs in 1975. I read it on the tube on the way to Queen's Park, a very short and powerful play, very different from and much harsher than his usual work.

You were born in Trinidad – were you writing plays when you were living there?

No. I came to England at twenty-one, with a lot of artistic ambitions, but no means of fulfilling them.

When you say artistic ambitions . . .

I wanted to be an architect at one time, or a painter, but I left school at an early age so I didn't have the academic qualifications. But I was interested in the arts. I'd been to the Royal Court, I'd seen Edward Albee's *Bessie Smith*, and that was very interesting to me. I was very much interested in the modern, the avant-garde, in what was happening at the time, and the Royal Court was it – and the French cinema was its equivalent in a different medium. As for how I began writing, I went to Rome, and I worked in a theatre there. Some expatriate black American actors from *Cleopatra* had stayed on in Rome, and they hired the Teatro Goldoni and put on *Shakespeare in Harlem*, by Langston Hughes – who did arrive, and was feted and so on. I got a job pulling the ropes for the curtains. So every night I watched that, and I think that went a long way towards inspiring me and showing me what to do. Then I came back to England and decided to give up show business and just start writing. So I started writing about my people, what I knew, and somehow my first plays were performed, and were well received. And so my reputation began spreading. Then I came into contact with Oscar Lewenstein and he linked me up with Donald Howarth, who liked my play, *Play Mas,* and directed it at the Royal Court. And it was a great and wonderful success. I remember John Osborne turning up one night in a little two-seater Mercedes, pink or red or something, him and Jill Bennett – the whole square stopped as they got out and walked in. Very grand, it was.

Where were your first plays done?

They were done at the ICA in a season of 'Black and White Power Plays'. I think they produced a play by David Mercer, and a short play of mine. And Roland Rees got together some of my plays and did a production of them.

They were all short plays?

Very short – very crude.

But had you never thought to write before that time in Rome?

Yes, I'd thought of writing, but not plays. I thought of maybe writing a novel or something. But what I always liked about novels was reading the dialogue. That told me. I'd skip all the fancy bits, the dialogue was what kept me interested. I remember being aware of that.

And in Trinidad, before you came to England, did you go to theatre?

Not really. There was some theatre, by ex-pat Brits, nothing interesting. Nothing indigenous.

So you were breaking new ground at that time.

Totally. My father was a motor-car salesman and my mother was a shop assistant. And my brother became a Dean of Psychology! We grew up really poor – it's a miracle how we did it.

But when you were in Rome, and you saw that play over and over again – something grabbed you about theatre?

I think so. I think it showed me a possibility. I don't like to give myself too much credit for things – I'd much rather trust in a way that they happen through divineness or something. But I do remember thinking, this is something I could do, I could go back to London and write. Sometimes it's as though you make a decision at the back of your mind that is sealed until you're ready to deal with it, but you know eventually it's somewhere you are headed and you will eventually get there.

And the process of writing, once you'd started, did you enjoy it?

Yes, I did, and I still do.

Because some people say, writing is such a pain and a trouble, and you wonder why they do it!

Oh no – when it's going well, there's nothing like it.

Tell me something about your time at the Royal Court.

One of the things about the Royal Court was that I was lucky, really lucky to meet Donald. Donald was an outsider like me. He was a maverick – he was subversive. Very subversive. And I liked that, it bonded us together. It was us against them.

But you came in at a good time, I think, having Oscar there as well. I think Oscar is not given enough credit for what he did. He took the theatre off in directions it hadn't really been before.

Yes, but he kept the tradition of the sacredness of the text, the word, which I think was a legacy I inherited. And there's a generation of directors, like Anthony Page, who still have that integrity to the text. I think that's part of the legacy, the tradition of the Court. But now I think it's gone for a sort of youth image. Would George Devine have approved?

He wrote somewhere that very young people can't write plays because they don't have anything to write about. So I don't think he would have gone for the cult of youth. One of the things he said that struck me was, 'I think that plays should be disturbing.' He hoped people would come out of the theatre thinking – which I believe they still aim for at the Court. Is that what you had in your mind when you were writing?

Oh yes. I wanted to shock people and grab their attention, and get them thinking. It's that anger and urgency you start with. And then you discover the art!

When you were talking about your early plays just now you said they were really crude.

Naive. Very unsophisticated. But real.

And they had the effect that you wanted them to have?

Yes, but I had no idea of that, really, when I was writing them. I didn't even think they would be produced, or performed – it was like a little hobby thing for me.

And how did they end up at the ICA? Did you send them to somebody?

No. I wrote them, and I showed them to a friend of mine. We were a sort of expatriate Trinidadian community – one was an actor, one was a director, and so we had a little sort of network. So I showed them to a friend who was a film director, and he mentioned them to Roland Rees, whom he knew. Because when Roland Rees was looking for works to put on in this Black and White season he had asked him if he knew any black playwrights, so he told him about me, and we met.

So it was almost like fortune shoved you in that direction.

It was. A big shove. And that's been the story of my life.

So when you first became associated with the Court you were almost still reeling from the shock of having your work put on at all?

I was. There was a lot of politics going on at the time, too. But the Court was a wonderful opportunity.

And Play Mas – *was that your first full-length play?*

No, *As Time Goes By* was also full-length. That was done Upstairs at the Court, and at the ICA too. *Play Mas* was the first one that opened Downstairs. And *Rum an' Coca Cola*, which Donald directed too.

And this one I read today, Black Slaves, White Chains – *that was done Upstairs.*

Yes, and as a lunchtime thing.

That's a very short play, but I was struck with it. It's not like your other work at all. Did you deliberately set out to write something different?

No, it just came in the shape and form that it came. I was sitting down one evening watching a film on television, and there was a guard, guarding a prisoner, in it – it must have been some old pirate film or something. So I thought, supposing the guard is dead, and this guy doesn't know. And it just came from that.

I found it very thought-provoking.

It's very basic, isn't it. I'm quite fond of it.

Yes, it's very basic, and it's quite scary – it seems to go to some big issues, without spelling them out. It's a profoundly political play.

Yes, it is. It says it all in a nutshell. It caused a lot of shock, too.

Donald was remembering this morning how funny your plays generally are. You do usually write comedy.

Yes – I like jokes.

But presumably you have something serious to say even when you're writing jokes.

I think I do. But maybe somewhere along the line I lost the idea that theatre can change the world – that what I say could change the world. In the sixties I thought it could cause a revolution. But the interest shifts to an interest in writing, and structure, and words, and so on – I mean I try to disguise any seriousness.

And you're talking about the whole of your writing life?

Yes. I think, possibly. I try to avoid the kind of obvious things, you know.

Terry Johnson said to me recently that comedy was thought of as a lower form in some way, but that it's just as serious and just as difficult to write.

Absolutely. You have to set up your joke – your punchline has got to be on time, and that takes some doing.

And just because you are putting it in the form of comedy doesn't mean you aren't saying something equally serious.

No – comedy is associated with country bumpkin, the thicko, ho ho ho – but it's not always like that. I once saw some French drama students and lecturers rehearsing something from the commedia dell'arte – door opening, pratfall sequence – and they spent all afternoon just doing that. And I was waiting with a group of young students, waiting to rehearse a play we were going to do that evening. And they spent the whole afternoon just rehearsing this one scene – open the door, bang someone with it, somebody on the other side gets hit – amazing.

My father really liked that sort of comedy. It takes some doing because of the timing.

Timing, yes, that's the word.

What did you want people to take away from those early plays?

I wanted people to know what was going on beyond Sloane Square.

To give a voice to people who had not been heard before?

That's right. I remember thinking at the time that this is a gap – this is a window – and how fortunate I was to have this opportunity, and that maybe I could get in there and widen it a bit for others to come.

Well, I think you did. Nowadays of course we think still about what kind of background, racially, people come from; and though there are many voices from different cultural groups, they may still be in the minority.

Yes. That's true. But I think Oscar should take a lot of credit for it. And I think a lot of anti-Oscar feelings went on afterwards. I had a perspective on it, through Donald and other factors.

It's only in the last couple of years that I have come to understand how important and serious a man Oscar was. He was not a popular man – he was not personally liked. He was not a physically attractive man. But what an amazing man he was – a lifelong communist, totally devoted to his principles, and he did all kinds of things at the Royal Court that hadn't been done before, and may not have been done if he had not appeared.

That's right. He had an international perspective.

Absolutely – so he should be given credit. His was a good moment. Now, tell me about this other play, A Dying Business, *that was put on at the Riverside. When Peter Gill was running it?*

Yes, they did a Play Umbrella season, following on from the Dance Umbrella season. Michael Joyce directed it.

And was it successful?

No, it wasn't. I didn't pay enough attention to it. It was all a rush – I was writing it when the season was announced.

So you sort of scrambled through it – and you weren't pleased with it?

The memory of it is not very satisfying. But I wrote it because I was fascinated by the West Indian funeral. My mother had died, and I had gone back there, and I was fascinated by the whole ritual of the funeral, and the greetings, old friends coming into the house, and they're all in black, and lace, and purple. That's what I got fascinated by. But it kind of got lost.

I was going to ask if there is one play closest to your heart?

I think *Play Mas*, you know. I like the masquerade, and the political dimension to it. I think it could be revived with a lot more colour and magic – it could be a musical. It could go into the West End! Why didn't I think of that before?

But you're still writing now, and your plays are getting done. But not at the Royal Court.

Yes, but not at the Royal Court. I think maybe I'm the baby that got thrown out with the bathwater. But I don't mind. They seem to have convinced themselves that they have developed an identity and that identity is young, challenging, and at the cutting-edge of teenage angst and so on. And that's fine. I suppose maybe the National has taken over the role of the Royal Court in some of the plays they put on. And why not? But I have a feeling that the directors I mention, like Anthony Page, maybe he is going to be the last of the directors of the old school, who pay attention to the text, and the character, and what's going on. I have a feeling some of that is going to be lost. I may be wrong. But that's what I feel.

And your plays from that period, do they get revived?

Not much. *Playboy of the West Indies* gets revived, it was revived recently at the Tricycle. That was a great success.

And that was from the eighties?

Yes, early eighties – no, middle. But my other plays don't get revived much. *Play Mas* was done at the University of the West Indies in the Virgin Islands.

Do your plays get done in Trinidad?

No! I'm a political hot potato in Trinidad. I'm not part of the artistic community down there. It's very cliquey. Anyhow, they don't like me – I'm a rebel.

Do you ever go back?

Oh yes. I usually go back every four or five years. I haven't been back for a while.

But your family originally was Indian?

My father was Indian. And I came back from India earlier this year – it was a very interesting experience for me. My grandfather was a Brahmin priest who left India and went to Trinidad. There are lots of Hindu temples in Trinidad, even more now than there used to be. And my mother was part-Scots, part-African, and my father was from the country, and came into town and met her. He converted to Christianity in order to marry her, because she came from an Anglican middle-class family.

And was his father still alive, the Brahmin priest?

Oh, I think he was. There was a big family problem over that. So he became alienated from his family, and she became alienated from hers, because he wasn't a catch. He was a chauffeur. It's a whole mini-world!

But all of that is somewhere in you, which in a sense represents what Trinidad is anyway.

Oh yes – I'm the walking Trinidad, exactly.

Interesting. Because my father was also not of any one nationality. His father was half-Irish and half-Greek, and his mother was Canadian. So he was not in any way an Englishman. And when he was young he used to feel more comfortable in Europe, he felt in some ways like a foreigner.

What did his parents do?

His father was a bank clerk and his mother was mad. Sad really. Hopefully it hasn't come down through the family too much.

You wish! George Devine's influence was very strong at the Court when I was there, and it was a happy place and a happy period for me. It was wonderful to be able to work in that environment.

Tell me about the process of writing a play. Seeing the guard on television – is an image like that how things usually come to your mind?

There is no formula.

So you don't know when something is going to come up?

No, you don't. But your writer's instinct tells you, rings a bell, and says – this has legs, or explore this, and then you start. You use your antennae.

And once that's happened, is it a quick process to get it down?

The initial process could be like an outpouring of a dam – it depends. Each idea has its own life and its own rules, and its own everything. But that is me. I know some people churn it out in a sort of formulaic way.

Everyone knows how David Storey writes – just puts pen to paper . . . and then writes very fast.

Unfortunately, with David Storey, critics sometimes use his speed of writing to criticise him. He was one of my role models. He was great stuff.

And when you've written, do you revise a lot?

I do now, but I never used to – hence the word 'crude'! I couldn't even bear to look at it once I had written it. But with experience you acquire certain structural and characteristic forms and shapes and you want to introduce them and you're more aware of possibilities – areas where you can take it.

And you said you had such a good experience working with Donald – have you ever had any really awful experiences working with directors?

Oh, I've had a few awful ones – let's not name names. I want to work!

Obviously this is a difference between plays and novels – when you write a play you hand it over to a whole lot of people who are going to make it either better or worse.

Well, I think my experience with Donald was so wonderful, and it made me realise that, yes, it is possible to do a play in harmonious surroundings, a good atmosphere, rather than one filled with tension and undercurrents and egos, and lack of unanimity and equality. The collaborative effect I very much like and enjoy. Working with Donald showed that was possible. And with my years I have learned to avoid the dark side and work with people who have the right charisma, because that's what makes great theatre. It has to come from there. You can't have a bitchy dressing room or rehearsal room and expect to have a great play. It's a showbiz myth that you can. That's what Archie Rice tells himself in *The Entertainer*. A wonderful play. That was my sort of introduction. The Royal Court was an automatic choice for me. Because of what was going on there.

I liked what you said at the beginning about good fortune . . .

Yes. I didn't plan to be a playwright.

It was sort of fortuitous, that things came together at the right time. It came right for you – which is great, isn't it?

Yes, wonderful.

Louise Page

Want Ad 1976
Salonika 1982
Falkland Sound 1983

Arranging an interview with Louise Page was easy because by good luck she was working at my own institution as the Royal Literary Fund Fellow, and her office was just a few doors away from mine. I'd never met her before she started at Edge Hill, but we got on well straight away. She was one of the first people I told about my idea for writing a book about the Royal Court, and one of the first people I interviewed, in my office, in late November 2004. Louise had read plays for the Court in the early 1980s, and we began by talking about her experience of the selection process.

Can you describe the process you used to go through, reading plays at the Royal Court?

You would pick up these scripts, knowing that on Friday morning you were going to go and talk about them. So it was really a way of giving writers a bit of extra money. At the Friday script meetings there would be Max Stafford-Clark, the assistant directors, the casting director and the literary manager – a whole lot of people. And you would discuss each script, and you would say, I think this play should be done, or this play needs rewrites, or this play doesn't work, the first half works but in the second half it just falls apart, and this character isn't developed enough, and all the other ways you think about scripts for production. And you'd discuss whether it was worth getting the writer to go further, or if it was already good enough to go on, and if so whether a bit of work would make it better. We would mark them A, B, C or D, but a decision wouldn't be made in one meeting. You'd go back the next week, and other people would have read them. Then sometimes you might just say, okay, I've changed my mind listening to you, I don't think it's as good as I thought it was – and all those personal things that come into play when you read scripts.

But when you say personal – that's the thing, isn't it? I mean, what criteria do you apply? Do you have in your mind a set of criteria that you want it to measure up to, or is it more an instinctive thing?

It depends who you're reading it for. Obviously, if I'm reading a play for a West End theatre, I've got to ask whether the audience is out there for it, whether it's economic to do it in the West End. Are you going to be able to get the casting you need? Are these good enough parts to offer to actors of the name you are probably going to require to get the audience? So you're thinking really in a much more commercial way, whereas for the Court, because it's subsidised, you'd be thinking in terms of what the play was like, and if it needed to be done there.

Did you actually formulate the question of whether this was a 'Royal Court play'?

I don't think we ever said that in so many words. I mean, the fact that we were sitting there in the Royal Court meant it was taken for granted anyway. I think the really hard thing was when you got plays by people who had had plays done at the Royal Court in the past, and twenty years later they were still writing the same play. That was very difficult. What you were discussing was what was interesting in the play, what it was about, what was the emotional impact, what was its focus. I think we were looking for what I'd call shaped pieces, but I wouldn't say necessarily well-rounded – it could have been a diamond or a triangle, or they could have been well-rounded, but actually it was the level of debate and passion that informed them. When I go to the theatre I want to be involved, and I want to be taken on journeys by plays. I don't care if it's not a pleasant journey, I want to go there.

You were also on the selection committee for the George Devine Award for a time. Were you applying the same kind of criteria when reading for that?

Well, I think you know within moments of starting to read a script whether it's good or bad – whether the writing's good or bad, that is. You get some scripts and you think, I just cannot believe that they can have written this! But we always used to say both at the George Devine Award and at the Royal Court script meetings that it's not the good and bad plays that are hard to spot, it's that wodge of plays that come in between. At the George Devine Award meetings we would actually get to a short list fairly quickly, but that was when the hard work came in. When you've got a short list of ten, everybody on the committee champions some and doesn't like others.

And then comes the really difficult question of how you make a decision, and what that decision is.

And that's when subjectivity comes in, I suppose.

I think it is. Also, you read plays from established writers in a different way to how you read plays by new writers. When you're reading plays by new writers you think, please let this be a really good play – it'd be just great if I'm reading a really, really good new play. That's what you want to happen. You don't start out saying, oh, we won't want to put this one on. It's quite different when you're reading plays by established writers. They come with a reputation, a track record, and I think sometimes that makes them very difficult to read objectively. With my own plays I've often thought to myself, I'd really like to send this play off anonymously, and see what people say. Because if it goes off somewhere and it's got my name on it, all sorts of preconceptions come into play, which are limiting.

So now we come on to you. Tell me about the first play you had produced.

The first play was *Want Ad*, which was produced in Birmingham in 1977. But before that it had a Sunday-night reading at the Royal Court. That would have been 1976, October or November.

So sometime before October 1976, you just sat down and said, for the first time, 'Now I'm going to write a play'?

No – no. Completely wrong. I had always known I was going to be a writer – always. I'd always loved going to the theatre, and I remember the first thing that really interested me in the theatre was when I went to Liverpool when I was three, to see *Noddy*. I was captivated by having a car indoors, and the whole experience of indoors being outdoors, and that is what I still love – I still love putting outdoors indoors. We always used to be taken to the theatre by my parents – not the panto, the theatre. Because then we lived in Sheffield, which had fortnightly rep. Also, at school we used to do plays, but I didn't want to act in them. I was the person standing at the side saying you go on there, and this is what you say when you go on, and quick, you come off, because you've said everything you need to say. The first time I can remember doing that I must have been about ten. And then I went to a theatre group in Sheffield. Also, I used to be allowed to go to the theatre every other Saturday afternoon. I got 1/9d. from my parents – 1/3d. for my seat, plus my bus money, and my choc ice. I used to sit there and see plays that were completely over my head. I would watch *Oedipus Rex* one week, *The Bed Sitting Room* the next week, and then the next time it'd be *The Silver Box* by John Galsworthy. I watched absolutely everything.

And that made you think of writing?

Yes, then I started writing real full-length plays. Of course the plays we studied at school were all Shakespeare, so the first things I wrote were three very long sub-Shakespearean epics. I was in the remedial English set at school, which meant that we were sent to the library rather than learning Latin. I was rather miffed at not learning Latin, and then one day I discovered this wonderful play in the library called *Chips with Everything*, by Arnold Wesker. So I made the school library buy all the plays of Arnold Wesker, and I just used to sit in these library periods reading plays. And then I went to see a play by John McGrath, called *Events While Guarding the Bofors Gun*, and I was so excited by that – it was like, God, plays can be about now.

How old were you then?

I must have been about fifteen or sixteen. I was going to do physics at university, right up to the point when I discovered you could do drama! But all the time I was thinking of myself as a writer, so I had sort of prepared myself. I'd given up A-level Maths to do typing, which horrified the school. But I kept saying to myself, well, as a writer, I'll need to be able to type. It'll be much more useful than A-level Maths. And I was lucky that at school I had teachers who encouraged my writing, and who later said to me, 'Well, we always knew you were going to be a writer.' I must have been absolutely obnoxious because I was completely determined and sure that I could do it. And by then I knew that I wanted to be a playwright, because when I went to university I did do drama, and I did playwriting on the drama course, and I wrote various plays. This was at Birmingham University, and David Edgar was teaching the course – he'd just had his first play done, and he was the playwriting tutor. He sent me off to interview all these people like Howard Brenton and Snoo Wilson and it was so wonderful. Here I was with all these people – they were like absolute gods to me.

So then you started sending plays around?

Yes. Over the summer after I'd finished my degree I sent my first piece of work, a play called *Rock*, off to the Royal Court, and they wrote back and said send us your next piece of work. So I sat down and wrote my next piece of work, which was *Want Ad*, and sent it off to them. Then I went to Cardiff to do my MA, and literally a week after I got there I got this phone call from the Royal Court saying, 'Would you like to come to London in two weeks' time and we'll do a Sunday-night reading of your play.' And then they said, 'Is it true that you're a student?' and I said yes. And then my mum phoned up (because I'd put my home address on the script) and said, 'You know, they just couldn't believe that you were a student.' So I went off to London to have a Sunday-night reading. But I used to go to London anyway, and go to the Court to see plays, so it wasn't the first time I'd been to the Royal Court. And after the Sunday-night reading of *Want Ad*, it sort of went from there. But also at the same time I'd written a play called *Lucy*, which I'd sent to the International Student Script Competition, and in the March of 1977 it won. So I'd got two things in pretty quick succession. But when they phoned me up from the International Student Script Competition and said, 'Is this your first play?' and I said that I'd had this reading at the Royal Court, they said, 'Oh, you're not the sort of winner we want!' And then I wrote a play for the Royal Court that they didn't do.

Did they commission it?

They did commission it, and I got £950. But by then I'd also written a play called *Tissue*, which is about breast cancer, that had been put on at the ICA in London, and then had been done all over the place, and in fact is still in production practically every week, which is interesting. I'd also done my first radio play. So actually by the time I was twenty-four I had quite a raft of writing, and I applied for the job of Writer in Residence at Sheffield University, and much to my surprise I got it. While I was there I wrote *Salonika* and sent it off to the Royal Court, and they said, yes, we're going to do it. And though looking back you think it couldn't have been as easy as that, somehow it was as easy as that. I wrote it in about nine days. I just sat there and I wrote and wrote until I got to the end of it. And when *Salonika* went on, it got fantastic reviews. I remember standing in the flat in London where I lived by then, and reading the *Observer*. I was looking at the end of the play review section, because that's where they always did the new plays, and I said to myself, well there's no review, that's very disappointing. Then Charlie, my flatmate, said, 'No, look, Louise, actually it's the lead review.' And it was just like, God, I can't believe it, I absolutely can't believe it. Then I won the George Devine Award with it.

It was really funny, because we were all sitting around in the flat saying, oh, we've got no money, what are we going to do? And I said, 'Don't worry, something always turns up' – and at that moment Christine Smith phoned up and said I'd won the George Devine Award! So I went out and bought a bottle of wine, which we hadn't been able to afford.

And do you remember what it was, how much it was?

Well, it seemed like a fortune – something like £1,000.

And it meant something to you? It made a difference to your life?

I think it's the psychological thing that makes the difference. I could win an award and my mortgage could be paid off, so it would make a material difference but, if I didn't think it was worth it, it wouldn't make a psychological difference. Being a writer, and being judged like that, it's how it makes you feel. It gives you confidence about your own writing. It's an arrogant profession, and I'm not somebody who feels naturally arrogant. But to be a playwright, you've got to be arrogant, because you're asking for people's money, and you're asking for their time, so you've got to believe that you've got something to say.

Yes – and also you're displaying yourself to them.

You are. I think that's another thing that actually limits a lot of people. I always say to students, if you want to be a writer, you're going to have to expose yourself. You're going to be really vulnerable, you're going to discover bits of yourself you don't want to know, you're going to discover areas you don't want to know, you are going to change your opinion about people. That's actually where you have to go to really push the writing. I don't think you can write up to the edge of the paper and pull back; you have to be aware that there are times when you have to go over the other side of the piece of paper, and it's like the dark side of the moon, you don't know what is there. There's writing that comes from the back of your brain and you don't know it's there.

What happens when you sit down to write a play? What's the process you go through? Is it always the same?

I'm a writer who tends to start at the beginning and keep going right on through to the end. I don't keep notebooks. If I had two pages of scrappy little notes, I'd think I'd done a lot of notes for a play. I have to insist to my students that they have notebooks, but I don't have a notebook myself, because that doesn't help me write.

What sort of subjects interest you?

Well, for one thing I'm interested in familial relationships.

And obviously issues to do with women are of interest to you.

Yes, because it's so much easier for me to write about women. After *Golden Girls*, which is about women athletes, people were saying, 'Why don't you write a play about male athletes?' But I'd say, 'I can't write about male athletes in the same way, because I can't be in the changing room with them.' I couldn't just sit in the changing room and listen, and I couldn't be that sort of fly on the wall.

But have you done that? Did you do that for Golden Girls?

Oh yes. I went on the track with them at six o'clock in the morning.

So you go in for a lot of hands-on observation.

I think it depends what you're writing about. It's so easy to get hooked on research – it's too easy to just sit in libraries, then you don't have to make people up. So what I usually do is to write a first draft, and then do the research to fill it out, rather than getting tons and tons of material and then trying to shape it. I try to get the shape of the play and then think, well, this is the information I need. Because I think with some plays – especially history plays – people have put in everything they have managed to garner about the subject. Then you go, well, this is rather more than we actually need. You're just showing us you've done the work. I think I'm a very concentrated writer. I sit down and I write and I don't get up and I don't wander round. But I'm not a private writer. I'd be perfectly happy – and I do it sometimes – sitting in public places to write. I've done it like that so people can see what writers do, and the way in which you go back over things, cross things out, delete things, change characters' names. So I'm not a sort of going-away, secretive writer. But I am a very concentrated, head-in-it writer. I can go to my office at eight in the morning and come out at four, having not been out of the office all day. I'm married to another writer and it seems to me he spends all day wandering around vacuuming, washing up, and I don't know how he ever gets anything done. But he writes in a completely different way. So I sit down to start, and I already know all about the characters and I know what the play's about.

So where does that come from, what it's about?

Often I set myself technical challenges. The play I've just written, I wanted to set in a room in real time. Because you don't see plays like that, plays that take place in ninety minutes' real time, and I wanted to see if I could sustain it. And I wanted to write about fathers and sons because I'm sick to death of being asked to write about mothers and daughters. Fathers and sons is an unexplored area, and I wanted to look at that territory. Also I wanted to talk about quite fundamental issues, like death. But once I've got that, my problem is that I've got two men in a room for ninety minutes, and they can't leave the stage, and I can't jump forward, or flashback. So then how do I write it? How do I keep the tension, how do I keep the momentum? Who controls the narrative? When does it pull back? How do you give your audience a breather, and when do you push it forward? All the technical things. I knew where it was going, I knew where it had to go; it was just the journey of getting it there.

So you always have an idea of something – a theme – something you want to explore, when you start writing?

I think so. I can see clearly that because *Salonika* was about a mother and daughter who'd always been together, I then wanted to write about a mother and daughter who'd always been apart. I'd found the character of the daughter interesting in *Real Estate*, and I'd also found women's ambition interesting in *Real Estate*. That was something you weren't really allowed to discuss under the rules of feminism at the time. We couldn't talk about having ambitious women, and yet you were surrounded by ambitious women all the time. And they were always saying, it's not right for women to be ambitious, we must be co-operative, or whatever. So then I wrote *Golden Girls*, which is about the ambition of those women who were individually ambitious but actually strongest working as a team. So you explore issues from different angles. I think as a writer you go, oh that's interesting, maybe I'll use it, or maybe it's not so interesting. There's a really interesting play that I'm not ready to write yet, which is about what I call the trapped generation of women. The ones who now have elderly mothers, and children who are expecting them to bail them out. I think you see it all the time. There's a whole generation, what I'd call that feminist generation of the 1980s, who have ended up with something more ghastly than they'd ever imagined possible. Because parents are living longer, and they're facing the responsibilities of having somebody with Alzheimer's. Also children now are expecting more from their parents, and not setting up independent lives. And it's women who are at the centre of it, which is really interesting. I've always been interested in generational things, in conversations between people of different age groups. I couldn't think of anything worse than writing a play about my own peer group. I was never interested in doing that, I was always interested in stepping out of it, of developing from it.

What are your feelings about having had plays done at the Royal Court?

Oh, it was like a dream. That was where everybody else had done it, and that was the dream, you got a play on at the Royal Court. And by the age of twenty-four I'd had my dream, which is sort of strange, really, because you're always told that's not what's going to happen. And that had happened – so what do you do after that? It's very interesting, the writers who stay writing, and the writers who don't. I certainly feel I've got loads of plays in me yet, and I don't feel jaded about it, and I don't feel that I dislike theatre. I still feel exactly the same way when I go to the theatre as I always have done. I'm always thinking, oh God, this is fantastic, what's going to happen when the lights go down? I don't go as often as I used to, because I really feel if I don't see *A Midsummer Night's Dream* again it's not going to break my heart – and I've never been to the theatre if I've been writing all day, because it's like going back to work. I don't like booking tickets in advance, I want to go when I feel like it, like getting my hair cut.

I know you also teach playwriting, and I'm interested in the question of how, or if, you can teach people to write.

You can give them time. But I think most of the students I now teach are surprised when I say that if you want to be a playwright you must go to the theatre. They think that somehow magically they can do it without ever having that experience. A lot of the students I teach – they've got no idea. They start off saying they want to write feature films, but then they say, oh, it doesn't work as a feature film so I've made it into a radio play. They have no notion about the different mediums. But I think with people who are going to become writers anyway, who have the talent, you can speed up the process.

Joe Penhall

Some Voices 1994
Pale Horse 1995
Dumb Show 2004

I talked to Joe Penhall in the Royal Court bar, in May 2005. I'd seen and enjoyed his play *Dumb Show*, which was done at the Court in the autumn of 2004. Although that was essentially a comedy, the other plays of his that I had read had all been quite dark and disturbing. I thought he might be a fierce or gloomy sort of person, but he is neither.

Can you remember the first time you ever went to the theatre?

Yes – the first time I ever saw drama was Arthur Miller's *Death of a Salesman*.

And when and where was that?

That was when I was a teenager, when I was probably about fourteen or fifteen, in a good little fringe theatre in Australia, where I grew up. We had this great teacher who was probably in his thirties, my age now, and he was determined he would bundle us all into a minibus, and put Led Zeppelin on, and take us to see his favourite play, at his favourite theatre. I hadn't seen any plays, and I was pretty impressed.

But you'd read plays, at school?

Yes, plays were on the curriculum, and I was at that age when you read plays, so I'd read Arthur Miller, and *Hamlet*, and *Macbeth*, and a few more contemporary things. But of course at that age you take the piss out of everything, you think they're all extremely pedagogic. So we were all having attention deficit disorder until we actually got to the theatre, and saw the play, which is about the naughty brother and the good brother, and the parent who let them down. I just connected with it in a huge way. And there was a guy playing trumpet in the background, and huge lights – you just think, this is the most fun I've ever had at school.

So you presumably weren't in a position to go to much theatre after that.

No. There weren't many plays on, and I wasn't encouraged. But after school I'd lived in Sydney for a while, and absorbed Joe Orton, and slavishly read his diaries, and his plays, and then gone on to Pinter. Basically I read all Joe Orton's influences. I heard he was influenced by Pinter, so I read Pinter. I heard he was influenced by Balzac – so bit by bit I went through those. Then when I was twenty-one I came back to London, and immediately realised, through the Royal Court, that this was a big important thing you could do, and you could do it for a living. They actually wanted you to do it for a living. It wasn't just a hobby, you could make a living at it and they would teach you how to do it, if you enrolled at the Royal Court Young People's Theatre in the Portobello Road. If you were lucky enough to get in, you went every Monday night, after whatever shitty job you were doing for a living.

You were a journalist?

I did all kinds of dead-end jobs first, like delivering pizzas – and then, after doing that for a couple of years and being at the Young People's Theatre, I was lucky enough to get a job as a journalist, by reviewing a Joe Orton play at the Lyric. I wrote this review and sent it to my local paper, and they said, yes, come in and do some work experience.

So when you joined the Young People's Theatre you had already started thinking you wanted to be a writer.

Yes, because I was massively influenced by the angry young man movement, and the Royal Court, and Joe Orton, and Pinter, and all the satellite writers. It all seemed very glamorous. And when you're that age, they articulate something for you. The cheekiness – I mean, Orton was cheeky, and Pinter was taciturn, and Osborne just blew his top all the time. And those are the very dramatic things you're interested in at that age – you're a drama queen when you're in your early twenties. So I was very soon writing. And this lot here took it seriously, and said yes, come in. And my first teacher was April De Angelis, who was so adorably encouraging – I've learned since then that I was lucky to have her; there aren't many people like her. And then Hanif Kureishi, who was a huge hero of mine, because that was the eighties, going into the nineties, and I adored *My Beautiful Laundrette*, and *The Buddha of Suburbia* was my bible – he was my teacher for a bit. I just thought, this is the most wonderful thing you could ever do in your entire life. These are the people I look up to.

Tell me about your first play.

I wrote a short play, about thirty-five or forty minutes long, which was done at the new writing festival at the Old Red Lion. But I was still always part of the Young People's Theatre. When I left to become a journalist, I was still writing – and I wrote a long play, which was *Some Voices*. I offered it to the Bush, and they didn't want it, and I offered it to the National Theatre and they didn't want it, and I offered it to Hampstead and they didn't want it, and I offered it to the Royal Court – and Stephen Daldry rang me up at work and said, 'Come in and talk to me.' And I said 'No, because I'm sick of it. I've talked to everybody, I've got work to do.' I didn't want a mug of stewed tea and more chat. And he said, 'I really think you ought to.' And I said, 'How serious are you?' And he said, 'Well, how serious do you want me to be over the phone, I can't really . . .' I was very young and bullish and awkward. So he said, 'Look, we can't really get into bed until we've had the foreplay.' That charmed me, and I came in, and he said, 'I love it – let's do it.'

I loved it too, though I didn't see it, I've only read it.

It was an awesome production that they did, with Ray Winstone and Lee Ross. It was on Upstairs, and it went on to be done everywhere, especially in France, where it was done on big stages, playing to five hundred people. It did a sort of Dylanesque never-ending tour of France playing to big, big houses. And in America it's been done off-Broadway three times now, in two- or three-hundred seaters. Then it was made into a movie.

And did you write the screenplay?

I wrote the screenplay. It was a little British movie. It was on in the directors' fortnight at Cannes, it played in cinemas for about three weeks, and now you can get it on DVD.

And did you feel satisfied with how it had been turned into a film?

About as satisfied as you could be, yes.

Did you have to make many changes?

I got the impression that the producer and the director wanted it to be a kind of off-beat romance rather than the story of a man drowning in mental illness. So to that end a lot of the rough edges were shorn off it, and a lot of the magic kind of went. Then when it was marketed it was determinedly marketed as a quirky love story. At the time I was annoyed, but

243

looking back you can't expect somebody to spend two million pounds on a film that's as volcanic and dark and hard to watch as that play was. So they probably did the only thing that they could. And it was a good film – I'm not saying that they completely cheesified it. It was just noticeably more a wacky love story and noticeably less about an everyman coming unstuck.

And the next one was Pale Horse – *I think that's a wonderful title.*

Yes, I like that title, it's my favourite title, and it was one of the easiest titles to choose. And Ray Winstone was the guy in that too. That was done Upstairs as well, and also went on to go all over Europe.

Why do you think they put it on Upstairs when the first one had been such a success?

I don't know. Because everything that came after that did tend to go on the main stage – I mean, now they do little tiny sixty-minute plays on the main stage.

I know there's a view here that the plays done Upstairs are often the most interesting, but I wonder how people feel about that. You can get writers who have had plays done on the main stage and their next play gets done Upstairs. But do they see that as some kind of awful demotion?

It's a mysterious process. There is a lot of flimflam about how the Upstairs is intimate, so it protects plays. And Downstairs is for plays that are more public. But none of that holds any water, because *Some Voices* was a very public play, and it's been done again and again – and in America, where they just don't understand the concept of social welfare, it's packed out two-hundred-and-fifty-seat theatres. So I did fall out with the Court about that, and they were careful not to make that mistake again. But I don't really understand it.

So your last one here was Dumb Show, *in 2004. But you've had plays done in other places – you're not solely a Royal Court writer.*

I've had a play done at the Bush, one at the Donmar, one at the National.

And these were commissions? Or you just offered them around?

The Bush was one I'd written for this lot, and they didn't want it, and the Bush did. The National one – *Blue/Orange* – I gave to the National because the Royal Court had been turning down my work. And with the Donmar one – *The Bullet* – I was halfway through writing it and Sam Mendes was really courting new writers, and was offering more money than any other theatre, and was crazy about this play I was writing. So I was seduced into going to the Donmar.

So you don't think, when you're writing a play, oh, I'm writing it for this theatre or that theatre, or this stage or that stage? You don't have that concept that if it's for the National, it's going to go on a bigger stage and have more people in it, or going to be somehow thematically different from a play that would go on at the Royal Court?

I didn't then, but now I am aware of it. I certainly don't sit down and start writing like that, but once I've done a bit of work on it, so I know what it is, I do have a clear idea of what is suitable for the Royal Court, for the National, for the Bush. And it's partly to do with the scale of the play – not just how many characters, but the scale of the ideas, and who you're addressing. So a play like *Dumb Show* was a comedy, and I didn't think it was saying anything particularly radical. It wasn't an idea that I thought was necessarily a big National Theatre idea – it didn't, hand-on-heart, address a huge constituency. I thought it was perfect for here because it was intimate and fun, and it's not very long. Whereas with *Blue/Orange* I would have been disappointed to do it for a few weeks here and then it would be gone. I did feel that that play addressed an enormous constituency, and said something that nobody else was saying, and that needed to be said, and seen by as many people as possible.

Dumb Show *was the first play of yours that I encountered, but then, going back to your earlier work, I saw that it was sort of uncharacteristically un-dark.*

Light! For want of a better word.

Are you conscious of there being some kind of underlying theme that you keep returning to – a common thread running through all your work?

Well, I am, because I'm constantly being told what it is. And the liberation of *Dumb Show* was to do something totally unexpected. I felt with *Blue/Orange* that it had become a huge machine – this kind of cottage industry of 'Joe Penhall speaks about the underclass', you know. 'Joe Penhall addresses the underprivileged constituency of inner London.' And I felt like I was becoming a tool of the Left. Because what attracted me to the ideas and the characters that are in all those early plays, which are all about schizophrenia and murder and disintegration and disenfranchisement, was that apart from anything else there's a lot of humour, and a lot of surrealism, and a lot of lateral tangential original thinking that's going on. And often those characters, and the people they're based on, for want of a better phrase, speak outside of the box.

That's exactly it, isn't it? I liked what you said in the introduction to your collected plays, that Some Voices *had started with this person that you knew and had thought was wonderfully creative and special, and that it was only many years later that you realised he was schizophrenic. And I think that sums it up for me – what's very exciting about that play, and feeds into other work of yours as well – you'd look at that guy walking down the street and probably run a mile, but at the same time if you had time to spend with him, you'd find there was a lot more going on.*

Yes, I find it very mysterious and enigmatic and intriguing. I'd had that idea for *Blue/Orange* for years about somebody being in a mental hospital, and you really don't know the truth about their sanity. Because the similarity between the delusions of a psychotic and the very fixed conviction of somebody who just has convictions, whether it be that Al Quaida are amongst us, or the aliens are amongst us, or whatever – there's almost no difference. I think that's been lost, in a way, because I found those ideas fascinating and intriguing and lots of fun, and they sparkled with possibilities – and it's all got reduced to this kind of lumpen worthiness. I felt like I was being expected to deliver dispatches from the trenches of worthiness, and that annoyed me. So I just wanted to write a play about a funny guy, a comedian, who's funny. But again, it was weird because the critics thought it must be a dispatch from the trenches of worthiness on the subject of the tabloid sting. And it wasn't at all.

And that's probably largely a result of its being by you, but also a result of its being on here. Everything's got to have a findable message.

Exactly. I mean one or two reviewers explicitly said, the Royal Court and Joe Penhall – what's the message here? Go figure. And it was meant to be just fun. I'd toyed with the idea of doing it at the Bush, but I didn't want to have just sixty people see it, I wanted lots of people to see it. But if it had gone on at the Bush it would have been perfect, because people would have just said, God, this is a really funny play about a funny guy and the mess he gets himself into. For me it was like a long weekend away from the heaviness of all the stuff I'd done before.

But where are you going now? Are you going back to darker plays?

There's always darkness in my ideas, I'll always go towards the darker stuff.

Can you say where the ideas come from? What's the actual process of writing like?

I think what a lot of people don't understand if they don't write plays, or stories, is that my plays tend to write themselves. They just arrive, very often in the middle of the night, so I wake up in the morning and there's an idea there. I don't really know why they've arrived, why I've chosen to write about that, why those ideas have presented themselves, until years later. I know now why I wrote *Blue/Orange* and *Dumb Show*, and why you have a huge dark play followed by a small light play. It's probably to do with deeply buried subconscious stuff, like about the death of my father, for example.

But you don't think that to yourself when you start writing.

I'm probably conscious of it on some level, but I'm not as aware of it as I'd like to be.

I've talked to a few people, not many, who have first to come up with an idea, a theme. Then they say, 'But the real writers . . .'

I think there is a certain type of writer who writes because they just have to. They have to release the valve. I'm like that. I hear all these voices in my head – I don't mean in any clinical sense, but a constant internal monologue which occasionally becomes a dialogue, and I have to get it down. It's a kind of weird thing. So to release the pressure I just write them down as much as I can.

So only later will that take a shape, or a narrative – or does that come along with it?

It's different every time. Sometimes you'll wake up in the morning with an idea and you'll think, I've got to get it all down. And you get it all down and it'll be a perfect scene, and you won't want to do anything with it, to change it – that'll be the scene that goes on in the theatre. Other times you can spend years with a load of material, that you know is good, and you know you like it, and you heard it in your head so you know it's real, but you can't shape it, it resists shaping, it resists crafting, and it takes years for it to finally untangle itself. *Blue/Orange* was like that. I had those elements in my head for years and years, and I'd written bits and pieces, but it wasn't until one stormy night that it came together. Then I wrote it

247

very quickly, in a couple of weeks. But I'd had it in my head for about seven years – attempting to write something and then thinking, oh, that's going nowhere, and leaving it. And very, very deep down, not even in my brain, probably down in my spine somewhere, there was that idea that was being carried around. But it wasn't until I directed a reading of another play, for fun, for the Royal Court, that suddenly it bubbled out and I knew exactly what I had to do. It literally sort of bubbled out. And first thing in the morning I got up and I wrote for two or three weeks solidly, and that was the play.

And when that happens, it's pretty complete and finished? You won't need to go back and revise?

It didn't take much revision, no.

And is that often the case?

I often do a lot of revision, and I'm happy for people to suggest revision, but I do find that the purest ideas – the ones I've been writing subconsciously for some time, that come out fully formed – don't need lots of revision.

I had a conversation with David Edgar recently, in which he invoked you! He said, 'Oh, Joe Penhall is so nice to us old writers.'

I'm nice to all writers – we're the same species. There's not many of us about. You respect them. And I like them, I just tend to like other writers, regardless of generation. I think there's a great brotherhood of writers attached to the Royal Court.

I get that feeling from talking to you all. April De Angelis was saying how writers feel so welcome here.

It's a wonderful thing in any profession to have colleagues and contemporaries you like and tend to respect. It's like a sort of secret society – it's great.

Anyway, David Edgar said he had the feeling that in the early days here, the play was treated as a sacred object, and no one would ever suggest revisions. That's the myth, anyway. But that's certainly not true now. Even established writers will often go through some sort of process here.

Yes – it's a good development process that they have here. And my experience of it is that it's very fair, and it's very right. I write for all sorts of media, film and TV and theatre, and various other theatres, and I think the process here is spot on. They'll come to you with a nice little collection of notes, not too many, not too few, and they'll always be extraordinarily good notes, astute notes, the kind of notes where you go, 'Oh, thank you! That's what I was trying to figure out.' And you go away and do it. They'll give you actors to hear it read, or whatever you need, that's part of the process. They're very good, and they're very supportive. It's not like TV or movies, where they're going, 'This is crap.' Here they'll pick away at your motivation for writing, and why you want it to be that way, couldn't be another way, and certain things could be clearer, could we clarify them, and so on. It's very gentle – firm but gentle. That's the way it should be.

In an interview, my father said, 'I want the theatre to be continuously disturbing. I want people to ask questions. I want to make them anti-conformist.' I take that to mean he wanted plays to shift people's preconceptions in some way. What do you think of that view? Do you think it applies to your plays?

I think that a play that shifts people's preconceptions is different from a play that disturbs people – slightly different. It's splitting hairs, I suppose, and in fact the dictionary definition of disturbing something is probably to shift it, I don't know. But the danger now is that there's a preconception that disturbing means 'disturbing' in the disturbing sense. And the lazier pundits have a view of the Royal Court as a nest of perverted radicalism. And it's not. So to answer the question about my own plays – I think I do write some plays that are intended to shift people's preconceptions. And occasionally I write plays that aren't intended to shift people's preconceptions, but just to entertain the audience, to entertain me. Occasionally you want a break from watching the news, you know.

Is your work classified as in-yer-face theatre? You're in the book!

Yes, I was put in the book, there's a chapter on me. He's kind of opportunistic, Aleks Sierz – and he opportunistically wrote, 'Joe isn't really part of the in-yer-face crowd, but I want to write about him anyway.' So, yes I was, in fact.

And how did you feel about that?

Well, it didn't bother me. It's just a writer trying to get a book deal, isn't it? So it's fine. If he's going to go to the trouble of writing a reasonably decent chapter about me, that's fine. I just thought he could have picked a better name than 'in-yer-face'.

Why write plays, rather than other kinds of writing?

Well, I have noodled about with other kinds of writing, but I think that the process from the page to the stage is like a chemical change of state. It's like liquid turning to gas, or gas turning to fire. There's an enormous release of latent energy of which nobody is aware till it happens. You can't quantify it on the page – you can't quantify it when you examine the liquid in the Petri dish – until that reaction has taken place. I find that reaction endlessly mysterious and exciting. You don't know how big the bang is going to be till it happens. I've started and abandoned novels a couple of times, and I do enjoy the control and all the rest of it, and I love reading novels, I devour them. But what strikes me is missing is that strange . . . not alchemy, but I'd say change of state – a very simple change from the page to the stage – live production. I would miss that. I find the mystery and the heat of that really seductive. And it's a lonely process, writing. If I went through that lonely process of writing and then just handed it to someone and they just read it quietly and went, yes, you know, good, I'd really feel robbed.

It's potentially risky, of course. Conor McPherson says he almost always directs his own plays because he wants to keep control of his initial vision. But most writers seem to like what happens to it when they hand it over.

Yes. I think I'm kind of torn really. The impulse to control is sometimes there, depending on what the material is. More often than not in the theatre, I know I can get a very good director and a very good cast, who will see it as their mission and their duty to serve you and the play, and who will do it with great dedication. Then I'm happy to hand it over because I can't wait to see what will be released, what change is going to take place. But with film and TV it's different, because you're effectively excluded from the process – you're practically fired once you've handed the script over. And then you're not a party to conversations with the director, and the designer, and the actors, and the musicians. And that is extremely unnatural and disturbing and worrying and so in those media I am not so happy about it.

Glyn Pritchard

Body Talk (participant) 1996

Glyn Pritchard is an actor, not a writer. But he'd been part of something I wanted to hear about, one of the Royal Court's relatively few experiments with verbatim theatre, *Body Talk*, which Stephen Daldry directed in the Theatre Upstairs in 1996. This was edited by Stephen from interviews done by the actors, in which the interviewees talked about their bodies, taking off their clothes as they did so. The actors were naked during the performance. I talked to Glyn at his house in Penge in November 2004.

Did you have an audition for this?

Yes. I don't think I really knew who I was going to see. Stephen Daldry was quite famous by then.

And did he explain to you at the audition what it was going to consist of?

Yes, he did. But I didn't bat an eyelid – if you're an actor you don't. If they say, 'Can you ride a horse?' you say, 'Yes,' so if they say, 'Will you take your clothes off?' you say, 'Yes, of course I will.'

But you didn't have to take your clothes off at the audition?

No, we didn't. He just checked that we didn't have any problems at all with that, and he explained what was going to happen. I feel I was telling the truth, that I really didn't have any problems with it.

And so then he gave you a list of questions? And did you find the people to interview?

There were five of us, six with Stephen Daldry, and he already had a pool of people to interview. But he said, if you can find people who'd be willing to do it, then bring in their names and phone numbers.

Who were the people he'd got?

People he knew – I think I interviewed one person he knew, and he had nothing to do with the theatre at all . . .

So it wasn't just the staff at the Royal Court!

No, and you never interviewed anyone you knew yourself.

So if you said, 'My friend Simon would be happy to be interviewed,' you wouldn't be the one to interview him.

That's right.

What sort of questions were you asking?

Well, I don't know if Stephen Daldry had done any kind of research into it – maybe he'd done a little bit. It was questions like, 'Tell me about your hair.' It started off like that and you worked your way down. So when you got to the arms you'd say, 'Can you take your shirt off?' so by the time you got to the feet they were completely naked.

And were you naked?

No, no. We rehearsed naked but we didn't interview . . . they were the only naked people. It was extraordinary to have naked people sitting there, but they got quite comfortable with it. I think people just like talking about themselves, really, whether they've got clothes on or not. But what I loved about it was, when you were talking to people, you saw them suddenly remember something they hadn't thought of for a long, long time – and a lot of people got quite emotional, because it became about more than the body, it was their association with their bodies, and that would obviously trigger a memory, and become something else.

What sort of thing?

Well, we would ask things like, 'Do you remember the first time you masturbated?' And you would get moments where people had obviously had some kind of sexual problems when they were children, maybe abuse from adults. They didn't go into it, it wasn't a big confession, but you could see there was pain in the way people talked about things. So you say, 'Tell me about your little finger,' and this incredible story comes out of it. It was fascinating.

So then what happened? You'd go home in the evening . . .

They gave you these little tape recorders, and you sat there in the evening with a pen and paper, transcribing. We had to write down everything that was said – obviously the important thing was to write it down completely verbatim.

So every 'um – um – um'?

Yes. And I worked out a system of how to measure pauses – not just seconds, but I used to put little marks for beats. I love this thing in theatre where instead of a pause of ten seconds they give you a pause of ten beats. So I remember doing all that because it was important as well. The length of pause someone gave before the next word became incredibly important. Because obviously, either they had a problem with that word, or maybe they just forgot what the word was, and you had to decipher which was which. And so it took a long time, all evening.

It must have been tremendously time-consuming.

Oh God, it was. I remember my son George was very little, and I would just come in and say hi, and go off into the cellar to write! So I wasn't seeing much of him then.

And then you'd go in with it in the morning?

That's right – and act it, exactly as they'd said it, in character, and hand Stephen the transcript, and talk about it. Basically he had complete control of what went in. So he said at the beginning, 'Don't get too attached to anything, because it could easily go.' It wasn't a democracy in that respect. And I think he was right – you have to have a director who's in control. But you didn't generally perform your own material, the stuff that you'd taken down.

So in the end he was the 'writer' – he made it into a play.

Yes, and originally he was going to do one with women, and then maybe perform them on the same night. But I don't know what happened with that.

Body Talk was done just before they started pulling the theatre apart and moved into the West End. It was the last performance at the Theatre Upstairs . . .

That's right. Because I remember it rained while we were doing the show, and the rain came in through the roof. We were all lying in baths anyway, so it was kind of handy. People thought it was part of the production.

Simon Stephens

Bluebird 1998
Herons 2001
Country Music 2004
Motortown 2006

As well as being a playwright, Simon Stephens is a tutor on the Royal Court Young Writers' Programme. I kept hearing his name from people who had been taught by him and who seemed to have learned a lot. He was almost the last person I interviewed, in June 2005. We sat in his office in the building which, in the early days of the Royal Court, used to be the London Transport café, where I had eaten many an egg and chips and drunk many a mug of strong tea. The building had just been converted to house the Young Writers' Programme, and the office was brand new and uncarpeted, so we struggled a bit with the smell of paint and the echo.

You've worked in other theatres as well as the Court, haven't you? How does this theatre compare?

As I get to know other places I get a sense that the Royal Court is in dialogue with itself much more than other theatres. The notion of what the Royal Court is, and what it does, and what it ought to do, is discussed much more fervently and much more heatedly – the artistic policy is discussed with more vigour – by people within and outside the institution than at any other theatre I've worked in.

That's good to know, isn't it?

I think it's really exciting. That's what lends itself to people being disappointed – people are disappointed with the Royal Court more than they are with other theatres. People aren't really disappointed with the Royal Exchange, or the Bush, because there isn't a clearly defined mission statement in those places which is cherished.

That's true. What else could you want? It would be dreary if it just went on doing what everybody thought it was going to do all the time.

Exactly.

Tell me about your first experience of theatre.

I come from Stockport – I lived there till I was eighteen. I never went to see new plays in the theatre. I rarely went to the theatre at all. When I was in sixth form I went to see Shakespeare twice with the school – *The Tempest* at the RSC, and a really exciting and subsequently quite famous production of *Macbeth* at the Royal Exchange that Braham Murray did with David Threlfall, set in a concentration camp – that was quite an explosive production. Outside school trips I went with my family two or three times. I remember going to see Michael Crawford in *Barnum* at the Manchester Palace, and another production, I think it was at the Palace, of *West Side Story*. But I never went to see a new play. The notion of a living playwright was slightly odd to me. I'd always wanted to write, but the notion of being a dramatist was not introduced to me as writing for theatre, it was introduced to me as writing for television. British dramatic writing for television in the 1980s, when I was a teenager, was stronger than it probably ever has been since. Writers like Alan Bleasdale, Dennis Potter, Alan Bennett were all writing for TV. Dennis Potter always said that the real National Theatre was BBC 1 – this was true in the 1980s, it's not any more. When I was fifteen or sixteen I also watched a lot of American films. Films by people like David Lynch and Martin Scorsese. But I never really went to see a serious *play* till I was at York University, doing a history degree. I always say this, but in a sense it is true – a lot of the most attractive girls at York University were aspiring actresses, so I used to go and watch them. Theirs were dreadful productions, at the Drama Barn, a place not much bigger than this office. But watching these plays I was struck by the notion that for the theatre it could be possible to write something with the force, or the anger, or the truth, or brutality, of David Lynch's or Martin Scorsese's films, or Alan Bleasdale's or Dennis Potter's TV plays. You could do that and you could keep people in the same room as the actors and the action. This was a hugely exciting idea to me. So knowing nothing about playwriting, nothing about the Royal Court actually, having only the sketchiest knowledge of what this place was, I started writing plays.

What did you think you would do after your history degree?

I always wanted to be a writer. I often wonder what my training as a historian has afforded me as a dramatist. I think the characters in my plays carry the burden of their past around with them, but I think that's true of all characters in all plays, probably. A notion of whereabouts in history the plays are taking place is quite important to me as well. I guess the historian, like the dramatist, fixates on behaviour and its causes and its consequences. It was a definite decision not to do an English degree, though. I loved literature and I wanted to continue to cherish it, not to dissect it. I remember reading Beckett for an A-level text without realising his plays were done here. I remember, too, reading James Joyce's *Dubliners*, and the poems of Dylan Thomas, and being staggered by those writers and thinking, I want to do something like that. For a long time I wanted to be a song writer. I was excited by people like Elvis Costello, and Shane MacGowan, and Tom Waits. These are songwriters who can really write. They wrote the most wonderful lyrics. Sam Shepard always said he only decided to be a playwright because he realised he was never going to be in the Rolling Stones. I can relate to that. I still try to find the lyricism of music in the stuff that I write, I think.

So you wrote a play. What did you do when you'd written it?

Actually, before university I did a school production of *Wind in the Willows*, in which I played a ferret. I became completely intoxicated with the process of being involved with the theatre – there was something amazing about doing a show. I remember feeling, I want to keep hold of that. Because when you do a show at school, it doesn't matter what year you're in, who your mates are outside the show – when you're doing the show, everybody's equal. And that spirit of collaboration, I'm still really fond of that in the work I'm doing now. The sense I had then, when the production finished, was, I want to do that again – I don't know how I'm going to. That, and this whole fascination with what a writer was, led me to write a one-man show, a dreadful dramatic adaptation of a song by Tom Waits called *Frank's Wild Years*. I wrote it, and I read it to my mates, and they told me it was great, and I put it away. I never did anything with it until I went to York, where I started hanging out with these people who'd all been to Harrow or other public schools. I gave them my play, and one of them directed a run of it for about two weeks. Altogether I wrote five other plays at York, and I put them all on in the Drama Barn. So I had the experience of sitting in the audience, watching the audience come to see them. I think one of the biggest and most dangerous myths about new writing at the moment is the myth of the first-time playwright. You've got all the media celebrating the discovery of this first-time playwright, and so there's an incredible pressure on their next play, and it's really unfair. I'm glad my career path wasn't like that, that I spent a long time writing plays at university, that were done, and learning from seeing them fuck up, basically.

So did any of these plays get done anywhere apart from York?

We took some plays to the Edinburgh Festival in 1992. I still didn't really know what the Royal Court was. I remember writing to Max Stafford-Clark and asking if he wanted to come and see these plays, and him saying, 'Send me a copy of the play, I'd love to see it.' But I couldn't afford to photocopy the script – it was quite expensive, and I didn't have any money at all. So in Edinburgh you get people paying to come and see it, and you learn very quickly what bores an audience. Joe Strummer said you learn more about playing music from a twenty-minute gig above a pub than you do from twenty years playing it in your own room. I think that's true about playwriting, too. I learned a lot from doing my plays in fringe theatres and seeing people leave, not because they were appalled but because they were bored. You just get to know what makes something alive.

And after university?

After I left York I went to live in Edinburgh. I worked in a café, much to my parents' despair. I was only the second member of my family to go to university and it wasn't easy for them to support those costs. I just wrote all the time. I made contacts with the university drama department and put a play on there, which transferred to the Traverse for three nights. And then I moved to London in 1994 and stopped writing plays. I got a job managing the bar at Riverside Studios, and started writing poetry. Gritty realist poetry that I published in small magazines and did readings of in bars and pubs. Then in 1997 Andrew Braidford, who runs a company called Young Blood at Riverside, asked me if I'd ever written any plays. So I gave him one called *Bring Me Sunshine*, and he invested a lot of his own money to take that play, with a company of thirteen actors, to the Assembly Rooms at the Edinburgh Festival in 1997. It was a really good festival, and I decided being a playwright was probably okay. I lived in a house with the company who were doing the play, spent a lot of time drinking with them and hanging out with them, and decided I was going to write another play for them. And weirdly that's something I've always carried on doing – I've always written for actors. When I imagine a character now, rather than seeing a completely fictional character I will imagine an actor playing that character. So I wrote another play.

And how did the idea for that come?

258

My girlfriend, who is now my wife, and I were having our first kid, and I thought, what's the worst thing a father can do? And I combined that with my experience of taking a lot of taxis when I was working late in the bar, and I wrote a play about a minicab driver who, seven years before the start of the play, had run over and killed his own daughter. It was called *Bluebird*, and I gave it to Andy, who said, 'This is really great and I'd love to do it, but I think you should send it out to other places – the Royal Court, for example.' So I did, and in 1998 I got a call from Graham Whybrow. I was watching the World Cup, having just finished my teacher training. And he said, 'We'd like to talk to you about your play.' And I was so excited, all I could think of to say was, 'Mexico are beating Germany!' Which was of absolutely no interest to Graham Whybrow at all. So we did a reading of it, and four months later my wife went to hospital to give birth to Oscar. And after a twenty-eight-hour labour, I walked in the door and five minutes later the phone rang, and it was the Royal Court saying they wanted to do my play.

And it went on Upstairs?

Well, it was when the Court were in the West End, so it went on at the Ambassadors, the Upper Circle.

Which was a slightly bigger space, so it was a good venue for it.

Yes, it was.

What a thing to happen – what a day!

Yes – a mate of mine turned up and said, 'Do you ever get the feeling you've just had the best day you'll ever have?'

So how did you get from that point to sitting in this office teaching the Young Writers' Programme?

After *Bluebird*, in 1998, Ian Rickson commissioned a new play from me. I didn't even know what a commission was, so I just said, 'Great!' I was working as a schoolteacher, and Oscar was in his first year of life, and I spent my days teaching, my afternoons marking and writing lessons, and my evenings playing with and bathing Oscar. So it took me a year to write my commissioned play, writing twenty minutes a night, absolutely fucking knackered. But I didn't have any choice. I could have said I wouldn't write at all, I'd only write in the summer holidays, but the notion of not writing seemed to me like an appalling betrayal of the privileged position

I'd got into. So I wrote this play, still very ignorant of what was going on in theatre. I couldn't really go to the theatre much because Oscar was really little and I was still teaching in the school. So – and this is really indicative of my naivety – I wrote a play about a pub three doors down from my house, this run-down East End pub, and four blokes spending an evening in this pub. And I didn't realise there was another play about four blokes . . . And then I went to see Conor McPherson's *The Weir* and thought – oh my God. Although it's very different from *The Weir*. So I gave them this play and they rejected it, and I was crestfallen. All this time writing it, and the commission. But they said the writing is beautiful, we really like the writing, but we don't really think you know how to create a drama. You're riffing, you're improvising, you're dependent on intuition rather than craft. So we can't really do this. But don't worry – we still believe in you, we still want to support you. A week later the phone rang, and it was Ian, and he said, 'Do you want to come in and have a chat? I don't want to tell you what it's about.' So I said okay. Then about twenty minutes later he rang again and said, 'I've changed my mind, I'll tell you. We want you to be our resident dramatist next year. So leave your teaching job, we'll get money for you, we'll commission another play and you can come and work in the theatre. You'll be surrounded by actors, and by directors, and you can learn your craft.'

That was good.

Yes – for him to take that leap of faith in a writer whose work he'd just rejected was extraordinary. So I spent the year 2000 as resident dramatist here. Sitting in script meetings with Max Stafford-Clark, Ian Rickson, Graham Whybrow, Stephen Jeffreys, James Macdonald, Dominic Cooke, as well as Elyse Dodgson and Katie Mitchell. I mean, I would never describe myself as an intellectual, but there've been rare times in my life where I've just thought, actually, Simon, you're just thick. I'd read three or four plays a week, get an opinion on them, and then go to one of these meetings and just feel cowed by how fucking clever those guys were. And then I kind of thought, well, I could go one or two ways with this. I could sink and just hide and stop going to meetings, or I could work my arse off and just try and get up to speed with that level of discussion. I remember talking to Graham, and to Stephen Jeffreys, and hungrily absorbing, learning, from them. And saying, 'What should I read, what should I read?' Graham gave me a reading list which was about sixty plays long, and I just read them, you know?

And you were writing as well?

Yes. One of the advantages of it was that I knew they were looking for a play for the Theatre Upstairs. So I was able to time the delivery of a play I was working on really cannily. A lot of the plays I read during my residency did one of three things with teenage or young characters. They would either have them offstage and referred to, or they would be onstage and silent, or they would be onstage and written in a way as if the writer had never met a teenager in their life. I'd just spent two and half years working with teenagers in Essex, and I decided I wanted to write a play that was about teenagers, but for adults – not a kids' play, but about kids. It struck me that there was a whole series of issues about young people, and representations of young people, that nobody was writing about, and I felt that I did need to write about. It struck me that we were living in a culture where for the first time adults were becoming scared of children, and there was something appalling about that, and something worth addressing. I was working with kids in Dagenham who were experiencing things aged twelve and thirteen that would floor me as an adult, and who managed to carry these experiences to school, and act as though they didn't happen. So I decided to write a play about them, and I wrote *Herons*, very quickly. And because I timed the delivery quite well they said, 'Yes, we'll do it.' So they did *Herons* in the Theatre Upstairs, and the job came up at the Young Writers' Programme, and it felt like the natural marriage of my two heads, being a teacher and being a writer.

So, you said to yourself, I'm going to write a play about teenagers – is that what happens when you start a play?

That's probably a simplification of the process.

What's it like writing a play? Is it always the same?

I was going to say I think every play is different, but I don't know that's true; seen from the outside I think it probably looks pretty similar. What I know for sure is that during the residency I changed my approach. When I wrote *Bluebird* and *Christmas* and all the nine student plays, I'd have a sense of place, and a sense of character, and I'd just start people talking. It would be like riffing, it's a musical analogy. I'd get pages and pages of dialogue, and when I thought I'd reached some kind of ending I'd go back through two hundred pages and sculpt the play out of it. But I changed my approach with *Herons*. I knew what I was good at was writing dialogue, that if you gave me a blank page I could just fill it with people talking. That was my strength. One of the analogies I use when I talk to students now is that all the muscles in the body are binary, and I think creativity is like that. When you make a work of art your intellect and your intuition have to work together. So, to pursue the analogy, you have to identify the muscle that is weak and work on it. And that's what I decided to do with *Herons*. I knew I could riff, depend on my instinct, but I thought, right, I'm going to work on the other part of the process, which is structuring and developing a play, crafting a story, 'wroughting' it rather than writing it.

So that's what you do now?

Since then, my process seems to be that I have an inkling that there's something there that in some way is interesting to me. So for the past six months, since the suicide of Corporal David Atkinson, I've had a sense that there's something interesting about soldiers. I've got a suspicion about it. So what I will tend to do is just sit on it for a while, not do anything about it, and then maybe after a while start researching. Go online, go to the library, maybe try and interview a few people. This morning I met a historian at Birkbeck College, a military historian who specialises in the history of killing. I went to talk to her about soldiers. But at the same time something I'm very big on is reading plays – I read a lot of plays. So for *Port*, which was staged at the Royal Exchange, I read plays by Robert Holman, for example, and for *Country Music* I read plays by Peter Gill, and by Franz Xavier Kroetz, the German writer, before I wrote a word.

Now most people would think that was a fantastically bad idea, wouldn't they?

A lot of people would, but a lot of people wouldn't. I think what happens is it gets filtered through my own perspective. When I wrote *On the Shore of the Wide World*, at the National Studio, I'd spent the month before that reading as many Eugene O'Neill plays as I could get my hands on. Just soaking up Eugene O'Neill. And on my first day at the Studio, I knew I wanted to write a big play about life in contemporary Stockport, so I got my desk, which was in a room a bit like this, and I sat down and I read Peter Gill's *Cardiff East*. But if you see the play, it's about a million miles away from either O'Neill or *Cardiff East*. It's my way of focusing, getting the structure.

Well, you're the first of all the writers I've spoken to who's said anything like that.

For the play I'm working on now, I've read over the past few weeks five or six of Gregory Motton's translations of Strindberg plays, and five or six plays by John Osborne. So in this play, if it ever manages to materialise, there'll be a tiny little grain of Strindberg and Osborne somewhere. I watch a lot of films, I go to a lot of galleries, I read a lot of novels and short stories; I read poems and listen to music. I identify which writer, which music is right for the play I want to write. Which pictures I need to see. Which films I need to watch. And I just absorb it, and make notes. And this will be a period that will last about six, seven, eight months. I went to a workshop by a Russian director when I was on my residency, and he explained how he chooses the plays he's going to direct. He said he asks two questions of them: 'What does this play say about my relationship to my world?' and 'What does it say about my relationship to myself?' When I'm developing a notion for a story I think about that a lot. What does this story say about the world, and what does it say about me? A good play for me should be driven by those questions. Then I do a lot of writing exercises, developing character. And then I plan – scene by scene, beat by beat. The final thing is writing the dialogue, and on the back of eight months' preliminary work, that might take just a few days. *Country Music* I wrote in four days, and *On the Shore of the Wide World*, a two-and-a-half-hour play, I wrote in three weeks.

As a teacher here, do you have any notion of what a Royal Court play is?

I get asked that all the time by students here. And what's exciting about this theatre is that I think the work your father did is still valid in defining what a Royal Court play is. It's instrumental and integral to the work of the place – the phrase he had of a play being challenging in either form or content. That letter that he wrote in 1954, the funding application letter, I read to every group of students that I teach. Kevin Elyot can be challenging in either form or content, as well as Leo Butler. Martin Crimp is, as much as Richard Bean. They're wildly different writers – they're not all smack-and-sodomy plays – but there's this sense of transgression in some way.

And what about your own work? Can you see any recurring themes, or does that strike you as an undergraduate kind of question?

Well, Methuen are doing a *Plays One*, which is lovely, and what that means is that I've just re-read four of my own plays this week. And yes, there is part of me that thinks that question is for the undergraduates to answer, not because I'm precious about it, but because in some sense I don't feel that I have a privileged authorial answer – it's just as impressionistic as everybody else's. What I did notice in reading the plays all in one go is that there are a lot of lines that recur, quite accidentally, and there are a lot of images and stories that recur. I think I'm drawn to stories of flight, to people trying to get out. I write about characters who carry the burden of the past around with them. So in *Bluebird* it was what this taxi driver had done six years before, in *Herons* it was the rape and murder of a teenager a year earlier, and in *Country Music* it was this character's whole past that he carries with him. And also – and this can be quite controversial here at the Court – I think in my plays there's a sort of spirit of redemption that I suspect a lot of people here think is sentimental. I really want to write with my guts – that's the non-analytical answer. I have a tremendous faith in humanity. I want to write plays that people who are non-academic, non-theatre, can come to and be changed by. I don't want to write for a theatre audience. I'm not bothered if my plays aren't learned, or ironic. I want to write plays that have heart, and passion, and guts – I don't know if I succeed, but that's what I want to do!

David Storey

Strangely enough I had never met David Storey before I went to interview him in his house in Camden Town in December 2004. Our paths must have crossed many times since 1963, when my mother designed the costumes for Lindsay Anderson's film of his novel *This Sporting Life*. His glorious period at the Royal Court had coincided exactly with my own disappearance from London, so I had not seen any of those celebrated plays when they were first performed. I'd seen him at Jocelyn Herbert's eightieth birthday party, where he had made a speech, but we had not spoken then or at any other time. But it became clear, as soon as I started to talk and think about writers and the process of writing, that David Storey was the writer *par excellence*, the legendary creative artist, who would sit down with a pen and paper and produce a play from nowhere, with no foreknowledge of what would come out. I was rather nervous, and in awe of the fact that I was finally going to meet someone equally talented as a painter, a novelist and a playwright, someone said to have such an unerring nose for good new writing, and someone so loved and admired by all who knew him. But I needn't have worried. He was kind, gentle and charming, and answered all my questions willingly though he must have been asked most of them many times before.

I know you've written about the first time you went to see a play. This was when your elder brother took you to see Hamlet, *wasn't it?*

Yes.

How old were you?

I was nine. We lived in Wakefield, and we took a bus to Leeds and saw *Hamlet* at the Grand Theatre.

And you weren't impressed.

All I remember is that there was a set, a row of arches made of canvas, and one of the characters was searching for another one along this row. But the whole audience could see the object of his search, clearly visible, downstage, reading a book. I was irritated by the pretence of it – it seemed absurd. The most interesting part of the evening was when we set off to walk home, having missed the last bus, and met two girls who had hastily got out of a car in which they had accepted a lift. We all walked home together through the night, with my brother carrying me on his back for part of the way, and found that my parents had reported us to the police as missing.

So how did it happen that you became a writer?

I had a Damascene experience at school. I was sitting in a French class listening to a poem by Verlaine and was mentally translating it into English when suddenly I had a vision of a straight railway line, with all the boys on a train going down it to set destinations – work, marriage, children, death. At the end of the line was a board with 'Death' written on it. I thought, 'I am not going down the line. I am going to be a painter and a writer.' I had been offered a place at university, but I told my father I wanted to go to art school. My father said no – he hadn't been down the mine all his life for his son to go off and be a painter. I could do that on a Sunday afternoon. To earn money I signed up as a player for Leeds Rugby League Club. But Leeds had a rule that you had to live within twenty-five miles of the club. To go to the Slade in London I would be in breach of the contract. I asked Leeds to give me time off, and they agreed to let me go. I continued to play football but went up for weekends, which was very uncomfortable, because in Leeds they thought I was a sort of homosexual aesthete, and had no place there, whereas in London I was seen as a sort of muddy oaf. It was only somewhere about Peterborough that I felt I was totally integrated as a human being. It was that division between those two that prompted me, even more, to write.

And This Sporting Life *came out of the experience of the football.*

Yes – it was about the seventh novel I'd written.

But the first to be published?

Yes. But it was rejected for many years. It was rejected fifteen times by publishers before it was taken – the result of that was that I went back to the first novel I'd written, in Wakefield, before coming to London, and rewrote it in three weeks, and they accepted it – the first novel I'd written, or attempted to write.

How long after This Sporting Life *was published did you meet Lindsay and start working on the film of it?*

I reneged on my football contract after I finished at the Slade, and had to pay back so much money, and I didn't play again. For four years I worked as a supply teacher in London.

And that was when you wrote the first play?

When I was schoolteaching I worked in seventeen different schools. At one school, in King's Cross, I was so depressed from the novels being rejected, I thought, perhaps I'm really a playwright. So one half-term, over three days, I wrote a play about a teacher cracking up. And then I didn't do anything about it. The year *This Sporting Life* was published, 1960, I met Lindsay Anderson, and he said, 'Have you ever written plays?' I'd been invited to write the screenplay. Lindsay had never directed a feature film before, and the producer, Karel Reisz, had never produced one, and the principal actor, Richard Harris, had never been a principal actor before, and the author had never written a screenplay. It was a bit of a nightmare for all of us. I told Lindsay I'd written a play, and I typed it out, and he gave it to George Devine at the Royal Court. It was suggested we should do it at the same time as the film, with Richard Harris. But Richard kept slipping away, eluding being pinned down to dates, with the net result that it wasn't done. So I wrote the screenplay of the film, and published further novels, and then about 1966, six or seven years after I'd given the play in at the Court, a young man wrote from the Traverse Theatre in Edinburgh saying he used to be an assistant at the Court, several years ago, and one day he'd taken down a play from a shelf, covered in dust, and he'd read it, and he said, 'If it's never been done, perhaps you wouldn't mind if we did it at the Traverse in Edinburgh.' This was the play about the schoolteacher, which was then called *To Die with the Philistines* – it was a rather tragic play at that time. I was so stimulated by this that I rewrote it, called it *The Restoration of Arnold Middleton*, and changed the ending.

Did he ask you to change the ending, or did you just think, oh, the ending needs changing?

I felt in an up period rather than a down period, so I felt, make it more positive . . . and it was then done at the Traverse. Just by chance a young assistant at the Court called Bob Kidd was on holiday in Scotland, because his family lived in Glasgow. He saw the last night of this play, and recommended it to Bill Gaskill. And they decided to do it. It was written in 1958 and was done about ten years later, in a short season of four writers. There was one by Donald Howarth – Joe Orton was one of them – I can't remember who the other one was. But it was a season of four plays, each to run for two weeks, though Donald Howarth very generously gave us one of his weeks. It was so lavishly praised, it transferred to the West End, and then it won the *Evening Standard* promising playwright award.

So did you think, oh, right, I'm going to write plays now? Was there some moment? When I ask people why they write plays, not novels, they sometimes say, rather disappointingly, 'Well, because I'm good at dialogue and I don't think I'd be any good at writing consecutive prose.' But in your case that's clearly not the answer, because you were a novelist already, and then having had that first success as a playwright, you went on and wrote a lot of plays very quickly.

I was excited by seeing the play at the Court. I think I was excited visually, because I also had been painting at the Slade and could quite easily have continued that career. I was interested in creating three-dimensional paintings, almost like reliefs, and seeing that play at the Court, and the three dimensions – going across, and in and out – was an invigorating experience and tied up with much that I had been doing. And I sat down and wrote five plays in no time at all. I'd also got stuck with a novel, so it was a welcome relief from struggling with that.

And you are somebody, I understand, who writes plays incredibly quickly.

All of them were written quickly. I think the first play I wrote was *The Contractor*, about erecting a marquee, which took me five days, and then I wrote *In Celebration*, which took three days, and then I wrote *Home*, which took two. I wrote two other plays, which were never produced because I didn't think they were any good.

You say it took three days – did you have any idea when you started where it was going? Did you have a sort of image of the finished product, or did you just start and see where it went?

I started with a first line, and, 'Let's see what happens.'

And every time that's what you did?

Plays that I've prepared beforehand, planning the structure, have always been no good. They turn out to be illustrations of a theme rather than organic experiences. The only ones that really work have been the ones that have started with a first line, when I don't know what's going to happen in the second. *Home*, for instance, started from the end of *The Contractor*, which ends with a bare stage with a white metalwork table. I thought, that's very much the setting of the beginning of a play rather than the end, and so I sat down and wrote, 'There's a white metalwork table on the stage.' And then I thought, there must be a chair there, perhaps two chairs, and somebody has to come and sit down on one of them. Somebody does, and then another person has to come and sit on the other. And until halfway through the first act of that play I thought they were sitting in a hotel, or a country mansion, and then I realised they were in a lunatic asylum.

I was interested when I saw it in Liverpool recently, because I knew the play, and I wondered how many of the audience did. It's a different kind of experience if you know. People were roaring with laughter all the way through, especially in the first act, and I was . . . well, I found it all rather moving. But where do the ideas come from?

They come out of the mist, as it were. I remember with *The Changing Room*, which I wrote later on, about a football team – I had been watching *The Contractor*, in the West End, one Saturday night, with a full audience. It was the second performance, there'd been a matinee. I'd been sitting in the green room with the actors, and I went to the back of the stalls and watched them come on and do the play, and suddenly had the idea of writing a play called *The Green Room*, about actors. But I thought, that's probably been written about before, and then I realised it would work very well with a rugby league team, if you had a changing room. That in a sense was a sort of preconception, because the title came first – I thought, *The Changing Room* because it was a changing room, but also, 'the changing *room*', because it is a room that changes, as people come into it and go out again.

Some playwrights would say that's real writing, that's what writing's supposed to be like. But many don't approach writing like that at all. Peter Gill, for instance, says he starts with language – that he'll have snippets of language and he'll only much later see how they form something. Other writers do masses of research. Do you think it's because you are a visual artist, perhaps, that the plays are more than just linear?

They feel like animated paintings – that's the experience I have when I'm writing them.

And you can see that with the great set-piece ones, with the marquee going up and coming down, or the changing room with people flowing in and out. But Home *is orchestrated in a different way – it's on a smaller scale, but you still have the sense of people coming and going, interacting and passing.*

Yes.

Looking at the plays as a body of work, could you say there's something in particular you're interested in exploring, or that there's a continuity between them, some recurring idea or theme, or is it just organic?

It seems to come out of that first line, which captures my imagination, and I follow it through.

You use language very precisely, and you have all these little bits of poetry.

I don't know . . .

The other thing I feel when I read them is a sort of sadness. Do you think that's there?

I think a sense of loss is characteristic. It's characteristic of the novels as well. They're all autumnal plays in a curious way, about life ending.

I liked the last one Ralph Richardson did, Early Days. *You could make such a dreary play out of that, and it was wonderful.*

That is the only play I've written for an actor, and it was a mistake, really, because when you're writing the play you can visualise the actor doing certain things and so you don't write them in, you leave them there for him to do.

Above all you worked with Lindsay Anderson, but with other directors as well – Anthony Page, for instance. Your relationship with Lindsay was one of the great partnerships.

It was rather a mystical experience, because he made his first films at the top of the housing estate where I lived in Wakefield. He made five documentaries there, and his first rushes were shown in the cinema at the end of our road. When he made a film about the town itself there were several people in it I knew. So he'd been working in Wakefield when I was living there, but we were unknown to one another. It was quite by chance that the novel, *This Sporting Life*, fell into his hands as a director for his first feature film. So there was this very strange, almost symbiotic relationship.

He must have been older than you?

He was ten years older.

Was it disappointing working with other directors? Did you feel they never measured up?

It was different. I worked with a quite young director who's revived some of the plays recently, and that was quite different from working with Lindsay. With Lindsay much of the relationship was unspoken, and when we rehearsed together we very much communicated by looks, and gestures. We seemed to know what each other was thinking.

And was it the same with Jocelyn Herbert, who designed several of the plays? Do you think the three of you working together . . .

Yes – it all went on underneath, as it were, so there was a connection you couldn't rationalise in any way.

Can you say which of your plays you're most happy with? Which you like the best?

I see them all as rather different experiences.

And do you still write now?

Yes, I've published about three novels in the past five or six years – I seem to have got back into novels, you know.

What about the Royal Court? It's a while since you've had a play done there.

I think the ambience of the Royal Court changed, to a degree. My last three plays were done at the National. I'd prefer to have done them at the Court.

Did the Court actually not want them?

I can't remember the circumstances. But over several years the Court were antipathetic to the plays, whereas the National were keen, so they ended up there.

The National seems traditionally to do the work of established writers, whereas the Court seems to have a commitment to new writers.

Well, that's a sort of responsible brief, in one sense. I think each artistic director thinks they've got to have their own school of writing, you know?

I want to ask about the many years you were on the committee for the George Devine Award.

I resigned each year, because I thought I was too old and they should get younger people in, and then Jocelyn Herbert would ring up at the appropriate time and say, 'We can't get anyone in so could you do it just one more year?' And one more year stretched into lots of one more years. It was interesting because each year we received – strangely – about seventy plays, and I found it kept me in touch with what younger writers were doing. We never made any real mistakes.

When I first went back to this I wondered, how do people choose plays, anyway? Is there a set of rules that one is expected to apply? But of course it doesn't work like that.

I found it too easy, that was the problem – because I rather looked at a play like sipping a glass of wine, you don't need to drink the lot to tell if it's any good. A page or two will be sufficient.

Bill Gaskill said to me recently that George Devine would be astonished that the Court was still in existence, still claiming to do what he said they should do, back in 1956.

It's broadly a humanist tradition. I think that's what holds them all together. They've had a stab at political theatre from time to time.

Yes – though you get the feeling that no one there has ever liked it much.

There was that sense that the audience were there to be instructed. A puritan ethic, basically. But I think it burgeoned beyond that, and broke the seals, eventually. I know when the two knights did *Home* they were terribly anxious, because they saw it as a theatre where you instructed the audience, whereas they were brought up in the Edwardian theatre, where you were there to entertain. That in fact gave the performances a strange dynamic, because you had these two perceptions of theatre suddenly fuse into this kind of strange demonstration – and it worked in a very magical way.

Timberlake Wertenbaker

I was looking forward to meeting Timberlake Wertenbaker. I had read her plays and enjoyed them a great deal. Also I was curious to hear about her experiences of working with Max Stafford-Clark in the 1980s, a period at the Court about which I knew little, though I'd read Max's book, *Letters to George*, describing his experiences of directing George Farquhar's *The Recruiting Officer* (1706) and Timberlake's new play *Our Country's Good*. I went to visit her on a cold day at the end of January 2005 at her house in Haringey, and we had a civilised interview drinking Earl Grey in front of a log fire.

Can you remember the first time you went to the theatre?

Yes I can, actually, very well. The first thing I saw was *The King and I* – I don't remember where. It could have been in New York, it could have been in London. But the next play I saw, when I was ten, was Jean Genet's *Deathwatch*.

That was in France?

No, that was in New York. I lived in France initially, and then we went to New York. I was with my mother and I was very homesick for France. This *Deathwatch* was being performed in French, so my mother, who did know about Genet – I mean she wasn't uneducated – thought, well, I'll take my ten-year old daughter. Now I don't know if you know the play, but this was extreme Genet – three men in prison. I remember it very well, because I was fascinated by it, by these three men very close – it was a studio theatre – absolutely fascinated. And they were speaking French. And she says the whole audience looked at her, and looked at me, horrified.

Because she had a child with her.

In fact I think it's what made me a playwright. Or I think the combination of the musical and that, made me a playwright. But I remember it so clearly. And not understanding much of it.

What aspect of it struck you so powerfully?

It must have been something about the shock of it, and the immediacy of it, because I remember it so well. It was a black box, really. I don't think there was any scenery, and there were these three men standing there. I don't remember any violence, but they talked, and I must have understood that they were about to be killed, or whatever. I haven't looked at it since. But it was very powerful – much more powerful than films. Then, because I grew up in the Basque country, there was a lot of street theatre, probably because it was a Catholic country, a lot of processions, a lot of public performances. So, that's not exactly theatre, but . . .

Did you always like writing, even when you were a kid?

I did write, but I really didn't want to become a writer, partly because my parents were writers. I thought it was an awful thing to do. It had no romantic connection. So I wanted to be anything but, and they wanted me to be anything but. And I backed into it, really. That's all I can say. I had a typewriter as a child, but I kind of backed into it.

And the first things you wrote, were they plays?

No. I wrote a novel and, while I was still trying not to write, I spent a year looking after horses, so I wrote about that. I wrote this and that. I wrote odd short stories. But then I was in Greece, working with some friends on plays for children, and that's when I suddenly started to write. I had never thought of writing plays, and I do remember, because it was one of those moments, when I thought, this is what I like. Really, this fits in some way. And we put on a couple of tiny plays I wrote.

When was the first moment you thought, 'I'm a playwright'?

I never said to myself, 'I'm a playwright' – I'm not sure I do now. But having written those plays in Greece – I did some plays for children, and then I did a couple of plays for grown-ups – I thought, well, I'm going to give this a year and see if I can get some plays on in London. It was very instinctive. So I moved from Greece to London and started sending my plays around, and I was quite lucky because the Soho Poly picked one up very quickly. And then very soon after that the Royal Court appeared.

And by that time Max Stafford-Clark was artistic director?

Yes, I think he had just come in. And Rob Ritchie was literary manager – he was terribly influential. I think before that the Court had gone into a bit of a dip, and in fact it was Stuart Burge who brought in Rob. I think Max was on the verge of taking over. But Rob read every script, and he did see that it was time for some women writers. I was part of the Writers' Union, and there was a lot of bad feeling among women at that time, that they were being dismissed by the Court – I mean really bad feeling – and Rob just reversed this. He had studied under Trevor Griffiths, or he had studied Trevor Griffiths, and he was very politicised.

At the moment you came in, there was that great upsurge of women writers.

But I think it came from Rob taking the trouble to go and see plays written by women, instead of saying, 'Oh, I'm not going to see that, I'm not interested,' which had been the attitude before, it really had been. So Rob went to see a play reading I had done – it wasn't even a play, it was a play reading – and he started to encourage me. And what he did was very good. If anybody called, a small company, saying we're looking for a play, he would send my play out, and a couple of other people's – because they weren't ready, they were little one-act plays – so that's how it started.

So he nurtured you, really.

He did. He really did.

And what was the first play of yours that went on at the Court?

The first play was this rather strange hybrid thing, *Abel's Sister*. Because I was then asked, I can't think by whom, to help this writer who was disabled, and who had been on a writing course, to help her write a play. So I did everything I could to help her write a play, but in fact what she wrote were tiny little paragraphs. And her life was interesting, you know? Who she was was interesting. After a time I realised there was not going to be a play, so I wrote a play myself.

Using her material?

No, not even that. But using her. And trying to imitate her voice a little bit. And it was given a double by-line, but in fact it was completely my play.

I've seen that listed as being by you and someone else.

Yes – afterwards I felt slightly resentful because it was my first play and I had in fact completely written it. So the by-line was wrong.

275

And did Max direct that?

No, it was directed by Les Waters. It had Linda Bassett in the main part, and it did pretty well. And from that I think people began to get a bit interested in me. Then Danny Boyle commissioned *The Grace of Mary Traverse.* So that was it. And then I became the resident writer. This was early 1980s. Even 1984, 1985.

And what was it like being the resident writer?

Wonderful. I read scripts, and I sat in on script meetings, which I loved. I think in those days I had not a bad nose for a play – you have it or you don't – and I did, then. I wouldn't say I had it now. I felt I 'discovered' an Irish writer, Anne Devlin. I loved her work. I used to discuss, and express my opinion very strongly – it was very democratic. And, I don't know if it's like that now, but then there really was a Royal Court tradition. You said what you thought, it was very passionate, people argued. Nobody cared, I mean nobody was protecting themselves. So there was no fear from anybody. It was great fun, and it gave me a sense of being part of something. And Max was there at the time, and I got to know him a little.

And as resident writer you were also expected to write plays.

I had to write – *The Grace of Mary Traverse* came out of that. I was given some money.

And you didn't do that as what we think of as a Joint Stock project?

No, that was absolutely individual – doing my own research.

But then fairly soon after that you did Our Country's Good?

I think it was about two years after, or a year and a half.

Which was a Joint Stock project. I've read Max's book about the writing of that and the production of The Recruiting Officer. *I think that people often have the wrong idea about Joint Stock.*

They do. People have asked me questions about it. They say, 'What was it like writing collaboratively?' Well, you know, I was sitting in my room writing and it was as lonely as anything else.

Really it's just a form of research, isn't it?

Yes, and it's quicker, and I like it very much. Because if you're doing historical research, books are fine, but contemporary research, when you're

276

the interviewer, you influence people, and as a playwright, you don't want to influence. Therefore to have these actors doing the interviewing and then bringing it back, maybe with their own influence – it gives you a much broader canvas, and that's what I really like about it. You're not influencing the outcome of the interview. You don't know what's going to come, whereas if you're interviewing yourself you know what you want to come out, and it's bound to turn the interview in a certain way. And the thing about being a playwright is to be surprised, of course.

But whether you're doing that or you're working on your own, you are somebody who does a tremendous amount of research, aren't you?

Yes.

I was interested in your play The Love of the Nightingale. *Did that get good reviews?*

Mixed. I've never had good reviews. *Our Country's Good* probably got the best reviews, but even that wasn't . . .

Why do you think that is? Do you think your plays are too clever?

I think the critics just don't like what I do. I mean they like it retrospectively, they just don't like it on the night.

Because it's too intellectual? Or because it's too experimental?

I don't know – you'd have to ask them.

Because it's both of those things, isn't it?

But I also think my plays are quite emotional, and I don't think critics like to go with that emotion. There are many university theses I get sent about why I get the reviews I do – maybe it's because I'm not part of a group – I don't know.

Do you find it painful?

Very. I'm still not used to it. I think *Our Country's Good* was the exception. But I don't think it's my best play, by any means.

Is there one thing that you are exploring in all your plays?

I think they are about identity.

And female identity in particular?

Not all of them. Some of them are about female identity, *The Grace of Mary Traverse*, for instance. But some are about male identity. *Credible Witness*, the last play I had on at the Court, was about national identity, but it was still about identity. There are different things that interest me at different times, but I think they tend to come back to that. *Our Country's Good* is about identity as well, and who you are, and how society then impinges on this, or crushes it, or whatever. It's a public–private kind of thing.

Do you think that when you were writing those early plays in the 1980s, the ones that are collected in your Plays: One, *that women were the issue, and that you've moved on from that? Caryl Churchill was also writing about women's issues at the time. And Louise Page. It seems to have been a period when there was a great explosion of plays by and about women.*

I think it was. There were a lot of questions about what it meant to be a woman in that period, what women were capable of, and also – which was what interested me – what happened to women in history, when were they in history, or what happened to them either imaginatively, as in *The Grace of Mary Traverse*, or in other circumstances. When they became public beings, what happened to them?

Is the process of writing always the same for you? Is it easy? Is it difficult? What happens when you sit down to write a play?

It's very difficult. I do a lot of research, as we've said. Eventually I sit down and write it, and it's always very difficult.

Somewhere you said that an image will come first. Is that right?

Yes – it can be an image or a character or an idea – usually a character or an image.

You say you do a lot of research, but at what point do you know what the whole thing is going to look like, or where it's going? Do you have a sense of that before you start writing?

I have an intuition. With *The Grace of Mary Traverse*, I knew something about her path. I knew with *Our Country's Good* that it was about humanity, the human dimension of the theatre. I knew that very, very quickly. In fact I remember when I discussed the thing with Max, I said this is what the play is about. I knew it immediately, by a kind of intuition. I knew that *Credible Witness* was about national identity and whether you hold on to it or reject it, and what that means. And after that, once that's there, in the process of writing the play things change a lot, and there's always that chance that you may lose it. You just glimpse something, somewhere out there, and then it's very very difficult to get it right.

Is it a slow and struggling business?

Yes – it's very slow, it's very struggling, it's very difficult.

And you do a lot of rewriting?

I do a lot of rewriting. I think people write in different ways, but the way I write, between the first draft to the final draft you could hardly recognise it. And it's a problem, because sometimes I send in first drafts, and people say, well, this can't be the same person who wrote that. I know what's going to happen to it, but I'm not quite clear – I don't know what's on the page and what's still in my head. I'll go through about ten drafts, at least.

And is a lot of that cutting out and paring down?

Cutting out and paring down, following different characters throughout the play. Sometimes as you follow one character, you realise you've left another character behind. So you have to then rewrite the play and put yourself into that other character. And then rewrite the play again and follow yet another character.

Has a director ever helped with that process, or is it very lonely?

No, I think by the time the director gets it, the first draft really, it's very nice to have some input. I like the input of the director, which is usually – in the case of Max, for instance – to say, 'Look, I don't understand.' And sometimes it may just be the process of me saying, 'Well, this is what this scene is about.' Max was very good at saying, 'Well, it's not in the scene yet, it's still in your head. Get it into the scene.' I would say, this scene is about this, and he'd say, but I can't see it, it's not there. Then I would know, right, it's not there, so I'll rewrite, I'll find a way of writing the scene so it's there. That kind of thing. How to distinguish between what's on the page and what's still in the writer's head.

That's good. I don't think all writers are happy to be so collaborative.

No, but I think it also depends how people write. Some people write just one draft and say, that's it.

David Storey does. But I think he's the exception.

I don't know. I read that Pinter is like that – he starts on page one and finishes where it's finished.

But it doesn't mean that the final product is better or worse?

I think it just depends whether the writer is working on paper or whether the writer is working in their unconscious, or whether the unconscious is on the paper, which is what I think I do. I have to find the play through the process of writing it. I don't find it and then write it. And if somebody's there to help me find it, that's great, and if they're not, they're not. But if you get a director who's an editor, it's very rewarding. If you get a director who's meddling . . .

Would you say that in your experience Max Stafford-Clark has been the most satisfactory person to work with from that point of view?

Yes, and Peter Hall, whom I worked with recently on *Galileo's Daughter*. He was lovely to work with as well. He has great respect for writers and that beautiful sense of language. But Max was terrific on two plays and not so terrific on the third play we did together, *The Break of Day*, which everybody forgets about. So it can work and not work. And I think he was more interfering in some way in the third play. We weren't on the right wavelength and the production wasn't a happy one. I've had six plays on at the Court altogether. *Credible Witness* was the most recent. That was directed by a very young director called Sacha Wares.

How was it working with somebody young and new?

It was fine. What's most important is the relationship between the actors and the director, and it can be more difficult if the director is new.

If you're lucky with the director it can be wonderful, but if you're unlucky you can feel . . .

Betrayed, yes.

That must be painful.

It's very painful – very, very painful. And you see this happening too late and there's nothing you can do.

In a sense it's out of your hands, and that makes it worse, I suppose.

It makes it much worse. It's often a breakdown of trust between the actors and the director, and then the actors come to you, and then you're in this difficult position where either the director gets undermined or you have to pull away and let them get on with it, which is difficult.

Because they're making something of it which you don't think is right?

Yes, and then you have that tension, a lot of tension in rehearsals. And if the director gets on very well with you but not with the actors, it's no good.

Can you say, of all your plays, which one is your favourite, the one you're most satisfied with?

No, I really can't. It's always the last one you've written. I forget about them, anyway. And I'm more interested in the next play, that should be the one I most care about, really. I'm not that attached to them, the plays. I don't go around watching productions of them, as some writers do. In particular *Our Country's Good*, which was put on all over the world – I was invited all over the world and I never went. I just got on with the next play. It's done, really, and there's not much you can do. I missed a lot of travelling, although I did go out to Mongolia, which was wonderful. But I don't like seeing the same play again and again.

What are plays for, anyway? My father said plays should be disturbing – now the buzzword at the Court seems to be oppositional, which has some-thing to do with the fact that plays should make you think. Do all writers believe plays are meant to make you think?

No, writers write for all kinds of reasons. But I would agree with that def-inition – I think that's as much as a play can claim to do. As much and as little as a play can claim to do. I always think of it as just shifting people slightly, you know?

Challenging their assumptions?

Yes, something like that. Making them a little bit uncomfortable. Not too uncomfortable, because then they won't follow the play, but just a bit uncomfortable so that they question – and I think a lot of plays may try to do that and fail. A lot of plays that call themselves political are not poli-tical. They just regurgitate what's happening in political events. All this thing now about the renaissance of political theatre – I'm quite sceptical.

Because it's like getting on a soapbox?

And it's not doing it. I mean, to be uncomfortable is something quite dif-ferent. And I think the Royal Court has had a tradition of that – I don't know if it still has it.

Do you think there is a notional idea somewhere of a Royal Court play? Challenging one's preconceptions – that it's doing something useful?

Yes. Of course the Court always reflects its artistic director, so what an artistic director finds challenging might not be very challenging to an audience, or the opposite – what they find challenging is so challenging to the audience that it's too much. I think the ideal of the Royal Court is that; and even if you have reservations, you know, it's always led the way into perceiving what would be challenging and what moves forward. And when the Royal Court doesn't do that, it's failing in what it's supposed to do. And I don't think it's shock, violence, blood and gore, although that can be part of it. I think it's very subtle. That thing of making people think, just shift a little bit.

Yes, I think that's good. I mean, if you said to somebody rather frivolously, 'What's a Royal Court play?' they'd probably say, 'Oh, social realism, gritty realism,' but that's not true.

No – it probably was, when social realism was disturbing. But it's not any more. And what is disturbing now is of course the big question. And the Court, in the last few years, hasn't quite found it.

I think that's what started me puzzling about it all, really – what is actually going on here? You had all that stuff in the 1990s, in-yer-face theatre, but that's not happening any more, and I would have a job putting my finger on exactly what is. Time will tell, perhaps.

Time will tell. If I think back to the plays I did, The Grace of Mary Traverse was very disturbing, because it was disturbing to have a woman like that on stage, and a woman writer, but that changes as well. And when Caryl did her *Cloud Nine*, that was uncomfortable. I think it's the big question, what's uncomfortable now? And I don't think the theatre has found the answer. Or if it's found it, it's not recognised it yet.

Arnold Wesker

Chicken Soup with Barley 1958
Roots 1959
I'm Talking about Jerusalem 1960
  (these three plays forming
  'The Wesker Trilogy')

The Kitchen 1961
Chips with Everything 1962
Their Very Own and Golden City
  1966
The Old Ones 1972

I think I met Arnold on the first Aldermaston March in 1958, but it was at Bill Gaskill's Writers' Group and the various parties associated with it, and on a trip to Bristol with Ann Jellicoe and Keith Johnstone to see some long-forgotten play, that I got to know him a little better. I also remember going, with my parents, to have dinner at his flat in Clapton. His mother was there and I was struck with the brightness of her eyes – they really shone, as Arnold's did and still do. I've seen him at the Court over the years, and I was happy to be going to talk to him, at his wife Dusty's house in Hove, in early December 2004. But I was also apprehensive, because Arnold has written a great deal about his life and work, and I didn't want to be thrashing over old ground. Then I jumped in at the deep end by raising a most sensitive issue.

I read your Shylock *and I think, this is an interesting, profound play and it was* not *done at the Court. I wonder why?*

That's my *cause célèbre* – I've been fighting to get it done on the London stage. It was done at Birmingham, and I did a workshop production at the Riverside, and it's been done in many other countries, but there is a resistance to it on the major stage. Even on the rep stage, no one will pick it up.

Writers like Stoppard and Frayn have gone on to become the grand names of English theatre. Why does that happen to some and not to others? I don't think it's because their plays are better, I think it's something else.

Well yes, it is something else, and it would be fascinating to try and identify it. It is to do with changing fashions, and one has to ask the question, was I a fashion or was I a playwright, and does that mean Stoppard was never a fashion but was a playwright? And is that why his work keeps getting done? Because he can't put a foot wrong, and David Hare can't put a foot wrong, and Pinter can't put a foot wrong. I will have, of course, all sorts of explanations, which are partly self-defensive and partly true and partly . . . I don't know. I've always been politically incorrect. The plays have always been different from what was expected. And Jews are not very popular these days because of the Middle East crisis.

You have written in your autobiography that you felt that my father didn't like the trilogy.

I don't know that he didn't like it, but he didn't understand it. That Jewish East End milieu was very, very alien to him. But the great thing about George was that he was prepared to admit he might not be right. And this is a modesty, a humility, that doesn't pervade among major directors today. So Nick Hytner turns down *Shylock*, saying, 'I don't believe in the relationship between Shylock and Antonio,' which is crazy, because for me that relationship is almost the strongest thing in the whole play. That extraordinary friendship between the two.

I quite agree – I think it's powerful.

So he's using it as an excuse. We'll never get to the bottom of it because it's so complex. And I mean – this might be strange for you – Hytner's Jewish, and there is a Jewish mentality, especially as you get on in the arts, that says, 'I'm not going to be seen favouring Jewish writers or Jewish scenes,' on the one hand, and on the other he says that he wants to get involved with the whole debate over the Middle East crisis, but he doesn't, because if you wanted to do that, you would put on *Shylock* as one side of an argument. I can remember there was one director who said the great thing about *Shylock* is that it presents different evidence, another set of evidence on the character and situation. So – I don't know.

One thing I thought I might find out when I started this project was what a Royal Court play is. I'm now beginning to realise that was naive. But the Court in its earliest incarnation is associated with social realism, isn't it? And really it was you, and Chicken Soup with Barley, *that started it off, wasn't it? The first working-class play?*

I wanted to affect people, certainly. One of my plays is called *Annie Wobbler* – it's one of a cycle of plays about one woman. I'd always sworn to myself that I'd never write a play about a writer. Nearly all first novels are about writers – *How Green Was My Valley*, you know. But I did. *Annie Wobbler* is in three parts, and the third part is about a novelist. She becomes successful with her fourth novel, and she's been interviewed silly. She's about to be interviewed by three more journalists, and she's rehearsing, and she thinks she's going to send them up. So first she rehearses being a very modest writer: 'It's the wind that blows through me, I have nothing to do with what I write.' In the second rehearsal she decides to try arrogance: 'I feel like the fucking queen. I know I can sit at those dinner tables and be taken notice of. I write for money, fame and power.' And in the third one, she is the real writer feeling vulnerable and third-rate, and that one day she is going to be found out. They're all asked the same questions, and one of the questions is, 'Why do you write?' And what she says is also true of me: 'I think I write because I want to affect other people the way the writers I read affected me.'

She's writing novels, you're writing plays. I know you want to affect people the way you were affected, but why do so in a play? Why not do it in a novel or an essay or a poem? What is it about plays particularly?

I have an answer for that. It's an answer I've given many times, though I don't know if it's true. But the world makes an impact on artists in different ways. It makes an impact on the painter in colours and shapes, with the sculptor it's solid form, and so on. And the world makes its impact on me in the way people talk to each other. The dynamic of dialogue is what interests me, perhaps because I came from a talking family. I've just finished writing my first novel, and I know what the critics are going to say about it. They'll say, 'You can tell this novel was written by a playwright because there's so much dialogue in it.' And it's true, I'm happiest in the novel when I'm writing dialogue and not when I'm writing prose. The other answer is that I don't really know how the English language is constructed. I don't know the parts of grammar. When I write prose, I keep my fingers crossed that I'm doing it the right way. I've learned over the years about the structure of the English language and prose form, and I look back now over my early journalism and I think, how on earth did those editors let this through? It's illiterate.

So can you remember your first experience of theatre?

The cinema. We couldn't afford theatre, so we went to the cinema. I nagged to go to the movies every day, and I suppose I was allowed, three times a week, to go to the Odeon cinema at the bottom of the road in the East End. I just went to movies, and I learned about drama. So I wrote a play that spanned twenty years because I knew you could span twenty years in drama, I'd seen it on the movies. I wrote a play that I didn't think was innovative – *The Kitchen* – having people work on stage. That didn't seem to me an innovation, because a) it was my experience, and b) I'd seen it on the movies.

And you were at film school when you wrote it, weren't you?

Yes.

But you must have been to the theatre by the time you started writing plays – because you were acting, as well.

As an amateur, yes. I wanted to be an actor.

And fate stepped in, and wouldn't let you?

No, but I had this histrionic streak in me. I think I probably had it in real life as well. I acted roles in my relationships, so that was always there. I suppose that was my first experience of theatre, as an amateur actor. My cousins were in the Query Players, and I went to see them, and then I became involved in the group. Professionally, the first play I saw, my sister took me to, at the Lyric Hammersmith. It was a Sean O'Casey play, *Red Roses for Me*. And I didn't know what it was about, I didn't understand anything, and I can't remember being impressed by it. The only other play I can remember seeing was *Brand*, by Ibsen. So it was the movies, and the novel. All those novels that span generations – I'd love to see them come back – A. J. Cronin and Howard Spring. That's where I got my sense of drama from.

When you write a play, you've not only got to find a theatre to put it on, you've also got to find a director, actors, who will do it justice. And your experience was that John Dexter was your man, and Bill Gaskill was obviously not your man.

No, he wasn't. That's not to say Bill's a bad director. Just not the right director for me.

But he was out of sympathy with what you were doing. So in a sense you could say writing a play is a riskier enterprise than a novel, because you are dependent on others and not just yourself.

Very much so. But I don't think I decide to write plays or prose because of that. I mean the books of stories that I wrote were because the material touched me, and came in the shape of stories. And I've always wanted to write a novel, so I didn't write the novel because I was fed up with theatre, and all the vicissitudes of that, even though I might be.

But just because that's how the material presented itself?

Yes.

I have read that you've said you have no imagination. And you also say you've got no memory! So if you've got no imagination and no memory, where the hell does all this stuff come from?

Well, the memory problem is solved because I make notes all the time. I've slightly changed from saying I have no imagination to saying I have no powers of invention. Which is different.

Because even if you've got a lot of material, you've got to do something with it?

Yes, you've got to imaginatively assemble it, and you've got to shape it. But I have difficulty in inventing. So one of the problems of writing this novel is that I couldn't invent a plot. So that's what I mean, a power of invention is what I haven't got. And memory is very selective.

All your early plays are founded on your own experience, whatever you made of it. You selected, you shaped. So they are about experiences that you've had. But they're not just about that, are they?

No. The other thing I say is that I never choose material that isn't more than itself. So that, for example, I've worked at lots of jobs, so why did I choose the kitchen to write a play about? Because it presented itself as a metaphor. That's something else that I say – if I have any talent, it's for identifying the metaphors life throws up to explain itself. So it presented me with the kitchen, which seemed to me to explain something about life. *Chicken Soup with Barley* is about something that has happened since time immemorial, the lost paradise, the failed ideal, the broken dream. I think I wouldn't have written about that if I hadn't realised that it was more than itself. Then *Roots* is about self-discovery.

I watched you interviewed by David Edgar on an old video, where he was trying to make you say that you were a political writer and you were saying you weren't. You don't like to be called a political writer?

No, because that suggests you start with ideas, and then you look around for characters to clothe them, and I don't. I start with people, but what animates me, what appeals to me, are people who are animated by ideas. But they have to be people to begin with. Tom Stoppard works the other way. He declares, 'I start off with an idea, and then think of the people with whom to explore that idea.'

This is one of the things that fascinates me, how the process takes place. Everyone I've spoken to has said something different. And I wonder if it's different every time. A long time ago you said you always wrote in longhand – is that still the case?

Yes. I prefer longhand because – well, I like looking at longhand. I like looking at the writing and then just saying, well, I've got to take it down to there. I mean, it's just fascinating visually.

And is it always the same, or could you look back over your plays and say, this one came just like that, but this one was a struggle?

Oh yes. *Chicken Soup* came very quickly. *Their Very Own and Golden City* took much longer. I went into eleven drafts. *Shylock* took a long time too. *Caritas*, which I thought would take ages, happened in a very strange period, when I was in my cottage in Wales. In the old days Dusty would take me to Wales and dump me there for two, four, six weeks. I'd have done preparation in London and I went there to break the back of it, or I'd do my reading there, research, and then come back to London and start the writing. But with *Caritas* I'd done my research over six months.

Because it was based on a true and frightening story?

Yes, the anchoress, who was walled up. So I'd read about Catholic mysticism, and anchoresses and anchorites, and their rituals and so on, and when I went to Wales it was a period when I used to do a number of things while I was there. I did a lot of gardening, I read more than I'd read in London, I drew, and I'd go for walks. I don't do any of that now – I just write! Oh, and the other thing I did was – this is the point of the story – I dieted. And I'd lose weight. On this occasion I dieted so severely that I was high. And I wrote *Caritas* in something like ten days. But not only *Caritas* (we're talking about first drafts) – as soon as I'd finished that, there'd been at the back of my mind an original film script, which I wrote, again, in a matter of days, called *Lady Othello*. And these two works came out white hot, in a very short period.

Did it need a lot of reworking, or less than usual?

I can't remember. I'm sure I did rework, but I can't remember exactly, and the manuscript is in Texas.

There is a tradition that something that pours out like that might spring out fully formed, like Mozart or Wordsworth.

I think a lot of it has remained. But it would be fascinating to go over it again, now that it's all over – to go through the manuscript. One of the reasons I regret selling it all to Texas is that it's such a long way away.

If someone said we're going to burn all Wesker's manuscripts except one, which would be the one?

Like which of your eight records? It would be a toss-up between *Shylock* and *Love Letters on Blue Paper.*

So though the rest of the world is wedded to the early plays, you're not?

No, not at all. The later plays hold much more interest for me.

Do you look back on those early plays and say, 'Oh, I couldn't write that now, I wouldn't want to write that now'?

Well, it's interesting. Yes and no. Two things. One, in the mid- to late-1970s I was commissioned to write a film script of the trilogy. And I made a decision that I was not going to adapt the three plays. I was going to use the three plays as material for one work. So I ditched a lot of stuff that's in the trilogy, and I remembered other material that I wanted to put in. So it was a film script that was going over the same ground, the same material, but I completely rethought it. And that's a film that needs to be made and is waiting for someone to discover it. And so that's the material in the trilogy. And the novel I've just written, *Honey*, is about Beatie Bryant from *Roots*. But again I've shifted it. Speaking strictly chronologically, the novel should begin in something like 1961, 1962, and therefore be set in the 1960s. But I set it in the 1980s for some strange reason, not that I have a feeling for the 1980s, but that's how it worked out. But the story is that Beatie Bryant goes back to education. Because the question at the end of the play is, she's discovered herself, so what's she going to do now? She goes back to education, and gets her Os and her As and goes to Oxford. So the novel begins when she leaves Oxford.

But you don't look at the early plays and think, these are awful?

No, I don't. And I'm going to have a chance to see *Chicken Soup* again at the Nottingham Playhouse in April 2005.

Don't they keep getting revived?

No, not really. Terry Hands revived *The Four Seasons* at Mold last year, and it was an excellent production. And Watford revived *Roots*, and the National revived *Roots*, the National revived *Chips with Everything*.

Of the trilogy, Roots *has been the most popular?*

Yes, of the trilogy. But the most popular play of all is *The Kitchen*, all around the world. At this moment it's on in France, a production in Lyons, it was on in Paris last year, in Gothenburg last year, and it's been bought for Korea and Japan. Romania, Hungary and Poland want to try a three-country production of it, and Italy has bought the film rights, and commissioned me to write the film script.

Wow. But it has been made into a film already, hasn't it?

Yes – not a very good film.

Why do you think that play is so hugely liked?

I think it's because of the spectacle, and its great challenge to directors. But you know I've seen lots of productions all round the world, and nothing compares to Dexter's production, and Jocelyn's brilliant idea of just taking everything up and leaving a bare stage.

It was absolutely wonderful. One can never forget it. I read somewhere that because you'd written it when you were at film school, it had a kind of filmic quality.

Yes, but that wasn't because I was at film school. As I told you, I was influenced by cinema.

The Journalists, *which I was reading on the train this morning, is also challenging in form.*

It's *The Kitchen* twelve years later.

Ann Jellicoe and Keith Johnstone were saying in the early days, let's throw out all this old stuff, Shaw and Galsworthy and all these boring old people who just write speeches, and let's have action. I'm not saying your plays don't have action, but they are quite ideas-heavy and speech-heavy, aren't they?

Curiously, I was also among those first writers who said the theatre's a place for action. So there's *The Kitchen*, and demonstrations in *Chicken Soup*, and the coke-stealing scene, without any words, in *Chips*.

Yes, you precede someone such as David Storey, who puts up a tent on stage. You bridge those two things, actions and speeches.

I like long monologues. I do like people to get their teeth into something.

And if we dismiss the thought that your plays are political, would you say there is one overriding thing that interests you, in life, which all your plays enact in different ways?

I think there probably is, and it's a mixture of two things. One is that I hate the thought of a wasted life. It is only one life. And the thought that it's lost for some people, that they don't make the most of it, that opportunities are taken from them, or not offered them, that they haven't made the best use of themselves – that, I suppose, drives me. The other thing will come out very strongly in the novel, but there are hints of it in the plays. The title of a collection of essays I wrote is *Fears of Fragmentation*. And the fragmentation of life – I don't know what other word to use – fascinates me, preoccupies me. The need to make a whole is very prevalent. So for example in *Annie Wobbler*, there are these three characters, and the actress has to move to each character without leaving the stage. First there's an old washerwoman, Annie Wobbler, who was based on a char-lady who did for us in the East End. We lived in an attic, so we didn't really need much cleaning, but my mother took pity on her. So Annie Wobbler is one. The second is a student who's just got her degree and is dressing up for her first date, with a new power in her. And there's the novelist. And Annie Wobbler says, and I think she says it more than once, 'They drew me wrong. Need to rub me out and draw me again.' Something's not quite right with her, she knows. The student is looking at herself in the mirror, dressing up. And she's saying, 'Something's wrong here. The top part doesn't belong to the bottom part. It doesn't match, it's not a whole.' The novelist, when she's doing her third part, the real writer, full of fears, talks about poetry, and what it is that makes a line work. You take away one syllable and the line falls to pieces. And she quotes a line and subsequently a verse of a Hardy poem, taking something out, and she says, 'Well, it doesn't work, does it? It's not the same.' So this assembly of words, that magic assembly, as she calls it, is what she strives for. And the anchoress in *Caritas* is also looking to be whole. And in the novel the Beatie Bryant character is thinking, 'What can I do with my life?' Something is nagging at her, and in the end she decides that what she wants to do is create an encyclopedia of parts. All the parts that we don't know. There's something wrong with your eye: what's that thing, that black thing? And the thing around the black thing? You look up 'eye' and it's broken down into all its parts. You want to describe a church but you don't quite know how – what's that thing at the top of the column? There's a name for it – look up 'church' and all its parts are there. So she has this need to reveal what the parts of everything are. So those are the things that preoccupy me, I think. But lots of other things also preoccupy me, like love, and death, and family relationships. Apropos of what we've just been saying, there's a lecture I once gave, about the DNA of a play. How you break a play down into its parts. And I asked the question, what makes a work of literature last through time, and cross frontiers – what is it? It can't be the language, because the great French novelists, or the great Russian novelists, are translated into English and we read them and admire them in English. So what is it? And in an attempt to find out what the answer is, I broke down the play into its parts, and I then tried to identify what I think is the one element that will make the play cross frontiers and pass through time – and I think it's perception. The artist's perceptions of life are what touch us, really.

No matter what he's perceiving, it's how he perceives it?

How he perceives it, how he perceives what is experienced. Which is not to dismiss technique or style, but in a way that's what you expect from a writer, just as you expect a carpenter to know how to cut wood.

I think this is fundamental. Having to judge a hundred and fifty plays in six weeks for the George Devine Award, I started asking myself, 'What criteria am I using here?' And I didn't know the answer. In the end it has to be, it grabs me or it doesn't. And it isn't the technique, because you can say, technically this doesn't work, but something can be done about that. It's more than that. Something that sort of reaches out to you, and is difficult to pin down. But it must be the way the writer is viewing life.

That's right – yes – he's touched it in such a way that you recognise a truth in your own experience.

Either a truth that you've always known or perhaps a truth that is obviously true even if you hadn't ever realised it.

And they've identified it.

I'm interested to know what you think about the Royal Court today. They claim that it is still the same kind of theatre that it was when it first started. What do you think?

I think there's an absence of passion. That was the great thing about John Osborne – some people thought it was bile, but I think it was passion. And you know I rarely go to the theatre now and find myself at the edge of my seat. I don't know if you think passion is what made the Royal Court hum, in those early days.

I don't know yet, because though I saw everything that was on there, I saw it as a child, or a young person growing up. And now I'm trying to think what it was about, and what it's about now. And there does feel as if there's a difference, that's for sure. Recently someone at the Court said to me, 'Those plays from the fifties and sixties, you can criticise them here or there, but they are still the most powerful thing you can think of. Those early plays had something which we have lost.' Perhaps he was talking about passion.

Yes – and there are very few directors today like John Dexter. I mean, for all that one quarrelled with him, he had a passion and an enthusiasm – he could animate actors and really get them going.

Roy Williams

Lift Off 1999
Clubland 2001
Fallout 2003

I first met Roy Williams in the spring of 2004 when we were both on the committee of the George Devine Award. I interviewed him early on, but my recording equipment let me down and the interview was unusable. So in the end he was the last person I talked to, in the Royal Court balcony bar, in September 2005. It was interesting to talk to him again, because I was able to get him to enlarge on some of the things he'd said before.

In our first interview, you told me that when you were at primary school some man turned up in a dress and sang songs with a guitar.

Yes, that's one of my earliest theatrical moments. I don't know how old I was – I must have been about seven, eight.

And was that Theatre in Education?

Yes.

It's such a worthy cause, and yet it seems to have more or less disappeared now.

I think it has. When I started acting in it, I think it was near to ebbing away. Active TIE companies now are very thin on the ground. That's a factor of the last Tory government, they just sort of got rid of them. It was a policy. I think they were accused of being too subversive – too left-wing and militant.

Ayub Khan Din said these actors turned up at school in Salford every year in clogs, and sang about the Industrial Revolution and everyone thought it was boring. So you think, what a pity, because it was a great opportunity.

Well, for me it was fun. Although we were still at school, it seemed like a day off from the usual routine. And whenever the van would pull up, we were curious who they were – these strangers coming to our school.

295

But what about plays, actual plays? Because you decided at some point to be an actor, didn't you? What age were you?

I was about seventeen, eighteen. Events sort of led me there.

What events were those?

Well, I knew I liked writing, and even by then I had an interest in theatre. And I think my brother was at college, and he gave me some flyers about a drama course at a particular college. So I thought, why not?

You must have encountered drama of a slightly more sophisticated kind in between the man in the dress and your decision to act!

Yes. I think what really did it for me was when I was eleven, and I was doing very badly at school. My mother arranged for me to have a private tutor who I would go and see every Saturday until my grades picked up. But he also ran his own theatre company, and he was a writer and director on the side.

That was a bit of fate, wasn't it?

Yes, it was. Just right place, right time, the right moment for me.

So did you look at plays with him, talk about plays?

Not at first. Whenever he couldn't do a full session with me on a Saturday because he had to work with his actors, I would tag along. And I would watch them act, rehearse, and sometimes I read in for an actor who wasn't there that day, or who was late. I'd join in the warm-ups, the vocal warm-ups, everything. And I just thought, this is the way to spend a Saturday morning – I liked that. I started reading scripts he was working on, which got me interested in plays. And at the time, at school, we were doing the usual kind of English, and learning about Shakespeare, and that made me appreciate his work more. So that was an influence.

Can you remember when you went to your first professional production?

Oh yes. I think my first play – and this is really going back – was at the Commonwealth Institute. They used to have a theatre, and the company my tutor worked for did a lot of plays there.

When I was a kid we used to be taken there, and see little films and things – it was brilliant. I learned a lot from that about the rest of the world.

When I was a teenager, with my mates, if we didn't have anything to do we'd just go there.

Was that the part of London you came from?

Yes – Holland Park, Notting Hill sort of area.

So then you acted professionally?

For a brief time, about two years.

And did you feel comfortable with it?

No, I never did.

You didn't feel you were really an actor?

That's the truth – I never did. It took me a bit of time to realise it, but I never felt I was. It felt like a chore. I enjoyed it, funnily enough, before I went professional, when I was doing youth theatre. That was when I really enjoyed it. But when I became professional I started to experience the hard-knock lives that actors have, and I just felt, no, this is not for me. It wasn't only the money side, I had stopped enjoying it. I mean the audition process and so on – I couldn't bear it, and I wanted to be on the other side of the table.

You were already thinking of writing?

I still wanted to be in the business, but on the other side. I wanted to be more in control.

Had you started writing at that time?

Not seriously, no. Just – more like, dialogue, and short stories.

You enjoyed the process of putting words on the page.

I enjoyed the process. I felt more at home.

So what got you thinking, 'I'm going to be a playwright now'?

I think it was during my acting time – I had a long period of unemployment, was out of work for about a year, and it just came to a stage . . . It helped me to make my final decision to give up acting because I thought, it's not going anywhere and I'm not doing anything with my life. So I had to think back to what I always liked, and that was writing. So I thought, why don't I get off my arse and try writing a play? And then I applied for a three-year degree course in playwriting at Rose Bruford.

Oh, that's right. Leo Butler was also on that course.

He was the year below me. Well, if I backtrack a little – when I was with the young people's theatre company, I was working with a couple of writers on their plays – Noel Greig and Lin Coghlan – and I just kind of felt, I want to do what you're doing. So working with them and being in their plays made me feel, I want to be where you are now.

Rose Bruford – you stuck it out for the three years? Because Leo didn't, I think he left. He was very dissatisfied with it.

It was a badly run course. We made a lot of complaints about how the course was set up. It was poorly handled, and it disbanded not long after we left. The college was in a bit of a mess as well. Staff were coming and going – the principal was fired while we were there, and a new one was brought in.

But nevertheless you must have felt that you got something from it.

Yes, I think we all felt, 'Let's just knuckle down and get our degree and get out of here.' You know, get what we can out of it.

Presumably by the end you had written a certain amount. Did you have to write a full-length play?

Yes, in our final year. That was part of our degree. It got produced at Stratford East. A tutor at the college, Gilly Fraser, who's also a writer – she had to mark it, but she suggested I should send it to new writing theatres. So I did – I sent it here, and to Hampstead Theatre, and to Theatre Royal, Stratford East. That was ten years ago.

And what was the response from the Royal Court?

They wanted to meet me. And so did Hampstead and Stratford East. It was pretty overwhelming, the interest in my very first play – these three companies all wanting to meet me. I didn't think the play was for the Royal Court, but they said, 'We like your writing, we want to commission you to write a play. We want you as part of our family.'

The first play that was done here was –

Lift Off. That was 1999.

So it took several years to get the Royal Court play staged?

Yes – well, the Stratford East one was 1996, and they commissioned me to write a second play for them, which took about two years to write. But by that time the commission got switched. They couldn't put it on any more because the theatre was closing for rebuilding, so the Tricycle picked it up, and they produced it in 1998. But during that time I was also trying to write a play for here.

And did Lift Off *go straight onto the main stage?*

No, it was done Upstairs. Indhu Rubasingham directed it, who'd directed my very first play, *The No Boys Cricket Club*, at Stratford East. My most recent Court play, *Fallout*, was staged in the main house.

And then there was the play at the National.

That was *Sing Yer Heart Out for the Lads*.

So consistently, since you stepped out into the world as a professional writer, you've been a success.

By and large, yes. I've had on average about a play a year.

That's a good record – some playwrights struggle for such a long time before anything takes off. Like Leo, who had a long period of nothing happening.

Well, as you know it's a funny business, very unpredictable. I would just thank God that it started off so well for me and ten years later I'm still here.

You say you've written short stories?

Long ago, yes.

But there came a point when you decided plays were what you wanted to write. But why plays?

Again it comes back to my tutor, whom I used to go and see – that had the biggest impact on me. Watching those guys on stage, I just thought, wow, this is powerful, this is in my face, this is live.

Because your words get transmitted outwards, instead of somebody just sitting down and reading them?

Exactly. It seems – it was exciting, it was powerful. Also, when I read my first play, I thought, wow, this is me – it was a play by Barrie Keeffe called *Barbarians*. And one by my namesake, Nigel Williams, called *Class Enemy*.

Oh yes – that was done here.

I was about fourteen when I read those plays, and I felt, yes, he's writing the way that we talk.

That's one thing that makes someone a playwright – it's dialogue that they respond to, it's something they can do. But it's not just that, is it? It's also the total experience of putting a play together.

Exactly, that as well. Though I have to say, if somebody commissioned me to write a novel, I think I would find that a struggle, for the same reason. I know I can write dialogue, but I don't know if I could write prose.

When you say to yourself, it's time to write another play, what is the first thing that happens? Where do the ideas come from?

What first comes to me – this is the process I've been going through this year for a play I've been writing for the RSC – are sort of flash images, almost what's in your head at the moment, what's going on in the world. And I sometimes just let that settle, and the stronger it gets, the more need I have to start writing something.

So those are visual images?

Visual images, yes.

And so the words come . . .

Much later. The whole thing starts with a strong visual image. Then possibly a theme, and then I try to find a voice, a character, who'll be my guide initially, who's going to lead me through telling the rest of the story. That's kind of how it works for me.

And do you make notes?

Mental notes, I do, yes.

So you don't put pen to paper until you have a clear idea?

I have to have a fairly clear idea, yes. It's strange, because I'm not physically working, I don't have a pen in my hand, but it's all going on up here, I'm working in here.

Do you write longhand?

Longhand, yes.

So by the time you start, are you clear about the whole shape of it?

Pretty much. As I begin to write, it starts changing again, but when I start I know ninety per cent of everything I need.

You know who the characters are?

Yes – and what their journeys are. But that could still change along the way.

And does it change because you suddenly think, 'Oh, this is wrong'?

Or I've got a better idea. I might make a start on a minor character who might grow to be a major character, or vice versa. That happens a lot. Or I take two characters and I create one person out of them.

And are you somebody who welcomes feedback from other people?

I think a new play is a very precious thing – it's like a new-born baby. You have to be extra careful about who you hand it to. I try to choose three people, and get their feedback. Usually I try to give it to another writer, a director, and someone who is not part of theatre at all, and see what they say. This is what I did with my last play, I gave it to a friend who's a writer and one who's a director.

And after that process, did you make changes?

I'm going to be making changes because, interestingly enough, they both said the same things.

Something like, 'This isn't very clear here'?

Things like, third act is too rushed, first act too long. Sometimes it will be that it's not clear, not strong enough.

So it's a matter of fine tuning.

Yes. I try to do a lot for myself. I do as many drafts as I can before I hand it in – their first draft is not my first draft.

At the Court, quite often suggestions are made and work is done with the play before it's thought to be ready to put on.

I'm fairly open to that. It's just whatever the play at the moment needs – what they think it needs. Also of course, as a writer you have to think, are they right in what they're saying?

Have you had happy experiences with your directors?

I think I've been very fortunate. I've had a few disagreements with a couple of them, but nothing major. The directors I've worked with have been very good, so far.

And when you have a play done here, you'll be part of the process – going to rehearsals and so on?

You can be there all the time here if you want, and that's great.

Is that true of all the theatres you've worked in?

By and large, yes.

And have you had work taken up and done abroad?

Only readings, not full productions.

Because I know some writers have experienced their play being done somewhere in Europe, and they think, God, what's this?

I went to Rome, where a theatre company did a reading of the play I wrote for the National, and that was quite strange, hearing it done in Italian. They treated it as a full production – they learned all their lines. They did it in the crypt of this old church. It was really great, really good.

And have you written for TV, or radio, or film?

I've worked in radio, and I've done a bit of TV as well; I'd like to do more. It's a very different kind of experience. You don't have the freedom of theatre – I always say to young writers, if they want to go and do telly, yes, that's fine, but you should know what it feels like – your work is not the centre. You get that in theatre but you don't get it in TV, good as TV can sometimes be.

Having experienced a number of theatres, would you be able to say there is anything about the Royal Court that is different from any of those other places?

It's different in the sense that, to me, it feels very communal. Every time I come here, it feels, and lives, and breathes, like it's a writers' theatre. Even when you're not on commission, or it's a while before you deliver your next play, it feels welcoming. Without disrespect to any other theatres, I think the Royal Court does what it says – it's the home of new writing. I'm not brown-nosing them, it's absolutely true.

Tell me something about the international programme. Where have you been with them?

The last place I went to was Brazil, Sao Paolo. We went over and worked with a writers' group over there.

How long did you spend with them?

The whole trip was ten days, and we spent pretty much every day with the writers. Reading their plays, and giving them feedback.

Was it a good experience for you?

Yes. I must admit that when I went there I was wondering, what can I do? Because it was clear that the three directors I travelled with would work on the plays . . .

So what did you do?

Well, I read the scripts and gave my thoughts, suggestions about what they could do with a piece, writing exercises they might want to try out. But I kind of felt, I'm where you guys are – I'm one of you, someone who sits all hours in front of that sodding computer screen.

And do you feel the group was valuable for those people?

It seemed to be. I was hoping it would be, and it seemed to be from what they said. So I was relieved.

Have you worked here with the Young Writers' Programme?

I've done some workshops for them, and also gone into schools and worked with schoolkids who've never done any writing at all, or who have a vague interest.

Is that something you enjoy doing? Because you wonder if you can teach people to write.

Well, you can't – you can just find that spark if they've got it in them.

If you have a commission from the RSC and a commission from the Royal Court, are you going to write two different kinds of play?

No. That's not how I write. I just write what I want.

Because I know that you and Richard Bean are Monsterists – that's such a great title – campaigning primarily about the kinds of venues that plays get produced in – is that right? The fact that new writers are usually shunted off into the little studio spaces and dead writers get done on the main stage?

Kind of, but also we would like more theatres to commission playwrights who've got big ideas – if they want to have large casts and so on.

So it's not just political – it is an aesthetic consideration.

It is, yes. We had a very good conference at Hampstead Theatre two months ago, and invited everybody – we had a debate about big plays, and also about where theatre is going.

I've been reflecting a lot recently on what sort of plays I'd like to see. I'm not knocking what goes on here – I see almost everything here now, and I think much of it is wonderful, but I have a hunger for something big.

Well, that's what we want, really.

I'd like to see some costumes, hear some music – a more total experience.

I think there's a myth about what we're saying, that we hate small plays. We don't, we feel too many new writers are encouraged to think small – just three or four characters.

But a lot of that must be a financial consideration.

Exactly. We discussed that. We're not having a go at theatres – they're constrained by financial pressures, which is why we had the conference. We were asking the question, is there anything we can all do about it?

And is there anything?

Well, we have a suggestion, a proposal, which is called the Dead Writers' Levy. Basically it's a funding thing – whenever a big company puts on a play by a dead playwright, the money that would have gone to that playwright if they were alive goes to this fund. So if a theatre wants to say, okay, we want to commission Richard Bean to write a big play, they can go to the Dead Writers' Levy to fund it. Obviously it's only writers who are out of copyright, who've been dead for over seventy years. It's all about encouraging new writers to remember they're working for theatre, not for TV. Because in theatre you can do so much. So it's very positive, what we're saying.

When we talked before, one thing you thought your plays were about was race.

Yes, but if you want to go further, I think they're about belonging. There always seems to be one character who's looking to belong somewhere.

But you don't sit down and think, okay, now I'll write another play about belonging.

No – it just comes through. I'm hoping there'll come a time when I write about something else! But it's asking universal human questions – what do we belong to, where are we going?

And do you think of yourself as a political writer in any sense?

I think so, to a certain degree. I don't think there's anything embarrassing about that. To me the best theatre is political – in a way I think all theatre is political. Even if I was to write a play and say, 'This has nothing to do with politics,' that act in itself is political. You can't get away from the fact that I'm black – that in itself adds a layer. I'm not ashamed if some people want to address me as that. I mean the word political is very complex, and I don't want to lose the complexity.

When I started this book, I was wondering if there was such a thing as Royal Court play. I've come to realise that's an impossibly superficial expectation. What do you think?

I don't know . . .

I don't think anybody knows. I have concluded there are things that are definitely not Royal Court plays. My father said he wanted to put on plays that made people think – he thought plays should be disturbing. Shifting people's preconceptions, I think he meant.

I can relate to a lot of that. That's the kind of theatre I like to see – something that does challenge misconceptions, and I try to do that in my work. And that's probably why I've had a few plays on here.

I think that is a fairly consistent thing in the plays here, in whatever way they choose to do it.

Also, to tell the stories that haven't been told anywhere else.

Exactly. Max Stafford-Clark said that he wanted to give a voice to people who had not traditionally had a voice.

Absolutely. That's good, yes.

Snoo Wilson

Lay By (collaboration) 1971	*The Pleasure Principle* 1973
England's Ireland (collaboration) 1972	*The Glad Hand* 1978
	The Grass Widow 1983

I first met Snoo Wilson when we were both on the committee for the George Devine Award in 2004. All I really knew of him, apart from the fact that he was a writer of wonderfully bizarre plays, was that his name kept cropping up in association with David Hare and Howard Brenton, because he took part in a venture called Portable Theatre in the early 1970s. This seems to have consisted of the three of them hurtling around England in a van, performing radical political theatre to an unsuspecting public. He was also part of the team responsible for two notorious collaborative efforts in the 1970s, *Lay By* (1971) and *England's Ireland* (1972). He was one of the first people I interviewed, in his house in Clapham on 19 November 2004.

Why did you decide to start writing plays?

I suppose it came rather naturally, because when I was very young I would do puppet plays, and I graduated from those to rather larger plays. Then when I was at university I was allowed to write and stage my own plays and reviews. So although I was interested in other media, theatre was the one that I knew and had access to, and a kind of instinctive empathy with.

Had you been to the theatre a lot when you were young?

Not a huge amount, but my father was a Shakespeare scholar, who taught English, and we used to do play readings at home in the days before television, and so it all felt absolutely natural. When I wanted to learn the piano they said no, but I was always encouraged in other directions.

So you were writing from a young age, and when you went to university it was just a continuation of that?

Yes, though I think that playwriting is more than just writing. You need a sort of three-dimensional sense, a kind of architectural sense. You have to be talented in more than just wordage. I think if you have just words then you become a novelist, but there are other aspects to playwriting, which are to do with cutting to the chase, and a journalistic attitude to the brevity of being able to convey emotion, which I find attractive. Because, you know, one is easily bored.

You were at the University of East Anglia on a creative writing degree?

It was before they had creative writing degrees there, but I was allowed to contribute my own writing as part of the final assessment.

So you weren't taught to write, you were just allowed to write.

I was allowed to write. But there was an extraordinary School of English there, and I got lots of encouragement from people like Angus Wilson, Malcolm Bradbury, Victor Sage, and Lorna Sage. I was terribly lucky to be there at that time.

I'm curious to know if it's possible to teach people to write. Do you teach, yourself, now?

I have done. I've taught creative writing in San Diego, and for the Arvon Foundation, and various other things. In one sense it isn't possible, because it's like teaching people to have perfect pitch – either you've got a spark there or you haven't. But plenty of people who apply themselves to creative writing courses are creative, though they may not be absolutely brilliant at writing, they may not have any prospect of writing award-winning plays or whatever. I've moved on from the rather snooty position of saying, oh, some people can make their living by writing and others should be dustmen. Actually it's an extraordinary gift which, if you've got any kind of wind of, you should be able to enhance, because it's one of civilisation's great achievements, writing.

How can you help people enhance it? Suppose somebody comes along and says, 'I want to write plays – here's one I've written,' and you look at it and think, okay, there's some spark here, but this clearly doesn't work in lots of different ways. What would you do?

It's usually fairly obvious if it doesn't work, because it becomes boring. A play is something that needs to be engaging, to have your continuous attention. If you start drifting off, or you don't get it, it's an easy mechanical process to point it out. You don't have to stick a dagger in their heart. Nowadays, because there are so many creative writing courses, I think the heat has gone out of that kind of character assassination – 'You can write', 'You can't'. I think that people who go to writing classes are people who genuinely want to learn to build sentences and so on. They have varying degrees of skills, and writing is an extension of their other life skills. Because to write plays you have to have some instinctive grasp of what a group of people is going to feel. So it's not foreign to the idea of civilisation, because rhetoric was one of the first things that was taught, after all, and in a sense playwriting is about rhetoric, it is about learning to pile up your case-making skills.

What was the first play you wrote that you felt was properly finished?

The first properly finished play was called *Pignight*, which was revived recently. Thirty-three years separates the two productions – the life of Christ. I wrote it stealing a lot of biography from my family, as one does, and using lots of fantasy, and also very much influenced by the film noir of the time, particularly by *Performance*. It was very nice to see it come back, and to work, for people who hadn't been born when I wrote it.

And can you describe to me the process of writing it? Where does the idea come from – can you even say that?

Well, to go back to *Pignight*, which is really my roots, the idea of humanoid pigs taking over the earth comes from horror magazines, comic magazines, and from that rather alarming Elizabethan illustration of the perfect servant, who was edible but brought you things as well, and from my own uncle's problems with small farming. So it came from a stew of things. What I was primarily concerned with was making something where you could have theatrical doubling. Because it's like a clown play, and that would keep the kind of comic horror of the thing alive, possibly unsettling an audience so that they would be compelled to laugh and then they would always be slightly off-balance. But of course I hadn't worked all that out in advance. I was making something which worked, something out of these characters I'd thought of, and working out how far the characters could see, and so on. At the time, I was stage managing a play of Howard Brenton's called *Fruit*, and we were staying in the middle of Holland, outside on this farm which had a theatre attached, so it was a very appropriate flat, sodden landscape. Well, I set it in the Fens, but certainly the spirit of the place, of the agricultural lowlands of Holland, is very much infused with that kind of grimness.

How long did it take to write?

I wrote out all the bits and pieces in longhand, which took a couple of weeks, and then I came back here and typed them up and that took another week or something. But it really was an assembly process. Does this fit, can you get away with that? So it already had that aspect of the theatre as a conjuring box, as a magic place where if you don't break the illusion you can move from one thing to another and still take the audience with you.

What are your plays actually about? What do you set out to do when you write a play?

I think it's to do with the sort of joyful illusion – we are the stuff that dreams are made on – and some of the best and most exciting moments in theatre are to do with the realisation we sometimes have that we are actually on the edge of nothing, you know, which is exciting. Stage illusion is perfect for that, because it is only two-dimensional, and everybody gets up and goes home at the end of it. I like the rules of theatre, and I've never been interested in changing them, only in extending them in the direction of wonder or something, or exploring different kinds of address, because in fact everything has already been done.

And have you had terrible struggles sometimes to get something to work?

Yes, I had a big problem with a play called *Glad Hand*, which I didn't know how to finish. I workshopped it while I was at the RSC, but none of the big directors came to see it and they weren't interested in forwarding it, although the actors were very interested, and had been buying their own props and so on. Actually Max Stafford-Clark staged it, and he script-edited it through to a finished product, a finished production.

I wonder how much help somebody else can be in producing a finished play. Max has a reputation for sending people out to do all kinds of things, workshops, interviews, so the play is a product of all that as well as of the writer. Have you ever been involved in that kind of project?

Not as such. The thing with Max is, he's very dexterous at mending imperfect plays. If he finds a play which he doesn't need to do anything with, I think he becomes rather frustrated. I had that experience with him too. So sometimes you can stand very close to a creative experience in one project and not at all in another. I did once do this collective play called *Lay By*.

Tell me about the writing of Lay By. *You were all in a meeting at the Court and David Hare said, 'Hands up who wants to go and write a play.' Is that right?*

It was definitely David. Something like that. And then we all went off and we used to meet periodically. There were 'assignments' given you, you know, as to who would write a particular scene.

So you'd come up in the first instance with a structure of sorts, an overall plan?

Well, there were areas to cover, but . . .

It was based on a real rape case?

Yes, it was based on a real case, but you could have any number of approaches to it. I eventually edited it, because I was directing it. It was a bit like *Pignight*, because whatever didn't fit hit the cutting-room floor, and you were left with sections that might have been disjointed, but that were certainly continuously interesting.

And did you go back to the other writers and say, 'Your bit doesn't work so I'm not using it'?

Well, as soon as the writer had contributed their bit, they were off the job, as it were. And I think I did some rewrites with David, but it was just a kind of collage, really. It all happened over a longish period because there were a lot of people involved. We would come together at weekends to either write on the spot or to further our allocations.

Did it work in the end as a coherent whole, or wasn't it supposed to be coherent? Was it supposed to look like a collage?

I don't think it was supposed to. I think David's idea originally – and this is an idea he has pursued through his professional life – was that theatre should engage with the journalistic events of the day. And these events, which were a wrongful conviction for rape, were electrifying if you reconstituted them in any kind of action. So it became a *succès de scandale*. But I don't recall any of us being particularly interested in whether justice was served afterwards. It was an exciting enough process in itself, but it wasn't pushing for a judicial review, because the material wasn't done like that, it was too off-the-wall.

And were you satisfied with it? There's a story that the Court didn't put it on because they didn't like it.

That's not true. What happened was that Michael Rudman commissioned it for the Traverse Theatre. He was prepared to stump up £400, which was a lot of money in those days, and that was the seed money, and that's where it was done. I think David may have drawn his original writers from writers who were attached to the Royal Court, but Michael Rudman put it on as a late-night show.

But it came to the Court after that.

Yes – I think Ted Whitehead and Tony Page came to see it, because there was such a big noise at the Fringe about it, and they grudgingly agreed to a Sunday night. It was a most peculiar product, then taken over by Charles Marowitz at the Open Space Theatre. Thelma Holt told me the amount of people it would hold and we made the actors' salaries depend on that. Unfortunately she rather misrepresented the number of seats and the actors were on starvation!

And was there ever a time when you felt like a Royal Court writer?

I suppose I felt like a Royal Court writer when I wrote *The Pleasure Principle*, which was actually commissioned by the Royal Court. David Hare directed it at the Theatre Upstairs.

And it meant something to you to be associated with the Royal Court?

It certainly had an enormous kudos, which I probably didn't understand properly at the time. I don't remember many reviews, but I do remember a review by Michael Billington which said it was one of the best things to come out of the Royal Court. You realised then that you were in some kind of cachet situation – I'm really bad at realising when I'm in a cachet situation – and that was nice. But in fact I'd really written it as a play for the West End. I thought at that time that I was going to write plays for the West End, and I didn't realise then that there was a gap between the way I saw the world and the way the people who went to Shaftesbury Avenue saw the world.

But you won the George Devine Award, didn't you?

No, I never won the George Devine Award. I think I was put on the committee because they were so bored with me sending in plays. I sent in lots of plays. I got the John Whiting Award, which I shared with David Halliwell, for *The Glad Hand*. But that's the only Royal Court writerly prize I've been honoured with.

Do you still feel an enthusiasm for writing plays?

I feel great enthusiasm for writing plays. It doesn't get any easier to get them put on. But I think good theatre is a fantastically electrifying and exciting thing to do – it's a gift.

I suppose you write as long as you've got something to say.

Yes, but we all know writers who keep on saying the same thing over and over again. You probably write as long as you think somebody's going to take an interest.

Nicholas Wright

Changing Lines 1968
The Gorky Brigade 1979

I was at drama school with Nicky Wright – LAMDA – and though he was in the year above me, we were both in the same social circle. It was rather curious, based in a flat in Earls Court, and composed mainly of homosexual men in their thirties and female drama students in their late teens. It sounds rather dodgy but was pretty innocent, with lots of card-playing and raucous mime games. He also started visiting my house and got to know my mother and the various frequent visitors like Bill Gaskill and Peter Gill. So in a sense I was responsible for his introduction to the Royal Court. A few years later, after my parents died, I rented him a room in the ground-floor flat at Lower Mall, where he lived surrounded by a lot of ex-hippies who were practising and teaching transcendental meditation. We have seen each other occasionally over the years since then, during which he has had a rather brilliant career, including a period as joint artistic director (with Robert Kidd) of the Royal Court.

Tell me about your first experience of theatre.

I have some ability to write, and I have some talent for mimicry as a writer, which is something – but apart from that the only real talent I have is a talent for the theatre. I mean I have an understanding of the theatre, a theatrical imagination, and I've always had it.

When you say always – you mean since you were born?

Since I could walk and talk. I acted as a child, I made little theatres, and I would save up my pocket money and buy books about the theatre.

I know you were brought up in South Africa. Did your parents take you to the theatre when you were little?

No, not very much.

But were they theatregoers?

No – my father wasn't there till I was five years old because he was in the war, and my mother and grandmother went to concerts, not to the theatre. So I don't know what the first play was that I ever saw . . . Oh, I remember exactly what it was! There were two boys who used to do plays at school in the lunch hour. They used to improvise plays, down on one of the rugby fields. I was about seven or eight. I saw this crowd of boys looking at something, and I assumed it was a fight, so I went and watched. But it wasn't a fight, it was two boys doing a funny play, about a schoolteacher and a schoolboy, that they were making up. And I was entranced by it. Completely entranced. And then I used to act on the radio, because I read very well. I acted with Gwen Ffrangcon-Davies and Marda Vanne when I was twelve. By this time I was convinced that I would become an actor because that was the only life in the theatre that I could imagine. I didn't really know about directors, and writing seemed so remote.

But did you write other kinds of things?

Yes, I was always quite good at writing. But when I grew up I turned out to be a terrible actor, and directing isn't my talent either. So for years and years I had to find different ways of surviving in the theatre, because I didn't have any other world to survive in. I never considered not being in the theatre, it was just a question of how to earn a living. Of course, not having a university education, having hardly any education at all really, made me an odd person to be literary manager, which I was much later at the National, or choosing plays like I was doing at the Court.

So you came to England to go to LAMDA.

Yes. And I worked a little bit as an actor, and did all sorts of other jobs, and then I got a job on a film. I met John Schlesinger at a party and I persuaded him to give me a job as a runner on *Far From the Madding Crowd*, which luckily for me was a huge epic film shot over something like seven months, in Dorset. I got £30 a week, which I thought was unbelievable riches. And then I discovered to my total amazement on the first Friday of my first week, that you didn't just get that £30 less tax, you also got another £35 in cash, for expenses. By the end of shooting I'd saved up £1,500, a huge quantity of money. So I thought, well, now I can become a writer. I thought, I'll go to Greece, with a typewriter, and write a play. I was walking down the King's Road to buy my ticket at Victoria Station, when I met someone who'd been on *Far From the Madding Crowd*, and he said, 'Oh, I've been looking for you! We want you to come and be on the next film.' I said, 'No. I'm going to go into the theatre.' He said, 'Well, okay, I think you're crazy, but there you are.' I've made only two decisions in my life, and that was one of them.

So the desire to write a play had been building up?

I just thought it was something I could do in the theatre. I've never had any impulse. I get unhappy and bad-tempered if I don't write, but I've never thought, oh, I must write this! I envy writers who have inspiration and can't wait to get it down.

So you did go to Greece with your typewriter?

Yes, and I wrote this play, which was pretty rotten, actually.

And that play was done as a Sunday night? Changing Lines?

Yes, which I haven't got a copy of. I've no idea where one might be. And then I went on working at the Court for a while.

And it was on the strength of that play that you worked at the theatre?

It was on the strength of that play that Bill took me on as casting director. I knew that he wouldn't give me a job otherwise, because he knew me too well. I was just this boy hanging round at your mother's. I knew he'd never take me seriously as a human being unless I could do something to show I had some ability, and that was really why I wrote the play, to convince Bill that I wasn't just a blond bombshell.

And was it difficult writing it?

No, it was quite easy. It was my first experience of how surprising it is, that you just start writing, not quite knowing what you're doing, and four hours later you've got a couple of pages.

So you didn't have a clear notion of what it was going to be about?

No, I don't think I did.

But it must have been of a reasonable enough quality?

Yes, I think it was reasonable.

Between Changing Lines *and* Treetops, *you didn't write anything at all?*

Not for ten years. Because I was working at the Court, and I was directing and running the Theatre Upstairs, which was the most incredibly interesting thing to do. When I was at Andy Phillips' funeral, I was reminded of how closely we all used to work together in those days, in terms of being there all day, from ten in the morning often till the pubs closed. In these tiny offices, squashed up against each other. But it was incredibly exciting. It wasn't something you wanted to stop doing, ever, because you felt you were at the most interesting place in the world, doing the most interesting things.

So the Theatre Upstairs came into being under your direction, is that right?

Yes. I think how it happened was that Bill had had a very successful season, and had a small financial surplus that he didn't want to give back to the Arts Council. So he decided to convert the restaurant upstairs, which had been run by Clement Freud. It had become semi-derelict, and people used to do plays up there in a scratch way. It was a very distinctive period, when a new kind of theatrical energy was appearing. Groups were playing in smaller places, challenging the traditional stage–auditorium relationship and all sorts of other things about the form. And Bill very presciently knew that the Court had to acknowledge this and accept this new movement but, rightly, he didn't want to alter his main stage. So the Theatre Upstairs was to accommodate this new wave of theatre, and he asked me to run it. It was direly unsuccessful for the first three plays, and then I asked Peter Gill to come and do *Over Gardens Out* and a revival of *The Sleepers' Den*. Both were tremendously good and he used the space wonderfully. I went away while Roger Croucher ran the theatre for a bit, and that was okay, and then I came back. This was the seventies, a very successful time, with *The Rocky Horror Show* and all that, and then it entered a different period of being more mainstream. I always thought of it as a sort of valve, for the stuff that wouldn't get on the main stage. In later years people like Lindsay didn't want that to happen. The great discovery we made was that even though the auditorium seated only about sixty people, the reviews that you got would take up just as much space as if you'd done the show at the London Palladium! You could create a really big media event, which was fantastically good for the writer. People heard about it, and you'd given him or her a remarkable launch.

And did you see your role also as nurturing writers? How much of that went on?

We didn't really nurture in a methodical way in those days. Playwrights would just turn up. But in the early seventies, when Ann Jellicoe was literary manager, she ran a young people's playwriting competition. And I had the

318

idea that you would take the plays of very young people and do them very seriously, with grown-up actors. Plays by schoolkids, ten-year-olds. I found it fantastically interesting. And a wonderful play came in by a girl who was about fifteen, Andrea Dunbar. A truthful, beautiful play called *The Arbor*, which Max Stafford-Clark did a very good production of. And that was when the Court really got the young persons oriented thing that it has now.

Did any of those very young writers go on and do anything interesting?

Well, one of them was Jack Bradley, who is now the literary manager at the National.

So once you stopped being artistic director, you decided to start writing again. And you wrote Treetops?

Yes, and it was done at Riverside. It was rather good. It wasn't very successful, but it's a rather charming play, about my childhood. John Burgess directed it.

Had you suddenly thought, 'Oh God, I'd better write another play now'?

Yes, it was the only thing I could think of to do, actually.

Because you left the Royal Court thinking things hadn't gone particularly well?

Oh, dreadfully.

Then you went through another stage of producing quite a lot of writing.

Yes, in the eighties. I did two plays for the RSC, one for Joint Stock, and then I started working at the National, and didn't write anything for the stage till *Mrs Klein* came out.

Did you work with Max Stafford-Clark for Joint Stock?

No, with Bill Gaskill.

And did you work in what we think of as the Joint Stock method?

Not really. It was not a very good project for the Joint Stock method. It was based on a novel, and a novel is smaller than life. The Joint Stock method always works well for approaching life itself, if you see what I mean. But in the end it sort of worked.

And then from 1997 onwards you've written a lot.

Because I've no longer had a job at the National. So I've had lots of time.

You've been very successful.

Well, it's really nice to be as old as I am and be paying my way. Not feeling that one has fallen off the bus and is never going to get back on it.

Of all these plays, could you say which is your favourite?

I like *Vincent in Brixton* the most, and *Mrs Klein* is good, and *Cressida* would be good if I'd done one more draft of it, very good. I know what it should be like. It just needs a radical reworking. But at the time I thought it was fine. You're so delighted when the play gets accepted.

Is there anything you are now really ashamed of?

No, but it's an interesting subject. Because there's that thing your father said about the right to fail. People use it to this day at the Royal Court, and I don't think they quite realise what it used to mean. I think what your father meant was the right to put on one or perhaps two plays which would be financially unsuccessful, and not actually have to close the theatre down, to go bankrupt. He was talking about a certain degree of financial security, which would allow you to do the programme you wanted, and not compromise too much, so you didn't have to put on *Look after Lulu*. But I think no one remembers how fragile the Court then was financially, so the phrase can easily come to mean the right to put on not very good plays. But looking back at some of my plays – *The Desert Air* is one, and *The Custom of the Country* – I like those plays, they have a lot of life and spirit, but I always think, how did I let anybody put on the play in that state? I think, this play could be really nice, there's a lot of fun in it, but it's about two drafts short of being ready. With *Vincent*, I wrote it and rewrote it. A lot of excellent playwrights don't do that. John Osborne didn't, David Hare doesn't do it, Caryl Churchill doesn't do it at all, and she's a wonderful writer. But that's how I have to work, just work it and work it and work it. So of my past stuff, there's nothing I don't like, but I wish my expectations of myself had sometimes been higher, that I'd been more demanding of myself, and not thought, hooray, the RSC's going to do it. I wish I'd thought, I don't care how much the RSC want to do it, they're not getting it until I'm happy with it.

What went wrong with The Gorky Brigade?

Oh, it's a pretty dull play.

320

But it went onto the main bill.

It shouldn't have done. What I think is odd about the Royal Court is that there are now many playwrights who are writing successfully well into middle age. But they tend not to be Royal Court writers. And I think one of the reasons is that working at the Royal Court was so exciting, and it felt such a magic period of one's life, that nothing can ever measure up to it. The romance was too great. After that nothing could ever be quite the same again.

Do you think you've got more plays that you're going to write?

Yes, too many, actually.

So ideas come, and you think, 'I'll do that sometime'?

Yes, and you end up with too many ideas. But I can't write imaginary plays. I can speculate endlessly, but the idea of making something up out of absolutely nothing – it's too arbitrary, I don't know how to do it. I need things that actually happened and then I can fantasise about them.

AFTERWORD

Graham Whybrow

Looking Back, Looking Forward

Graham Whybrow has been the literary manager of the Royal Court since 1994. I started talking to him about this book when I first had the idea of writing it, and his input has been invaluable. We have had many conversations but never managed to record a formal interview until October 2005, when I went to see him to try to get some brief quotations to put into the introduction. When I read back over what I had recorded then, it seemed a good idea to include the interview in its entirety, for the perspective it gives on the past, the present and, to some extent, the future of the Royal Court.

I sometimes wonder about my father's original vision for the Royal Court. If you read what he wrote in his proposals before the English Stage Company was launched, you get the impression that he didn't envisage it as a theatre that would be solely devoted to new writing, or that would focus mainly on British writing. He mentions a number of European writers, some of whom were well established by then.

But if I can identify the quotation you're referring to, he says that this should be a theatre in which all the experimentalists of the modern era should be seen, from Brecht to Ionesco to Pirandello and so on. And I suppose that, in the grey post-war world of ration-book 1950s England, continental Europe was very exciting for its modernism in the theatre. It was austere, and challenging, and disturbing, and strange and imaginative, in a way that the West End didn't seem to be. So I think for me there is a very simple remit and artistic policy expressed there, which you can define as a dream of having a writers' theatre. You could equally say that the mixture, in those early days, of new plays, foreign plays, and classic plays, was a healthy one. But the context has changed, and there is now a National Theatre, an RSC, and a fringe, so the Court has become a specialist theatre for new plays. I hope that over the last decade the Royal

Court has seized the initiative again in making the play the thing, against the systematic attacks in the 1980s of physical theatre, of dance, mixed media, devised work and so on, which try to usurp the playwright. It's my belief that in every theatre culture there's a place for a writers' theatre. It's not the only way of making theatre, but an institution needs to defend it in the name of playwrights, because the artist is outside the organisation. So to enshrine a theatre as a theatre for new plays and new playwrights is very important. And it becomes part of the duties and responsibilities of the artistic director and literary manager to discover the defining plays of our time. If they don't, then they're failing to do their job.

But are the plays always there to be discovered?

It's my belief that the theatre is responsible for creating a vibrant playwriting culture. When you travel, you find that in many countries people say, 'Yes, the Royal Court – but this model wouldn't work in our country because in our country there are very few new plays and those plays are very bad.' I must have heard that twenty times. I would argue that the theatre firstly, guided by this vision, has to be open, receptive, curious and creative in relation to existing and aspiring playwrights. It needs to respond to the present and anticipate the future, and try to bring the future into the present. It's a very strange thing. You can't simply be guided by the principles of the past. If you use your values, or mine, you will be out of sync with the emerging young writers, who will see the world in a different way and have a different pattern of thought and feeling and expression. There's a risk that this may not be valued by theatre management, who will be that much older. You can work with established playwrights – you can treat them as artists and offer to put their plays on or not. But there's a whole band of untrained playwrights who are trying to write plays. They don't have a lot of experience but they do have a distinctive voice, or style, or vision, that needs a lot of creative support. But not interference. The role of the literary manager particularly is to know when to step back and to facilitate, and when to help a writer realise their intentions, without resort to laws or rules or formal study or theories of playwriting. You will have picked up from your interviews that it's quite a delicate negotiation, and I see it as a matter of the relationship between the theatre and the writer. There's potentially an imbalance of power, and writers may easily try to please us in order to get the play on. You can only measure it by the results you get artistically, the vibrancy of the programming, and the sense of confidence and range among new playwrights particularly. An artistic director and literary manager really should not have the attitude that we know and they don't. If you've got your wits about you, you can see that they know, and you need to respect that.

Be open to it.

Yes. I am particularly averse to the over-professionalisation and formalis-ation of this, because it could easily become too fixed, too ossified. The ethos has spread enough for people to realise that you're proceeding on the basis of respect. You're reading a play, which is not easy – reading a play for performance, that is, understanding it, seeing its potential, seeing what its strengths and weaknesses are, speculating on what the writer's intentions are. Because unlike a work of literature that's handed down to you from the canon, this isn't a fixed thing. A literary manager is in a sense a writer's manager – what you're responding to is a person, as well as a script, and if you have questions, then the writer is in a sense their own first reader and their own first audience member. But they may not themselves be a skilled reader. So by asking questions you are, I think, helping to ensure that the artistic choices they have made are within their control, and achieve the effects they want to achieve. That's the guiding principle for a discussion, a negotiation between the writer's intentions and what they've written. But you need to have the discretion to stand back and wave through, and not interfere, when it's great work. You should not be carving out a role as a script adviser or justifying your position by interfering for the sake of it. A new play by Harold Pinter or Caryl Churchill or Sarah Kane never went through a process. It was pro-duced. But new playwrights, or playwrights who've worked in another medium and are going back to the theatre, may need advice and support.

And do you feel confident that you always make the right choices?

I've been here an exceptionally long time, as literary manager – twelve years in 2006, almost a quarter of the theatre's history. Over two hundred new plays have been done in that time, by probably fifty or sixty new playwrights. But actually that has not led me to fixed or brittle values. In a sense the more you work as a literary manager on new plays the less conviction you can have except for the guiding principles.

What are the guiding principles?

I don't like using special expertise when I meet writers because I might have ideas about the genre or style they're trying to write in which are not relevant. It's highly likely, certainly, that the theatre is going to be more experienced and better read in new plays than first-time playwrights are. But you have to respect them – they are making something artistically, and rigging something technically, and you have to help them to discover how they can find a dramatic form for their material. What we're valuing here is not simple technical excellence but certain unusual things like originality, an individual voice and so on. The guiding principle for me is helping a writer to make the play more like itself, which is a question only they can answer, ultimately. Not trying to make the play more like previous plays you've read.

So you've got to have a great willingness to be surprised. You've got to be open to the possibility of what could be done.

Yes – and that means, if there is subjectivity in the process of reading a play, you have to make sure it's their subjectivity, not yours.

My father famously said that the theatre was a temple of ideas, and I have thought of suggesting that the Court might be called a theatre of ideas. But is that right, do you think?

Well, if it is, it's a cold climate for ideas.

Why do you say that?

Because I think that literature and theatre are seen as quite separate in England, as compared to other countries. If you go to Germany, or Ireland, or Russia, they don't distinguish. You are just a writer. They don't understand this capital-L concept of literature and then theatre. It's a cause of some frustration to senior playwrights who feel that they're not taken seriously as literary artists. Also contemporary playwriting hasn't particularly attracted intellectuals in recent times. You can go to other periods of history where you would see that there were intellectuals who were trying to work in the theatre. But the writers who come forward now very often have had particular strengths with character, language, social world and so on which they can observe or imagine or write about but it's very specific, not an intellectual matter.

I just felt that these are plays that have something to say, which may not be an intellectual statement – but that something is being said somewhere.

Yes – which raises the question of what is the play's relationship to the world. You pick up on a distinction in the introduction, which is that some writers say openly that they set out simply to entertain – to play, to tickle, to amuse – while others set out to disturb, to provoke and to question. They have a more complex, abrasive relationship with the audience. The founding moment of the Royal Court was a theatre in opposition to commercial managers setting out to please and win an audience. If the theatre had an abrasive relationship that upset the critics and emptied the house, but the work was felt to be of enduring value, that was the thing to do. Now that's the austere side of the Royal Court's remit. It can't do it all year round – it would be miserable. It understands that there's a place for politics, a place for art, and a place for humour.

Indeed. But that's what's good about many of the plays here – they strike a balance between the two. For example, Richard Bean's play Harvest *was really funny, but actually Richard has a very powerful agenda: he has things to say in that play about farming, and about the state of the country in general, that are wholly serious.*

That's right. But you could see the simple triangle or pendulum that the theatre functions in as having the theatre at the top, and at the bottom left-hand corner 'art' and at the bottom right-hand corner 'audience'. If you decide to be purely minority, coterie-art led, you will be elitist and lose your audience, but if you're nakedly populist and commercial, you'll lose your art. And there's a sense in which the theatre swings from one to the other across the season or across the year.

But is that a deliberate plan? Do you sit there and say, okay, this one is art so we've got to have a bit of fun in there as well?

No. I think, because of the English theatre tradition, which has been strong in being popular and anti-literary, that there's a popular tradition that can do poetry and art but also reach a larger audience. It's something specifically English in theatre, and indeed in our language – we can go Latinate, we can go Anglo-Saxon, we can go highfalutin, we can go ridiculous – we constantly shuffle between those things. We can translate everything we say into something formal, articulate and intelligent, and then puncture it at any time into something coarse and crude and base, but we're using the same language. It's not like in Germany where one's a written and one's a spoken language – we're not like that. That's the brake on severe, or austere, modernism in England. If England becomes too high-minded, it's quickly deflated as being pretentious or clever or highfalutin, and it's knocked off its pedestal – people don't like too much of it. I don't think

England could sustain a great art theatre in the way that they can in Moscow or Berlin or Bucharest. But the Royal Court exists in this strange mixed economy, mixed value system of challenging yet entertaining, of innovating but continuing a tradition. It's riddled with contradictions, which at best help propel it forward. Which means that guided by these simple principles, artistic directors and literary managers of the future need to be open and receptive to their time. And the choices aren't obvious, that's all I can say, having seen both the programming and the back of the tapestry – all the plays that we've rejected – which is full of aspiring writers whose plays weren't achieved enough, or weren't suitable for this theatre. But that leads you to constant questioning. It doesn't lead to any facile convictions about what a play should be.

So, where's it all going? It has seemed to me, looking at the whole fifty years, that one could identify phases in which certain things were happening. We look back for instance to the nineties, when what was called in-yer-face theatre was happening – there seems to have been a great outpouring of a certain kind of play then. But now in the past few years it seems much more diverse – it's much harder to pin down a certain type of play that you could put a label on. Do you think that's right?

Well, from 1994 onwards the field was wide open to discover and produce a large number of new playwrights and to create quite a purposeful sense of a new generation coming through. We were aware of it at the time, as the story unfolded, then it was retrospectively grouped together through some rather simplifying categories.

That always happens, I suppose.

We are constantly monitoring or watching the impulses of aspiring writers, good and bad, and creating hypotheses about the direction British theatre is taking. And there are patterns. There are patterns in the emotional structure and life of a play, there are patterns in its gesture, in its imagery, in its way of thinking. For example there might be a spate of plays that are entirely present-tense action plays, where characters who don't know each other encounter each other through skirmishes – they have no family, they have no history, they have no context. And then you might pick up a new play from Ireland, and immediately you have a sense of home, literally or metaphorically, of place, of setting, of a family, an extended family, a community, a landscape, an emotional landscape, all of which are infused with feeling and atmosphere. You immediately see what a contrast there is between, say, Conor McPherson's *The Weir*, and the in-yer-face play from London in 1997 that is full of violent gesture and sex and rape and so on. What you learn from this is how culturally specific the preoccupations and techniques of writers are. So the wider your range, the more precise your ability to identify what is specific about that particular play or writer. I think it's very healthy for us to be internationally minded, and to be reading plays by aspiring writers that are sent to the theatre. For me, it's like a dipstick into an engine. When you read not just the twenty plays we put on each year but the three thousand plays that are sent to us each year, you actually see what people are preoccupied with. And there are patterns. What does it mean that characters are trapped – literally or metaphorically – unable to move, living at home, trying to murder a parent, without freedom of movement – what does this mean, personally and politically? Then twenty years later there might be a much stronger liberating ideology that infuses the plays, where the characters are open, they have much more freedom of choice, the settings are multi-locational, with a happy, free use of time scheme, or they are inspired by cinema and start using multiple narratives, or concurrent narratives plaited together, or narratives that are connected by theme. You begin to spot these patterns, but you can't fold writers into the pattern. All it does is help you to be alert to the direction that writers are reaching towards, and therefore when you see something that at first sight seems very strange and very odd, but that fully realises that direction, you wave it through. That's the alertness I've been talking about. Because innovations in the theatre will always be truant, or transgressive – they will always go astray from received forms or styles. If in the visual arts you use the values of traditional portraiture and Picasso comes in with one of his Cubist paintings, using those values you will say, well this picture fails because it doesn't respect the classical norm of the human figure and it doesn't follow traditional rules of perspective, which have dominated portraiture since the Renaissance. But you have to recognise that it's the next new thing in painting, and you have to wave it through, not go and tell him to repaint. You don't tell artists to repaint, though you do seem to tell playwrights to rewrite. So it's vital to respect somebody who presents themselves like that. Because the producer or the curator of the international art gallery has to be the one that sees it, recognises it, values it, and produces or presents it, not the one that blocks, thwarts, stigmatises and discredits. That's the responsibility in a nutshell.

The generation of writers that included David Hare and David Edgar say exactly that about Lindsay Anderson. He didn't value their work because

331

he had preconceptions about what a play should be. But what they were writing was what people were doing then and it needed to be given some credit.

Yes. When you look back through the history of the Royal Court you see that those writers are not well represented here. There's a perceived blockage of those senior playwrights and it's absurd because by that time they had the Theatre Upstairs, which should have been the most vibrant second stage in the country. Many of those writers, especially the self-declared political playwrights of the late sixties and early seventies, felt disenfranchised.

They did.

But anyway – summarising the principles does mean that you can pass the baton on to other artistic directors and literary managers in the future, leaving them creative freedom and suppleness and flexibility in their approach, but putting it squarely on them to maintain the Royal Court's responsibility in leading and taking responsibility for discovering playwrights. If you remove that, you let them off the hook and they can easily blame others for the lack of talent or lack of new plays, and I think that would be galling. In my experience it's fairly and squarely the theatre's responsibility. You can't be the sexiest theatre all the time – you can't be high-profile all the time. Sometimes you can put it out there and it might be very extrovert, other times you are more reflective and introvert, but maintaining the principle will ensure that you stay one step ahead. That's harder now with a field of more theatres producing more plays. We are also in the grip of the media, which is mostly hype – you have 'young British artists' and you have 'young British playwrights' and you have 'blood and sperm plays' and 'in-yer-face' – it's all sexed up. But once the whole river of time has gone, there may be plays of enduring value which we produced which weren't particularly valued at the time. So the two things sit side by side – the honourable task of discovering the defining plays of our time, but also a producers' imperative to discover plays which will keep the programme exciting and varied.

Further Reading

Berney, K. A., and N. G. Templeton, eds (1994) *Contemporary British Dramatists*, London, Detroit, Washington DC: St James Press

Doty, Gresdna A., and Billy J. Harbin, eds (1990) *Inside the Royal Court Theatre, 1956–1981: Artists Talk*, Baton Rouge and London: Louisiana State University Press

Dromgoole, Dominic (2000) *The Full Room*, London: Methuen

Findlater, Richard, ed. (1981) *At the Royal Court: Twenty-Five Years of the English Stage Company*, Ambergate: Amber Lane Press

Gaskill, William (1988) *A Sense of Direction*, London: Faber and Faber

Griffiths, Trevor R., ed. (2003) *The Ivan R. Dee Guide to Plays and Playwrights*, Chicago: Ivan R Dee

Johnstone, Keith (1979) *Impro: Improvisation and Theatre*, London: Faber and Faber

Lesser, Wendy (1997) *A Director Calls: Stephen Daldry and the Theatre*, London: Faber and Faber

Rebellato, Dan (1999) *1956 and All That: The Making of Modern British Drama*, London: Routledge

Richardson, Tony (1993) *Long Distance Runner: A Memoir*, London: Faber and Faber

Roberts, Philip (1986) *The Royal Court Theatre, 1965–1972*, London: Routledge

Roberts, Philip (1999) *The Royal Court Theatre and the Modern Stage*, Cambridge: Cambridge University Press

Sierz, Aleks (2000) *In-Yer-Face Theatre: British Drama Today*, London: Faber and Faber

Stafford-Clark, Max (1997) *Letters to George: The Account of a Rehearsal*, London: Nick Hern Books

Trussler, Simon (1981) *New Theatre Voices of the Seventies*, London: Eyre Methuen

Tschudin, Marcus (1972) *A Writers Theatre: George Devine and the English Stage Company at the Royal Court, 1956–1965*, Bern and Frankfurt/M: Lang

Wardle, Irving (1978) *The Theatres of George Devine*, London: Cape